GREECE
AND
ROME

A Bacchante

GREECE
AND
ROME

H. A. GUERBER

SENATE

Greece and Rome

First published in 1907 by George G. Harrap
& Company Ltd

This edition published in 1994 by Senate, an imprint of
Studio Editions Ltd, Princess House, 50 Eastcastle Street,
London W1N 7AP, England

Copyright © this edition Studio Editions 1994

Reprinted 1994

ISBN 1 85958 002 5

Printed and bound in Guernsey by
The Guernsey Press Co. Ltd.

PREFACE

THE myths of Greece and Rome have inspired so much of the best thought in English literature that a knowledge of them is often essential to the understanding of what we read.

"When Byron calls Rome," says Thomas Bulfinch, "'the Niobe of nations,' or says of Venice, 'She looks a Sea-Cybele fresh from Ocean,' he calls up to the mind of one familiar with our subject illustrations more vivid and striking than the pencil could furnish, but which are lost to the reader ignorant of mythology." Literature abounds in such poetic borrowings from the classics, and it is impossible to enjoy fully the works of some of our best writers if we cannot immediately appreciate their imagery.

Again, expressions such as "the heel of Achilles" are part of the common language, but their meaning is lost upon those to whom the myths from which they are derived are unfamiliar.

But apart from the practical utility of the myths, as necessary to the comprehension of much that we read and hear, they have a great æsthetic value, presenting, as they do, a mine of imaginative material whose richness and beauty cannot fail to appeal even to the colder sensibilities of this more prosaic age. It would be difficult, indeed, to exaggerate the importance of these old-world stories, with their wonderful admixture of pagan faith and riotous imagination, in correcting the tendency to mere utilitarianism in the education of the young, and there is need to lay stress upon this because of the increased attention now being given to science and modern languages at the expense of the classics.

Translations of the exquisite writings of the Greek

and Latin poets cannot, of course, convey the same rich impressions. They are, at the best, weak and imperfect vehicles for reproducing the literary and imaginative wealth of a golden age; but they are, nevertheless, capable of imparting something of the atmosphere of the great originals, and, in whatever tongue they may be told, the stories themselves cannot easily be spoilt; they will assuredly appeal to thousands to whom the ancient languages of Greece and Rome are as a sealed book.

The writings of many of the great English classical translators, it may be added, are instinct with the spirit of the ancients. We might fancy that they, too, had caught sight of Proteus rising from the sea, and had heard

"Old Triton blow his wreathèd horn."

But properly to understand even these translations we first require a knowledge of mythology which it would take a lifetime to acquire piece by piece from general reading, and the aims, therefore, of this book are: first, to present outlines of the stories in a simple form pleasurable to the reader who has no desire further than to obtain a general knowledge of the myths, or to be entertained; and, second, to furnish a practical guide for the student who wishes to prosecute his mythological studies, and who desires to acquire the means whereby he will be enabled to follow intelligently the allusions to other myths which meet him at every turn, and to know something of the origin and significance of the stories.

The numerous quotations throughout will show the way to the noble pasturage from which these "flowers of Parnassus" have been culled, and they will enable the reader to appreciate the great influence of the myths upon our literature. The large selection of repro-

PREFACE

ductions from famous pictures and statuary, also, will show something of the debt which art, both ancient and modern, owes to the same inspiration.

The myths are told as graphically and accurately as possible, great care being taken, however, to avoid the more repulsive features of heathen mythology ; and when two or more versions of the same myth occur, the preference has invariably been given to the most popular, that is to say, to the one which has inspired the greatest works.

Both the Latin and the Greek forms of proper names are given, but the Latin names are usually retained throughout the narrative, because more frequently used in poetry and art.

The closing chapter includes an analysis of myths by the light of philology and comparative mythology, and the philological explanation of the stories related in the preceding chapters.

A map, genealogical table, and complete glossary and index adapt this volume for constant use in the library, the school, and the arm-chair.

Thanks are due to Messrs. Longmans, Green and Co. for permission to include numerous quotations from Mr. Conington's translation of the " Æneid," and to Sir Lewis Morris and others whose works have similarly been placed under contribution.

CONTENTS

CONTENTS

1

LIST OF ILLUSTRATIONS

LIST OF ILLUSTRATIONS

xii

LIST OF ILLUSTRATIONS

CHAPTER I : THE BEGINNING

Myths of Creation

MYTHOLOGY is the science which treats of the early traditions, or myths, relating to the religion of the ancients, and includes, besides a full account of the origin of their gods, their theory concerning the beginning of all things

Among all the nations scattered over the face of the earth, the Hebrews alone were instructed by God, who gave them not only a full account of the creation of the world and of all living creatures, but also a code of laws to regulate their conduct. All the questions they fain would ask were fully answered, and no room remained for conjecture.

It was not so, however, with the other nations. The Greeks and Romans, for instance, lacking the definite knowledge which we obtain from the Scriptures, and still anxious to know everything, were forced to construct, in part, their own theory. As they looked about them for some clue to serve as guide, they could not help but observe and admire the wonders of nature. The succession of day and night, summer and winter, rain and sunshine ; the fact that the tallest trees sprang from tiny seeds, the greatest rivers from diminutive streams, and the most beautiful flowers and delicious fruits from small green buds,—all seemed to tell them of a superior Being, who had fashioned them to serve a definite purpose.

They soon came to the conclusion that a hand mighty enough to call all these wonders into life, could also have created the beautiful earth whereon they dwelt. These thoughts gave rise to others ; suppositions became certainties; and soon the following myth or fable was evolved, to be handed down from generation to generation.

THE CLASSICAL MYTHS

At first, when all things lay in a great confused mass,—

> " Ere earth and sea, and covering neavens, were known,
> The face of nature, o'er the world, was one ;
> And men have called it Chaos ; formless, rude,
> The mass ; dead matter's weight, inert, and crude ;
> Where, in mix'd heap of ill-compounded mould,
> The jarring seeds of things confusedly roll'd."
>
> *Ovid (Elton's tr.).*

The Earth did not exist. Land, sea, and air were mixed up together ; so that the earth was not solid, the sea was not fluid, nor the air transparent.

> "No sun yet beam'd from yon cerulean height;
> No orbing moon repair'd her horns of light ;
> No earth, self-poised, on liquid ether hung ;
> No sea its world-enclasping waters flung ;
> Earth was half air, half sea, an embryo heap;
> Nor earth was fix'd, nor fluid was the deep ;
> Dark was the void of air ; no form was traced ;
> Obstructing atoms struggled through the waste ;
> Where cold, and hot, and moist, and dry rebell'd ;
> Heavy the light, and hard the soft repell'd."
>
> *Ovid (Elton's tr.).*

Over this shapeless mass reigned a careless deity called Chaos, whose personal appearance could not be described, as there was no light by which he could be seen. He shared his throne with his wife, the dark goddess of Night, named Nyx or Nox, whose black robes, and still blacker countenance, did not tend to enliven the surrounding gloom.

These two divinities wearied of their power in the course of time, and called their son Erebus (Darkness) to their assistance. His first act was to dethrone and supplant Chaos ; and then, thinking he would be happier with a helpmeet, he married his own mother, Nyx. Of course, with our present views, this marriage

2

was a heinous sin ; but the ancients, who at first had no fixed laws, did not consider this union unsuitable, and recounted how Erebus and Nyx ruled over the chaotic world together, until their two beautiful children, Æther (Light) and Hemera (Day), acting in concert, dethroned them, and seized the supreme power.

Space, illumined for the first time by their radiance, revealed itself in all its uncouthness. Æther and Hemera carefully examined the confusion, saw its innumerable possibilities, and decided to evolve from it a " thing of beauty"; but quite conscious of the magnitude of such an undertaking, and feeling that some assistance would be desirable, they summoned Eros (Amor, or Love), their own child, to their aid. By their combined efforts, Pontus (the Sea) and Gæa (Ge, Tellus, Terra), as the Earth was first called, were created.

In the beginning the Earth did not present the beautiful appearance that it does now. No trees waved their leafy branches on the hillsides ; no flowers bloomed in the valleys ; no grass grew on the plains ; no birds flew through the air. All was silent, bare, and motionless. Eros, the first to perceive these deficiencies, seized his life-giving arrows and pierced the cold bosom of the Earth. Immediately the brown surface was covered with luxuriant verdure ; birds of many colours flitted through the foliage of the new-born forest trees ; animals of all kinds gambolled over the grassy plains ; and swift-darting fishes swam in the limpid streams. All was now life, joy, and motion.

Gæa, roused from her apathy, admired all that had already been done for her embellishment, and, resolving to crown and complete the work so well begun, created Uranus (Heaven).

3

THE CLASSICAL MYTHS

This version of the creation of the world, although but one of the many current with the Greeks and Romans, was the one most generally adopted.

> " Her first-born Earth produc'd,
> Of like immensity, the starry Heaven ;
> That he might sheltering compass her around
> On every side."
>
> *Hesiod (Elton's tr.).*

Another popular version stated that the first divinities, Erebus and Nyx, produced a gigantic egg, from which Eros, the god of love, emerged to create the Earth.

> In the dreary chaotical closet
> Of Erebus old, was a privy deposit,
> By Night the primæval in secrecy laid ;
> A Mystical Egg, that in silence and shade
> Was brooded and hatched ; till time came about :
> And Love, the delightful, in glory flew out."
>
> *Aristophanes (Frere's tr.).*

The Earth thus created was supposed by the ancients to be a disc, instead of a sphere as science has proved. The Greeks fancied that their country occupied a central position, and that Mount Olympus, a very high mountain, the mythological abode of their gods, was placed in the exact centre. Their Earth was divided into two equal parts by Pontus (the Sea,—equivalent to our Mediterranean and Black Seas) ; and all around it flowed the great river Oceanus in a " steady, equable current," undisturbed by storm, from which the Sea and all the rivers were supposed to derive their waters.

The Greeks also imagined that the portion of the Earth directly north of their country was inhabited by a fortunate race of men, the Hyperboreans, who dwelt in continual bliss, and enjoyed a never-ending springtide. Their homes were said to be " inaccessible by land or

4

by sea." They were "exempt from disease, old age, and death," and were so virtuous that the gods frequently visited them, and even condescended to share their feasts and games. A people thus favoured could not fail to be happy, and many were the songs in praise of their sunny land.

> "I come from a land in the sun-bright deep,
>   Where golden gardens grow ;
> Where the winds of the north, becalmed in sleep,
>   Their conch shells never blow.
>
> "So near the track of the stars are we,
>   That oft, on night's pale beams,
> The distant sounds of their harmony
>   Come to our ears, like dreams.
>
> "The Moon, too, brings her world so nigh,
>   That when the night-seer looks
> To that shadowless orb, in a vernal sky,
>   He can number its hills and brooks.
>
> "To the Sun god all our hearts and lyres
>   By day, by night, belong ;
> And the breath we draw from his living fires
>   We give him back in song."
>
> *Moore.*

South of Greece, also near the great river Oceanus, dwelt another nation, just as happy and virtuous as the Hyperboreans,—the Ethiopians. They, too, often enjoyed the company of the gods, who shared their innocent pleasures with great delight.

And far away, on the shore of this same marvellous river, according to some mythologists, were the beautiful Isles of the Blest, where mortals who had led virtuous lives, and had thus found favour in the sight of the gods, were transported without tasting of death, and where they enjoyed an eternity of bliss. These islands had sun, moon, and stars of their own, and

5

were never visited by the cold wintry winds that swept down from the north.

> " The Isles of the Blest, they say,
>   The Isles of the Blest,
> Are peaceful and happy, by night and by day,
>   Far away in the glorious west.
>
> " They need not the moon in that land of delight,
>   They need not the pale, pale star ;
> The sun is bright, by day and night,
>   Where the souls of the blessèd are.
>
> " They till not the ground, they plough not the wave,
>   They labour not, never ! oh, never !
> Not a tear do they shed, not a sigh do they heave,
>   They are happy, for ever and ever ! "
>
> *Pindar.*

Chaos, Erebus, and Nyx were deprived of their power by Æther and Hemera, who did not long enjoy the possession of the sceptre; for Uranus and Gæa, more powerful than their progenitors, soon forced them to depart, and began to reign in their stead. They had not dwelt long on the summit of Mount Olympus, before they found themselves the parents of twelve gigantic children, the Titans, whose strength was such that their father, Uranus, greatly feared them. To prevent their ever making use of it against him, he seized them immediately after their birth, hurled them down into a dark abyss called Tartarus, and there chained them fast.

This chasm was situated far under the earth; and Uranus knew that his six sons (Oceanus, Cœus, Crius, Hyperion, Iapetus, and Cronus), as well as his six daughters, the Titanides (Ilia, Rhea, Themis, Thetis, Mnemosyne, and Phœbe), could not easily escape from its cavernous depths. The Titans did not long remain sole occupants of Tartarus, for one day the brazen doors were again thrown wide open to admit the Cyclopes—Brontes (Thunder), Steropes (Lightning), and Arges (Sheet-lightning),—three later-born children of Uranus and Gæa, who helped the Titans to make the darkness hideous with their incessant clamour for freedom. In due time their number was increased by the three terrible Centimani (Hundred-handed), Cottus, Briareus, and Gyes, who were sent thither by Uranus to share their fate.

Greatly dissatisfied with the treatment her children had received at their father's hands, Gæa remonstrated, but all in vain. Uranus would not grant her request to set the giants free, and whenever their muffled cries reached his ear, he trembled for his own safety. Angry beyond all expression, Gæa swore revenge, and descended into Tartarus, where she urged the Titans to conspire against their father, and attempt to wrest the sceptre from his grasp.

All listened attentively to the words of sedition; but none were courageous enough to carry out her plans, except Cronus, the youngest of the Titans, more familiarly known as Saturn or Time, who found confinement and chains peculiarly galling, and who hated his father for his cruelty. Gæa finally induced him to lay violent hands upon his sire, and, after releasing him from his bonds, gave him a scythe, and bade him be of good cheer and return victorious.

Thus armed and admonished, Cronus set forth, came upon his father unawares, defeated him, thanks to his extraordinary weapon, and, after binding him fast, took possession of the vacant throne, intending to rule the universe for ever. Enraged at this insult, Uranus cursed his son, and prophesied that a day would come when he, too, would be supplanted by his children, and would suffer just punishment for his rebellion.

Cronus paid no heed to his father's imprecations, but calmly proceeded to release the Titans, his brothers and sisters, who, in their joy and gratitude to escape the dismal realm of Tartarus, expressed their willingness to be ruled by him. Their satisfaction was complete, however, when he chose his own sister, Rhea (Cybele, Ops) for his consort, and assigned to each of the others some portion of the world to govern at will. To Oceanus and Thetis, for example, he gave charge over the ocean and all the rivers upon earth; while to Hyperion and Phœbe he entrusted the direction of the sun and moon, which the ancients supposed were daily driven across the sky in brilliant golden chariots.

Peace and security now reigned on and around Mount Olympus; and Cronus, with great satisfaction, congratulated himself on the result of his enterprise. One fine morning, however, his equanimity was disturbed by the announcement that a son was born to him. The memory of his father's curse then suddenly returned to his mind. Anxious to avert so great a calamity as the loss of his power, he hastened to his wife, determined to devour the child, and thus prevent him from causing further annoyance. Wholly unsuspicious, Rhea heard him inquire for his son. Gladly she placed him in his extended arms; but imagine her surprise and horror when she beheld her husband swallow the babe.

Time passed, and another child was born, but only to meet with the same cruel fate. One infant after another disappeared down the capacious throat of the voracious Cronus—a personification of Time, who creates only to destroy. In vain the bereaved mother besought the life of one little one: the selfish, hard-hearted father would not relent. As her prayers seemed unavailing, Rhea finally resolved to obtain by

8

THE CHILD-HOOD OF ZEUS

FROM THE PAINTING BY G. F. WATTS

BY PER-MIS-SION OF MR. FRED-ERICK HOLLVER

Enceladus under Mount Ætna

stratagem the boon her husband denied ; and as soon
as her youngest son, Jupiter (Jove, Zeus), was born,
she concealed him.

Cronus, aware of his birth, soon made his appearance,
determined to dispose of him in the usual summary
manner. For some time Rhea pleaded with him, but
at last pretended to yield to his commands. Hastily
wrapping a large stone in swaddling clothes, she handed
it to Cronus, simulating intense grief. Cronus was
evidently not of a very inquiring turn of mind, for he
swallowed the whole without investigating the real
contents of the shapeless bundle.

> " To th' imperial son of Heaven,
> Whilom the king of gods, a stone she gave
> Inwrapt in infant swathes ; and this with grasp
> Eager he snatch'd, and in his ravening breast
> Convey'd away : unhappy ! nor once thought
> That for the stone his child behind remain'd
> Invincible, secure ; who soon, with hands
> Of strength o'ercoming him, should cast him forth
> From glory, and himself th' immortals rule."
>
> *Hesiod* (*Elton's tr.*).

Ignorant of the deception practised upon him, Cronus
then took leave, and the overjoyed mother clasped her
rescued treasure to her breast. It was not sufficient,
however, to have saved young Jupiter from imminent
death : it was also necessary that his father should
remain unconscious of his existence.

To ensure this, Rhea entrusted her babe to the
tender care of the Melian nymphs, who bore him off to
a cave on Mount Ida. There a goat, Amalthea, was
procured to act as nurse, and fulfilled her office so
acceptably that she was eventually placed in the heavens
as a constellation, a brilliant reward for her kind ministrations. To prevent Jupiter's cries being heard in
Olympus, the Curetes (Corybantes), Rhea's priests,

uttered piercing screams, clashed their weapons, executed fierce dances, and chanted rude war-songs.

The real significance of all this unwonted noise and commotion was not at all understood by Cronus, who, in the intervals of his numerous affairs, congratulated himself upon the cunning he had shown to prevent the accomplishment of his father's curse. But all his anxiety and fears were aroused when he suddenly became aware of the fraud practised upon him, and of young Jupiter's continued existence. He immediately tried to devise some plan to get rid of him ; but, before he could put it into execution, he found himself attacked by his son, and, after a short but terrible encounter, he was signally defeated.

Jupiter, delighted to have triumphed so quickly, took possession of the supreme power, and aided by Rhea's counsels, and by a nauseous potion prepared by Metis, a daughter of Oceanus, compelled Cronus to produce the unfortunate children he had swallowed; *i.e.*, Neptune, Pluto, Vesta, Ceres, and Juno.

Following the example of his predecessor, Jupiter gave his brothers and sisters a fair share of his new kingdom. The wisest among the Titans—Mnemosyne, Themis, Oceanus, and Hyperion—submitted to the new sovereign without murmur, but the others refused their allegiance ; which refusal, of course, occasioned a deadly conflict.

> " When gods began with wrath
> And war rose up between their starry brows,
> Some choosing to cast Cronus from his throne
> That Zeus might king it there, and some in haste
> With opposite oaths that they would have no Zeus
> To rule the gods for ever."
>
> *E. B. Browning*

THE GIANTS' WAR

The Giants' War

Jupiter, from the top of Mount Olympus, discerned the superior number of his foes, and, quite aware of their might, concluded that reinforcements to his party would not be superfluous. In haste, therefore, he released the Cyclopes from Tartarus, where they had languished so long, stipulating that in exchange for their freedom they should supply him with thunder-bolts,—weapons which only they knew how to forge. This new engine caused great terror and dismay in the ranks of the enemy, who, nevertheless, soon rallied, and struggled valiantly to overthrow the usurper and win back the sovereignty of the world.

During ten long years the war raged incessantly, neither party wishing to submit to the dominion of the other, but at the end of that time the rebellious Titans were obliged to yield. Some of them were hurled into Tartarus once more, where they were carefully secured by Neptune, Jupiter's brother, while the young conqueror joyfully proclaimed his victory.

> "League all your forces then, ye powers above,
> Join all, and try th' omnipotence of Jove;
> Let down our golden everlasting chain,
> Whose strong embrace holds heaven and earth and main:
> Strive all, of mortal and immortal birth,
> To drag, by this, the Thunderer down to earth
> Ye strive in vain! if I but stretch this hand,
> I heave the gods, the ocean, and the land;
> I fix the chain to great Olympus' height,
> And the vast world hangs trembling in my sight!
> For such I reign, unbounded and above;
> And such are men and gods, compar'd to Jove."
>
> *Homer (Pope's tr.).*

The scene of this mighty conflict was supposed to have been in Thessaly, where the country bears the

imprint of some great natural convulsion; for the
ancients imagined that the gods, making the most of
their gigantic strength and stature, hurled huge rocks
at each other, and piled mountain upon mountain to
reach the abode of Jupiter, the Thunderer.

> "Mountain on mountain, as the Titans erst,
> My brethren, scaling the high seat of Jove,
> Heaved Pelion upon Ossa's shoulders broad
> In vain emprise."
>
> *Lowell.*

Saturn, or Cronus, the leader and instigator of the
revolt, weary at last of bloodshed and strife, withdrew to Italy, or Hesperia, where he founded a
prosperous kingdom, and reigned in peace for many
long years.

Jupiter, having disposed of all the Titans, now fancied
he would enjoy the power so unlawfully obtained; but
Gæa, to punish him for depriving her children of their
birthright, created a terrible monster, called Typhœus,
or Typhon, which she sent to attack him. This
Typhœus was a giant, from whose trunk one hundred
dragon heads arose; flames shot from his eyes, nostrils,
and mouths; while he incessantly uttered such blood-
curdling screams, that the gods, in terror, fled from
Mount Olympus and sought refuge in Egypt. In
mortal fear lest this terror-inspiring monster would
pursue them, the gods there assumed the forms of
different animals; and Jupiter became a ram, while
Juno, his sister and queen, changed herself into a
cow.

The king of the gods, however, soon became ashamed
of his cowardly flight, and resolved to return to Mount
Olympus to slay Typhœus with his terrible thunderbolts. A long and fierce struggle ensued, at the end
of which, Jupiter, again victorious, viewed his fallen

foe with boundless pride ; but his triumph was very short-lived.

Enceladus, another redoubtable giant, also created by Gæa, now appeared to avenge Typhœus. He too was signally defeated, and bound with adamantine chains in a burning cave under Mount Ætna. In early times, before he had become accustomed to his prison, he gave vent to his rage by outcries, imprecations, and groans; sometimes he even breathed forth fire and flames, in hopes of injuring his conqueror. But time, it is said, somewhat cooled his resentment ; and now he is content with an occasional change of position, which, owing to his huge size, causes the earth to tremble over a space of many miles, producing what is called an earthquake.

> " 'Tis said, that thunder-struck Enceladus,
> Grovelling beneath the incumbent mountain's weight,
> Lies stretched supine, eternal prey of flames ;
> And, when he heaves against the burning load,
> Reluctant, to invert his broiling limbs,
> A sudden earthquake shoots through all the isle,
> And Ætna thunders dreadful under ground,
> Then pours out smoke in wreathing curls convolved,
> And shades the sun's bright orb, and blots out day."
>
> *Addison.*

Jupiter had now conquered all his foes, asserted his right to the throne, and could at last reign over the world undisturbed ; but he knew that it would be no small undertaking to rule well heaven, earth, and sea, and resolved to divide the power with his brothers. To avoid quarrels and recriminations, he portioned the world out into lots, allowing each of his brothers the privilege of drawing his own share.

Neptune thus obtained control over the sea and all the rivers, and immediately expressed his resolve to wear a symbolic crown, composed exclusively of marine shells and aquatic plants, and to abide within the bounds of his watery realm.

Pluto, the most taciturn of the brothers, received for his portion the sceptre of Tartarus and all the Lower World, where no beam of sunlight was ever allowed to find its way ; while Jupiter reserved for himself the general supervision of his brothers' estates, and the direct management of Heaven and Earth.

Peace now reigned throughout all the world. Not a murmur was heard, except from the Titans, who at length, seeing that further opposition would be useless, grew reconciled to their fate.

In the days of their prosperity, the Titans had intermarried. Cronus had taken Rhea " for better or for worse " ; and Iapetus had seen, loved, and wedded the fair Clymene, one of the ocean nymphs, or Oceanides, daughters of Oceanus. The latter pair became the proud parents of four gigantic sons,— Atlas, Menetius, Prometheus (Forethought), and Epimetheus (Afterthought),—who were destined to play prominent parts in Grecian mythology.

The Story of Prometheus

At the time of the creation, after covering the new-born Earth with luxuriant vegetation, and peopling it with living creatures of all kinds, Eros perceived that it would be necessary to endow them with instincts which would enable them to preserve and enjoy the life they had received. He therefore called the youngest two sons of Iapetus to his aid, and bade them make a judicious distribution of gifts to all living creatures, and create and endow a superior being, called Man, to rule over all the others.

Prometheus' and Epimetheus' first care was, very naturally, to provide for the beings already created

THE STORY OF PROMETHEUS

These they endowed with such reckless generosity, that all their favours were soon dispensed, and none remained for the endowment of man. Although they had not the remotest idea how to overcome this difficulty, they proceeded to fashion man from clay.

> "Prometheus first transmuted
> Atoms culled for human clay."
> *Horace.*

They first moulded an image similar in form to the gods; bade Eros breathe into its nostrils the spirit of life, and Minerva (Pallas) endow it with a soul; whereupon man lived, and moved, and viewed his new domain.

Justly proud of his handiwork, Prometheus observed man and longed to bestow upon him some great power, unshared by any other creature of earth, which would raise him far above all other living beings, and bring him nearer to the perfection of the immortal gods.

> "Of Prometheus, how undaunted
> On Olympus' shining bastions
> His audacious foot he planted,
> Myths are told and songs are chanted,
> Full of promptings and suggestions.
>
> "Beautiful is the tradition
> Of that flight through heavenly portals,
> The old classic superstition
> Of the theft and the transmission
> Of the fire of the Immortals."
> *Longfellow.*

Fire alone, in his estimation, could effect this; but fire was the special possession and prerogative of the gods, and Prometheus knew they would never willingly share it with man, and that, should any one obtain it by stealth, they would never forgive the thief.

15

Long he pondered the matter, and finally determined to obtain fire, or die in the attempt.

One dark night, therefore, he set out for Olympus, entered unperceived into the gods' abode, seized a lighted brand, hid it in his bosom, and departed unseen, exulting in the success of his enterprise. Arrived upon earth once more, he consigned the stolen treasure to the care of man, who immediately adapted it to various purposes, and eloquently expressed his gratitude to the benevolent deity who had risked his own life to obtain it for him.

From his lofty throne on the topmost peak of Mount Olympus Jupiter beheld an unusual light upon earth. Anxious to ascertain its exact nature, he watched it closely, and before long discovered the theft. His anger then burst forth, terrible to behold ; and the gods all quailed when they heard him solemnly vow he would punish the unhappy Prometheus without mercy. To seize the offender in his mighty grasp, bear him off to the Caucasian Mountains, and bind him fast to a great rock, was but a moment's work. There a voracious vulture was summoned to feast day by day upon his liver, the tearing of which from his side by the bird's cruel beak and talons caused the sufferer intense anguish. All day long the vulture gorged himself ; but during the cool night, while the bird slept, Prometheus' suffering abated, and the liver grew again, thus prolonging the torture, which bade fair to have no end.

Disheartened by the prospect of long years of unremitting pain, Prometheus at times could not refrain from pitiful complaints ; but generation after generation of men lived on earth, and died, blessing him for the gift he had obtained for them at such a terrible cost. After many centuries of woe, Hercules, son of

16

Jupiter and Alcmene, found Prometheus, killed the vulture, broke the adamantine chains, and liberated the long-suffering god.

> "Thy godlike crime was to be kind,
> To render with thy precepts less
> The sum of human wretchedness,
> And strengthen man with his own mind."
>
> *Byron.*

Epimetheus and Pandora

The first mortals lived on earth in a state of perfect innocence and bliss. The air was pure and balmy; the sun shone brightly all the year; the earth brought forth delicious fruit in abundance; and beautiful, fragrant flowers bloomed everywhere. Man was content. Extreme cold, hunger, sickness, and death were unknown. Jupiter, who justly ascribed a good part of this beatific condition to the gift conferred by Prometheus, was greatly displeased, and tried to devise some means to punish mankind for the acceptance of the heavenly fire.

With this purpose in view, he assembled the gods on Mount Olympus, where, in solemn council, they decided to create woman; and as soon as she had been artfully fashioned, each one endowed her with some special charm, to make her more attractive.

> "The crippled artist-god,
> Illustrious, moulded from the yielding clay
> A bashful virgin's image, as advis'd
> Saturnian Jove.
>
> .   .   .   .   .
>
> "But now when the fair mischief, seeming-good,
> His hand had perfected, he led her forth
> Exulting in her grac'd attire, the gift
> Of Pallas, in the midst of gods and men.
> On men and gods in that same moment seiz'd
> The ravishment of wonder, when they saw
> The deep deceit, th' inextricable snare."
>
> *Hesiod (Elton's tr.).*

Their united efforts were crowned with the utmost

success. Nothing was lacking, except a name for the peerless creature; and the gods, after due consideration, decreed she should be called Pandora. They then bade Mercury take her to Prometheus as a gift from heaven; but he, knowing only too well that nothing good would come to him from the gods, refused to accept her, and cautioned his brother Epimetheus to follow his example. Unfortunately Epimetheus was of a confiding disposition, and when he beheld the maiden he exclaimed, " Surely so beautiful and gentle a being can bring no evil ! " and accepted her most joyfully.

The first days of their union were spent in blissful wanderings, hand in hand, under the cool forest shade; in weaving garlands of fragrant flowers; and in refreshing themselves with the luscious fruit, which hung so temptingly within reach.

One lovely evening, while dancing on the green, they saw Mercury, Jupiter's messenger, coming towards them. His step was slow and weary, his garments dusty and travel-stained, and he seemed almost to stagger beneath the weight of a huge box which rested upon his shoulders. Pandora immediately ceased dancing, to speculate with feminine curiosity upon the contents of the chest. In a whisper she begged Epimetheus to ask Mercury what brought him thither. Epimetheus complied with her request; but Mercury evaded the question, asked permission to deposit his burden in their dwelling for safe-keeping, professing himself too weary to convey it to its destination that day, and promised to call for it shortly. The permission was promptly granted. Mercury, with a sigh. of relief, placed the box in one corner, and then departed, refusing all hospitable offers of rest and refreshment.

He had scarcely crossed the threshold, when Pandora expressed a strong desire to have a peep at the contents

18

of the mysterious box ; but Epimetheus, surprised and shocked, told her that her curiosity was unseemly, and then, to dispel the frown and pout seen for the first time on the fair face of his beloved, he entreated her to come out into the fresh air and join in the merry games of their companions. For the first time, also, Pandora refused to comply with his request. Dismayed, and very much discouraged, Epimetheus sauntered out alone, thinking she would soon join him, and perhaps by some caress atone for her present wilfulness.

Left alone with the mysterious casket, Pandora became more and more inquisitive. Stealthily she drew near and examined it with great interest, for it was curiously wrought of dark wood, and surmounted by a delicately carved head, of such fine workmanship that it seemed to smile and encourage her. Around the box a glittering golden cord was wound, and fastened on top in an intricate knot. Pandora, who prided herself specially on her deft fingers, felt sure she could unfasten it, and, reasoning that it would not be indiscreet to untie it if she did not raise the lid, she set to work. Long she strove, but all in vain. Ever and anon the laughing voices of Epimetheus and his companions, playing in the luxuriant shade, were wafted in on the summer breeze. Repeatedly she heard them call and beseech her to join them ; yet she persisted in her attempt. She was just on the point of giving up in despair, when suddenly the refractory knot yielded to her fumbling fingers, and the cord, unrolling, dropped on the floor.

Pandora had repeatedly fancied that sounds like whispers issued from the box. The noise now seemed to increase, and she breathlessly applied her ear to the lid to ascertain whether it really proceeded from within. Imagine, therefore, her surprise when she distinctly

19

heard these words, uttered in the most pitiful accents: "Pandora, dear Pandora, have pity upon us! Free us from this gloomy prison! Open, open, we beseech you!"

Pandora's heart beat so fast and loud, that it seemed for a moment to drown all other sounds. Should she open the box? Just then a familiar step outside made her start guiltily. Epimetheus was coming, and she knew he would urge her again to come out, and would prevent the gratification of her curiosity. Precipitately, therefore, she raised the lid to have one little peep before he came in.

Now, Jupiter had malignantly crammed into this box all the diseases, sorrows, vices, and crimes that afflict poor humanity; and the box was no sooner opened, than all these ills flew out, in the guise of horrid little brown-winged creatures, closely resembling moths. These little insects fluttered about, alighting, some upon Epimetheus, who had just entered, and some upon Pandora, pricking and stinging them most unmercifully. They then flew out through the open door and windows, and fastened upon the merry-makers without, whose shouts of joy were soon changed into wails of pain and anguish.

Epimetheus and Pandora had never before experienced the faintest sensation of pain or anger; but, as soon as these winged evil spirits had stung them, they began to weep, and, alas! quarrelled for the first time in their lives. Epimetheus reproached his wife in bitterest terms for her thoughtless action; but in the very midst of his vituperation he suddenly heard a sweet little voice entreat for freedom. The sound proceeded from the unfortunate box, whose cover Pandora had dropped again, in the first moment of her surprise and pain. "Open, open, and I will heal your wounds! Please let me out!" it pleaded

20

Pandora

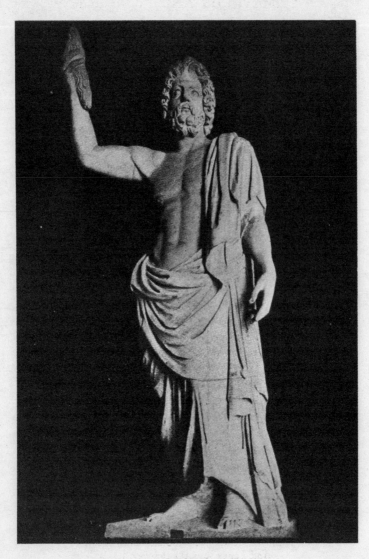

Jupiter

EPIMETHEUS AND PANDORA

The tearful couple viewed each other inquiringly, and listened again. Once more they heard the same pitiful accents; and Epimetheus bade his wife open the box and set the speaker free, adding very amiably, that she had already done so much harm by her ill-fated curiosity, that it would be difficult to add materially to its evil consequences, and that, perchance, the box contained some good spirit, whose ministrations might prove beneficial.

It was well for Pandora that she opened the box a second time, for the gods, with a sudden impulse of compassion, had concealed among the evil spirits one kindly creature, Hope, whose mission was to heal the wounds inflicted by her fellow prisoners.

> "Hope sole remain'd within, nor took her flight,
> Beneath the vessel's verge conceal'd from light."
>
> *Hesiod (Elton's tr.).*

Lightly fluttering hither and thither on her snowy pinions, Hope touched the wounded places on Pandora's and Epimetheus' creamy skin, and relieved their suffering, then quickly flew out of the open window, to perform the same gentle office for the other victims, and to cheer their downcast spirits.

Thus, according to the ancients, evil entered into the world, bringing untold misery; but Hope followed closely in its footsteps, to aid struggling humanity, and point to a happier future.

> "Hope rules a land for ever green:
> All powers that serve the bright-eyed Queen
> Are confident and gay;
> Clouds at her bidding disappear;
> Points she to aught?—the bliss draws near,
> And Fancy smooths the way."
>
> *Wordsworth.*

THE CLASSICAL MYTHS

During many centuries, therefore, Hope continued to be revered, although the other divinities had ceased to be worshipped.

According to another version, Pandora was sent down to man, bearing a vase in which the evil spirits were imprisoned, and on the way, seized by a fit of curiosity, raised the cover, and allowed them all to escape.

Little by little the world was peopled ; and the first years of man's existence upon earth were, as we have seen, years of unalloyed happiness. There was no occasion for labour, for the earth brought forth spontaneously all that was necessary for man's subsistence. " Innocence, virtue, and truth prevailed ; neither were there any laws to restrict men, nor judges to punish." This time of bliss has justly borne the title of the Golden Age, and the people in Italy then throve under the wise rule of good old Saturn, or Cronus.

Unfortunately, nothing in this world is lasting ; and the Golden Age was followed by another, not quite so prosperous, hence called the Silver Age, when the year was first divided into seasons, and men were obliged to toil for their daily bread.

> " Succeeding times a silver age behold,
> Excelling brass, but more excell'd by gold.
> Then summer, autumn, winter, did appear,
> And spring was but a season of the year ;
> The sun his annual course obliquely made,
> Good days contracted, and enlarg'd the bad.
> The air with sultry heats began to glow,
> The wings of winds were clogg'd with ice and snow;
> And shivering mortals into houses driven,
> Sought shelter from the inclemency of heaven.
> Those houses, then, were caves or homely sheds,
> With twining osiers fenc'd, and moss their beds.
> Then ploughs, for seed, the fruitful furrows broke,
> And oxen labour'd first beneath the yoke."
>
> *Ovid (Dryden's tr.).*

EPIMETHEUS AND PANDORA

Yet, in spite of these few hardships, the people were happy, far happier than their descendants during the Age of Brass, which speedily followed, when strife became customary, and differences were settled by blows.

But by far the worst of all was the Iron Age, when men's passions knew no bounds, and they even dared refuse all homage to the immortal gods. War was waged incessantly; the earth was saturated with blood; the rights of hospitality were openly violated; and murder, rape, and theft were committed on all sides.

Jupiter had kept a close watch over men's actions during all these years; and this evil conduct aroused his wrath to such a point, that he vowed he would annihilate the human race. But the modes of destruction were manifold, and, as he could not decide which would eventually prove most efficacious, he summoned the gods to deliberate and aid him by their counsels. The first suggestion offered, was to destroy the world by fire, kindled by Jupiter's much dreaded thunderbolts; and the king of gods was about to put it into instant execution, when his arm was stayed by the objection that the rising flames might set fire to his own abode, and reduce its magnificence to unsightly ashes. He therefore rejected the plan as impracticable, and bade the gods devise other means of destruction.

After much delay and discussion, the immortals agreed to wash mankind off the face of the earth by a mighty deluge. The winds were instructed to gather together the rain clouds over the earth. Neptune let loose the waves of the sea, bidding them rise, overflow, and deluge the land. No sooner had the gods spoken, than the elements obeyed: the winds blew; the rain fell in torrents; lakes, seas, rivers, and oceans broke

23

their bonds ; and terrified mortals, forgetting their petty
quarrels in a common impulse to flee from the death
which threatened them, climbed the highest mountains,
clung to uprooted trees, and even took refuge in
the light skiffs they had constructed in happier days.
Their efforts were all in vain, however ; for the waters
rose higher and higher, overtook them one after
another in their ineffectual efforts to escape, closed over
the homes where they might have been so happy, and
drowned their last despairing cries in their seething
depths.

> " Now hills and vales no more distinction know,
> And levell'd nature lies oppress'd below ;
> The most of mortals perish in the flood."
>
> *Ovid (Dryden's tr.).*

Deucalion and Pyrrha

The rain continued to fall, until, after many days,
the waves covered all the surface of the earth except
the summit of Mount Parnassus, the highest peak in
Greece. On this mountain, surrounded by the ever-
rising flood, stood the son of Prometheus, Deucalion,
with his faithful wife Pyrrha, a daughter of Epimetheus
and Pandora. From thence they, the sole survivors,
viewed the universal desolation with tear-dimmed
eyes.

In spite of the general depravity, the lives of this
couple had always been pure and virtuous ; and when
Jupiter saw them there alone, and remembered their
piety, he decided not to include them in the general
destruction, but to save their lives. He therefore bade
the winds return to their cave, and the rain to cease.
Neptune, in accordance with his decree, blew a resounding blast upon his conch shell to recall the wandering
waves, which immediately returned within their usual
bounds.

24

DEUCALION AND PYRRHA

Deucalion and Pyrrha followed the receding waves step by step down the steep mountain side.

> " At length the world was all restor'd to view,
> But desolate, and of a sickly hue ;
> Nature beheld herself, and stood aghast,
> A dismal desert and a silent waste."
>
> *Ovid (Dryden's tr.).*

As they talked upon how they should repeople the desolate earth, they came to the shrine of Delphi, which alone had been able to resist the force of the waves. There they entered to consult the wishes of the gods. Their surprise and horror were unbounded, however, when a voice exclaimed, "Depart from hence with veiled heads, and cast your mothers' bones behind you !" To obey such a command seemed sacrilegious in the extreme; for the dead had always been held in deep veneration by the Greeks, and the desecration of a grave was considered a heinous crime, and punished accordingly. But, they reasoned, the god's oracles can seldom be accepted in a literal sense ; and Deucalion, after due thought, explained to Pyrrha what he conceived to be the meaning of this mysterious command.

"The Earth," said he, " is the mother of all, and the stones may be considered her bones." Husband and wife speedily decided to act upon this premise, and continued their descent, casting stones behind them. All those thrown by Deucalion were immediately changed into men, while those cast by Pyrrha became women.

Thus the earth was peopled for the second time with a blameless race of men, sent to replace the wicked beings slain by Jupiter. Deucalion and Pyrrha shortly after became the happy parents of a son named Hellen, who gave his name to all the Hellenic or Greek race ; while his sons Æolus and Dorus, and grandsons Ion

THE CLASSICAL MYTHS

and Achæus, became the ancestors of the Æolian, Dorian, Ionian, and Achaian nations.

Other mythologists, in treating of the diluvian myths, state that Deucalion and Pyrrha took refuge in an ark, which, after sailing about for many days, was stranded on the top of Mount Parnassus. This version was far less popular with the Greeks, although it betrays still more plainly the common source whence all these myths are derived.

> "Who does not see in drown Deucalion's name,
> When Earth her men and Sea had lost her shore,
> Old Noah !"
>
> *Fletcher.*

CHAPTER II : JUPITER

The Power of Jupiter

JUPITER, Jove, or Zeus, king of the gods, supreme ruler of the universe, the special deity of mankind, the personification of the sky and of all the phenomena of the air, and the guardian of political order and peace, was the most prominent of all the Olympian divinities : the others were obliged to submit to his will, and trembled at his all-powerful nod.

> " He, whose all-conscious eyes the world behold,
> The eternal Thunderer sat, enthroned in gold,
> High heaven the footstool of his feet he makes,
> And wide beneath him all Olympus shakes."

> " He spoke, and awful bends his sable brows,
> Shakes his ambrosial curls, and gives the nod,
> The stamp of fate and sanction of the god :
> High heaven with trembling the dread signal took,
> And all Olympus to the centre shook."
>
> *Homer (Pope's tr.)*

The Fates and Destiny alone dared oppose Jupiter's sovereign will, and they continued to issue their irrevocable decrees, even after he supplanted his father and began to rule over all.

In common with all other Greek and Roman divinities, Jupiter, though immortal, was subject to pleasure, pain, grief, and anger, and a prey to all the passions which rule the hearts of men.

It was he who presided at the councils held on the top of " many-peaked Olympus," and summoned the gods whenever he wished to discuss with them any matter of importance, or to indulge in a sumptuous repast, when they ate the celestial ambrosia and quaffed the fragrant nectar.

He is generally represented as a fine majestic figure,

27

with long curling hair and beard, clad in flowing
drapery, his redoubtable thunderbolts or sceptre in one
hand, and a statue of Victory in the other. The world
is his footstool; and the eagle, emblem of strength
and power, is usually seen close beside him.

His Attendants

Jupiter had his own special attendants, such as
Victoria, or Nice, the goddess of victory, who was ever
ready to obey his slightest behest, and it is said her
master loved her so dearly that he generally held an
image of her in his hand.

The hundred-tongued goddess of fame, Fama,
trumpet in hand, proclaimed, at his bidding, anything
he wished, never questioning whether it were true or
false.

> " Fame than who never plague that runs
>   Its way more swiftly wins :
> Her very motion lends her power :
> She flies and waxes every hour.
> At first she shrinks, and cowers for dread ;
>   Ere long she soars on high :
> Upon the ground she plants her tread,
>   Her forehead in the sky."
>   *Virgil* (*Conington's tr.*).

Close by Jupiter's side was sometimes seen Fortuna,
goddess of fortune, poised on a constantly revolving
wheel, whereon she journeyed throughout the world,
scattering with careless hands her numerous gifts, and
lavishing with indifference her choicest smiles ; while
Hebe, or Juventas, the goddess of youth, was ever
ready at his wish to pour out the nectar, in which the
gods were wont to pledge each other.

> " Hebe, honoured of them all,
> Ministered nectar, and from cups of gold
> They pledged each other."
>   *Homer* (*Bryant's tr.*).

PHILEMON AND BAUCIS

But this fair goddess awkwardly tripped and fell on a solemn occasion, and was forced to resign her office. To replace her, the father of the gods was obliged to go in quest of another cup-bearer.

To facilitate his search, he assumed the form of an eagle, and winged his flight over the earth. He had not flown far, before he beheld a youth of marvellous beauty, alone on a neighbouring hill. To swoop down, catch him up in his mighty talons, and bear him safely off to Olympus, was but a moment's work; and there the kidnapped youth Ganymede, the son of a king of Troy, was carefully instructed in the duties he was called upon to perform in the future.

> " And godlike Ganymede, most beautiful
> Of men ; the gods beheld and caught him up
> To heaven, so beautiful was he, to pour
> The wine to Jove, and ever dwell with them."
>
> *Homer (Bryant's tr.).*

Philemon and Baucis

Solicitous for the welfare of mankind, Jupiter often visited the earth, taking great care to assume some disguise which would enable him to ascertain all he wished without any risk of detection. One day he and Mercury, his special messenger and favourite among the gods, took the forms of needy belated travellers, and entered the lowly hut of a worthy old couple, Philemon and Baucis.

Eager to offer their best to the strangers, these poor people decided to kill their sole remaining goose ; but their efforts to secure it were vain, and finally the persecuted fowl took refuge between Jupiter's knees. Touched with their zeal, yet anxious to prevent the death of the confiding goose, Jupiter revealed himself to his faithful worshippers, and in gratitude for their intended sacrifice bade them ask any boon, promising

by the great river Styx—the most binding and
solemn oath a god could utter—to grant their
request.

Contrary to the custom current in similar cases,
Philemon and Baucis made a modest and judicious
choice, and proffered a timid request that they might
serve the gods as long as life and strength endured,
and finally die together. This most reasonable wish
was immediately granted; and Jupiter, moreover,
changed their humble abode into a superb temple,
where they could offer daily sacrifices on his altars.

> " Their little shed, scarce large enough for two,
> Seems, from the ground increased, in height and bulk to grow.
> A stately temple shoots within the skies,
> The crotches of their cot in columns rise ;
> The pavement polish'd marble they behold,
> The gates with sculpture grac'd, the spires and tiles of gold."
>
> *Ovid (Dryden's tr.).*

After many years of faithful service, when age had
made them long for death, Philemon and Baucis were
transformed into majestic oaks, which stood for many
a century in front of the temple, monuments of the
love and faith which had bound the pair through
life.

Although married to Juno, Jupiter often indulged in
love affairs with other goddesses, and even with mortal
maidens. The ancients themselves did not practise
polygamy, but their gods were supposed to be able to
indulge all their passions with impunity. As the
personification of the sky, Jupiter, therefore, consorted
at times with Juno (the Atmosphere), with Dione
(Moisture), with Themis (Justice), &c., without
incurring any reproach; for these marriages, in their
estimation, were all symbolical.

The Story of Europa

But Juno being of a jealous disposition, Jupiter was forced to conduct his courtships with great secrecy and circumspection, and therefore generally adopted the precaution of a disguise. To win Europa, the fair daughter of Agenor, for instance, he became a bull.

> " The gods themselves,
> Humbling their deities to love, have taken
> The shapes of beasts upon them. Jupiter
> Became a bull, and bellow'd."
>
> *Shakespeare.*

One day Europa was playing in her father's meadows with her three brothers, Cadmus, Phœnix, and Cilix, when she suddenly saw a white bull coming towards her ; not with fiery eyes and lowered horns, but gently, as if to express a mute request to be petted. The maiden, delighted, stroked the beast, and decked him with bright garlands of meadow-blossoms. Then, seeing him kneel, as if to invite her to mount, she lightly sprang upon his broad back, calling to her companions to follow her example ; but, before they could do as she wished, the bull had risen to his feet, and galloped off towards the sea with his fair burden on his back.

Instead of turning when he saw the foam-crested waves, he plunged into the midst of them, and in a few minutes disappeared from view, so rapidly did he swim away. To reassure the frightened girl, the bull now spoke in gentle accents, bidding her dismiss all fear, for he was the great Jupiter in disguise.

> " Take courage, gentle maid ! nor fear the tide :
> I, though near-seen a bull, am heavenly Jove :
> I change my shape at will."
>
> *Moschus (Elton's tr.).*

Pleased with the novelty of her situation, and flattered by the god's evident admiration, Europa ceased to struggle, wound her arms more closely round the bull's neck to prevent the waves from washing her off her perilous seat, and allowed herself to be carried away.

Jupiter finally deposited his fair burden upon the shores of a new land, to which he gallantly gave her name, Europe. He then resumed his wonted form, explained at length his reasons for so unceremoniously kidnapping her, and finally won her consent to their union. Their three sons were Minos, Rhadamanthus, and Sarpedon. The two former were subsequently appointed judges in the Infernal Regions, while the third found an early but glorious death during the Trojan war.

All unconscious of their sister's fate, the young princes had returned in haste to their father's palace to announce her sudden involuntary departure. Agenor, whose favourite she had always been, rent his garments in grief, and bade his sons go forth and seek her, and not to return till they had found her. Accompanied by their mother, Telephassa, they immediately set out on their journey, inquiring of all they met if they had seen their sister. Search and inquiry proved equally fruitless.

At last, weary of this hopeless quest, Phœnix refused his further aid, and allowed his sorrowing relatives to continue without him, remaining in a land which from him was called Phœnicia. Cilix, too, soon followed his example, and settled in a fertile country which they had reached, hence called Cilicia; and finally Telephassa, worn out with grief and fatigue, lay down to die, charging her eldest son to go on alone.

Cadmus wandered on till he came to Delphi, where

The Delphic Sibyl

Arachne

he consulted the oracle; but, to his great dismay, the only reply he received was, " Follow the cow, and settle where she rests."

In deep perplexity he left the temple, and, from force of habit, journeyed on, patiently questioning all he met. Soon he perceived a cow leisurely walking in front of him, and, mindful of the oracle, he ceased his search and followed her. Urged by curiosity, many adventurers joined him on the way, and, when the cow at last lay down in the land since called Bœotia, they all promised to aid Cadmus, their chosen leader, to found their future capital, which was to be called Thebes.

Parched with thirst after their long walk, the men then hastened to a neighbouring spring, but, to Cadmus' surprise, time passed and still they did not return. Armed with his trusty sword, he finally went down to the spring to discover the cause of their delay, and found that they had all been devoured by a huge dragon, which lived in the hollow. The prince raised his sword to avenge their death, and dealt the dragon such a deadly blow upon the head, that he put an immediate end to its existence.

While Cadmus stood there contemplating his lifeless foe, a voice bade him extract the dragon's teeth, and sow them in the ground already broken for his future city. No human being was within sight : so Cadmus knew the order proceeded from the immortal gods, and immediately prepared to obey it. The dragon's teeth were no sooner planted, than a crop of giants sprang from the soil, full grown, and armed to the teeth. They were about to fall upon Cadmus, when the same voice bade him cast a stone in the midst of their close-drawn phalanx. Cadmus, seeing the giants were almost upon him, and that no time was to be lost, quickly threw a stone. The effect produced was almost instantaneous; for the giants, each fancying it had been thrown by his neighbour, began fighting among themselves. In a few minutes the number of giants was reduced to five, who sheathed their bloodstained weapons, and humbly tendered their services to Cadmus. With their aid, the foundations of the city were laid; but their labour was not very arduous, as the gods caused some of the public buildings to rise up out of the ground, all complete, and ready for use.

To reward Cadmus for his loving and painstaking search for Europa, Jupiter gave him the hand of the fair princess Harmonia, a daughter of Mars and Venus, in marriage. Cadmus, the founder of Thebes, is supposed to have invented the alphabet, and introduced its use into Greece. Although his career was very prosperous at first, he finally incurred the wrath of the gods by forgetting, on a solemn occasion, to offer them a suitable sacrifice; and, in anger at this dereliction of duty, they changed him and Harmonia into huge serpents.

Jupiter was, of course, very widely and generally worshipped by the ancients; and his principal temples —the Capitol at Rome, and the shrine of Jupiter Ammon in Libya—were world-renowned. He also had a famous temple at Dodona, where an oak-tree gave forth mysterious prophecies, which were supposed to have been inspired by the king of gods; this long-lost shrine has recently been discovered.

> " Oh, where, Dodona ! is thine aged grove,
>   Prophetic fount, and oracle divine ?
> What valley echoed the response of Jove ?
> What trace remaineth of the Thunderer's shrine ?
> All, all forgotten ? "
>
> *Byron.*

A magnificent temple at Olympia, on the Peloponnesus, was also dedicated to Jupiter; and here every

fifth year the people of Greece were wont to assemble
to celebrate games, in honour of Jupiter's great victory
over the Titans. These festivals were known as the
Olympian Games; and the Greeks generally reckoned
time by olympiads, that is to say, by the space of
time between the celebrations. Within the temple at
Olympia stood a wonderful statue of gold and ivory,
the work of Phidias. Its proportions and beauty were
such, that it was counted one of the Seven Wonders
of the ancient world. It is said, too, that the artist,
having completed this masterpiece, longed for some
sign of approval from heaven, and fervently prayed for
a token that the god accepted his labour. Jupiter, in
answer to this prayer, sent a vivid flash of lightning,
which played about the colossal image, illuminating it,
but leaving it quite unharmed.

The Greeks were indebted to Phidias for many of
their most exquisite statues of the gods; but none of
the others equalled this figure of Jupiter in size, dignity
of attitude, or elaborate finish.

> " Wise Phidias, thus his skill to prove,
> Through many a god advanc'd to Jove,
> And taught the polish'd rocks to shine
> With airs and lineaments divine ;
> Till Greece, amaz'd, and half afraid,
> Th' assembled deities survey'd."
>
> *Addison.*

CHAPTER III : JUNO

The Consort of Jupiter

JUNO (Hera, Here), queen of heaven, and goddess of the atmosphere and of marriage, was the daughter of Cronus and Rhea, and consequently the sister of Jupiter ; but, as soon as the latter had dethroned his parents and seized the sceptre, he began to look about him for a suitable helpmate. Juno won his affections by her great beauty ; and he immediately began his courtship, which he carried on in the guise of a cuckoo, to infuse a little romance into it. He evidently found favour in her sight, and won her consent to share his throne ; for shortly afterward their wedding was celebrated with great pomp on Mount Olympus. It was on this solemn occasion that the immortal conclave of the gods declared that Juno should be henceforth honoured as goddess of marriage.

> " Juno, who presides
> Supreme o'er bridegrooms and o'er brides."
> *Virgil (Conington's tr.).*

But although in the beginning this union seemed very happy, there soon arose subjects for contention ; for unfortunately Jupiter was inclined to be faithless, and Juno jealous, and, like the element she personified, exceedingly variable in her moods. On such occasions she gave way to her violent temper, and bitterly reproached her husband, who, impatient of her censure, punished her severely, and, instead of reforming, merely continued his numerous intrigues with renewed zest.

Callisto and Arcas

On one occasion he fell deeply in love with a maiden named Callisto, gentle, fair, and slender ; but, in spite

36

of all the precautions which he took when visiting her, Juno discovered the object of his affections. Night and day she thought and planned, until she devised a species of revenge which seemed adequate. The graceful girl was suddenly bereft of speech, changed into a rough, ungainly bear, and driven out into the solitudes of the great forests, which were from that time forth to be her home. Jupiter vainly sought his absent mistress, and it was only long afterward that he discovered her and her little bear son Arcas. In pity for all they had suffered, he transferred them both to the sky, where they are still known as the constellations of the Great and Little Bear.

Juno, like her husband, had also her special attendant, Iris (the Rainbow), whom she frequently employed as messenger,—a task which this deity accomplished with as much celerity as Mercury. Her flight through the air was so rapid, that she was seldom seen ; and no one would have known she had passed, had it not been for the brilliant trail her many-coloured robe left behind her in the sky.

> " Like fiery clouds, that flush with ruddy glare,
>   Or Iris gliding through the purple air ;
>   When loosely girt her dazzling mantle flows,
>   And 'gainst the sun in arching colours glows."
>   *Flaccus (Elton's tr.).*

Juno is the mother of Mars, Hebe, and Vulcan, and is always described and represented as a beautiful, majestic woman, clad in flowing robes, with a diadem and sceptre. The peacock and cuckoo were both sacred to her, and are therefore often seen at her side.

Her principal places of worship were at Mycenæ, Sparta, Argos, Rome, and Heræum. She had also numerous other sanctuaries scattered throughout the ancient world, and was worshipped in the same temples as Jupiter. Many fine statues of this goddess were found in Greece and Italy, some of which are still extant, and serve to show the ancients' exalted conception of the Queen of Heaven.

Cleobis and Biton

Juno's festivals, the Matronalia, in Rome, were always celebrated with great pomp. Less important feasts were held in each city where a temple was dedicated to her. On one of these occasions an old priestess was very anxious to go to the temple at Argos, where she had ministered to the goddess for many years, and which she had left only to be married. The way was long and dusty : so the aged woman, who could no longer walk such a distance, bade her sons, Cleobis and Biton, harness her white heifers to her car. The youths hastened to do her bidding ; but, although they searched diligently, the heifers could not be found. Rather than disappoint their aged mother, who had set her heart upon attending the services, these kind-hearted sons harnessed themselves to the cart, and drew her through the city to the temple gates, amid the acclamations of all the people, who admired this trait of filial devotion.

The mother was so touched by her sons' affection, that, as she knelt before the altar, she fervently prayed Juno to bestow upon them the greatest boon in her power. At the conclusion of the services the ex-priestess went into the portico, where her sons had thrown themselves down to rest after their unwonted exertions; but instead of finding them merely asleep, as she expected, she found them dead. The Queen of Heaven had transported them while asleep to the Elysian Fields, the place of endless bliss, where such as they enjoyed eternal life.

CHAPTER IV : MINERVA

The Birth of Minerva

ALTHOUGH immortal, the gods were not exempt from physical pain. One day Jupiter suffered intensely from a sudden headache, and, in hopes that some mode of alleviation would be devised, he summoned all the gods to Olympus. Their united efforts were vain, however ; and even the remedies suggested by Apollo, god of medicine, proved inefficacious. Unwilling, or perchance unable, to endure the racking pain any longer, Jupiter bade one of his sons, Vulcan, cleave his head open with an axe. With cheerful alacrity the dutiful god obeyed ; and no sooner was the operation performed, than Minerva (Pallas, Athene) sprang out of her father's head, full-grown, clad in glittering armour, with poised spear, and chanting a triumphant song of victory.

> " From his awful head
> Whom Jove brought forth, in warlike armour drest,
> Golden, all radiant."
>
> *Shelley.*

The assembled gods recoiled in fear before this unexpected apparition, while at the same time a mighty commotion over land and sea proclaimed the advent of a great divinity.

The goddess, who had thus joined the inhabitants of Olympus, was destined to preside over peace, defensive war, and needlework, to be the incarnation of wisdom, and to put to flight the obscure deity called Dulness, who until then had ruled the world.

> " Ere Pallas issu'd from the Thund'rer's head,
> Dulness o'er all possess'd her ancient right,
> Daughter of Chaos and eternal Night."
>
> *Pope.*

39

Minerva, having forced her unattractive predecessor to beat an ignominious retreat, quickly seized the sceptre and immediately began to rule in her stead.

Not long after her birth, Cecrops, a Phœnician, came to Greece, where he founded a beautiful city in the province since called Attica. All the gods watched his undertaking with great interest; and finally, seeing the town promised to become a thriving place, each wished the privilege of naming it. A general council was held, and after some deliberation most of the goɑ. withdrew their claims. Soon none but Minerva and Neptune were left to contend for the coveted honour.

To settle the quarrel without evincing any partiality, Jupiter announced that the city would be entrusted to the protection of the deity who would create the most useful object for the use of man. Raising his trident, Neptune struck the ground, from which a noble horse sprang forth, amid the exclamations of wonder and admiration of all the spectators. His qualities were duly explained by his proud creator, and all thought it quite impossible for Minerva to surpass him. Loudly they laughed, and scornfully too, when she, in her turn, produced an olive tree; but when she had told them the manifold uses to which wood, fruit, foliage, twigs, &c., could be applied, and explained that the olive was the sign of peace and prosperity, and therefore far more desirable than the horse, the emblem of war and wretchedness, they could but acknowledge her gift the most serviceable, and award her the prize.

To commemorate this victory over her rival, Minerva, gave her own name of Athene to the city, whose inhabitants, from that time forth, were taught to honour her as their tutelary goddess.

Ever at Jupiter's side, Minerva often aided him by her wise counsels, and in times of war borrowed his

THE STORY OF ARACHNE

terrible shield, the Ægis, which she flung over her
shoulder when she sallied forth to give her support to
those whose cause was just.

> " Her shoulder bore
> The dreadful Ægis with its shaggy brim
> Bordered with Terror.   There was Strife, and there
> Was Fortitude, and there was fierce Pursuit,
> And there the Gorgon's head, a ghastly sight,
> Deformed and dreadful, and a sign of woe."
>
> *Homer (Bryant's tr.).*

The din of battle had no terrors for this doughty
goddess, and on every occasion she was wont to plunge
into the thickest of the fray with the utmost valour.

The Story of Arachne

These virile tastes were, however, fully counter-
balanced by some exclusively feminine, for Minerva
was as deft with her needle as with her sword.   In
Greece there lived in those olden times a maiden by
the name of Arachne.   Pretty, young, and winsome,
she would have been loved by all had it not been for
her inordinate pride, not in her personal advantages, but
in her skill as a needlewoman.

Arachne, in her conceit, fancied that no one could
equal the work done by her deft fingers, so she boasted
far and wide that she would not hesitate to match her
skill with Minerva's.   She made this remark so loudly
and so frequently, that the goddess finally was annoyed,
and left her seat in high Olympus to punish the maiden.
In the guise of an old crone, she entered Arachne's
house, seated herself, and began a conversation.   In a
few minutes the maiden had resumed her usual strain,
and renewed her rash boast.   Minerva gently advised
her to be more modest, lest she should incur the
wrath of the gods by her presumptuous words; but

41

Arachne was so blinded by her conceit, that she scorned the well-meant warning, saucily tossed her head, and declared she wished the goddess would hear her, and propose a contest, in which she would surely be able to prove the truth of her assertions. This insolent speech so incensed Minerva, that she cast aside her disguise and accepted the challenge.

Both set up their looms, and began to weave exquisite designs in tapestry : Minerva choosing as her subject her contest with Neptune ; and Arachne, the kidnapping of Europa. In silence the fair weavers worked, and their webs grew apace under their practised fingers. The assembled gods, the horse, the olive tree, seemed to live and move under Minerva's flashing shuttle.

> " Emongst these leaves she made a Butterflie,
> With excellent device and wondrous slight,
> Fluttring among the Olives wantonly,
> That seem'd to live, so like it was in sight :
> The velvet nap which on his wings doth lie,
> The silken downe with which his backe is dight,
> His broad outstretched hornes, his hayrie thies,
> His glorious colours, and his glistering eies."
>
> *Spenser.*

Arachne, in the meanwhile, was intent upon her swimming bull, against whose broad breast the waves splashed, and upon a half-laughing, half-frightened girl, who clung to the bull's horns, while the wind played with her flowing tresses and garments.

> " Sweet Europa's mantle blew unclasp'd,
> From off her shoulder backward borne :
> From one hand droop'd a crocus : one hand grasp'd
> The mild bull's golden horn."
>
> *Tennyson.*

The finishing touches all given, each turned to view her rival's work, and at the very first glance Arachne was forced to acknowledge her failure. To be thus

42

Varvakeion Statuette
Antique copy of the Athena of Phidias

Latona and Her Children

outstripped, after all her proud boasts, was humiliating indeed. Bitterly did Arachne now repent of her folly ; and in her despair she bound a rope about her neck, and hung herself. Minerva saw her discomfited rival was about to escape : so she quickly changed her dangling body into a spider, and condemned her to weave and spin without ceasing—a warning to all conceited mortals.

Minerva, the goddess of wisdom, was widely worshipped. Temples and altars without number were dedicated to her service, the most celebrated of all being the Parthenon at Athens. Naught but the ruins of this mighty pile now exist ; but they suffice to testify to the beauty of the edifice, which served, in turn, as temple, church, mosque, and finally as powder magazine.

> " Fair Parthenon ! yet still must Fancy weep
> For thee, thou work of nobler spirits flown.
> Bright, as of old, the sunbeams o'er thee sleep
> In all their beauty still—and thine is gone !
> Empires have sunk since thou wert first revered,
> And varying rites have sanctified thy shrine.
> The dust is round thee of the race that rear'd
> Thy walls ; and thou—their fate must soon be thine ! "
>
> *Hemans.*

Statues of Minerva—a beautiful, majestic woman, fully clothed and armed—were very numerous. The most celebrated of all, by the renowned Greek sculptor Phidias, measured full forty feet in height. Festivals were celebrated in honour of Minerva wherever her worship was held—some, the Greek Panathenæa, for instance, only every four years ; others, such as the Minervalia and Quinquatria, every year. At these festivals the Palladium, a statue of the goddess, said to have fallen from heaven, was carried in procession through the city, where the people hailed its appearance with joyful cries and songs of praise.

The Beautiful God

THE most glorious and beautiful among all the gods was Apollo (Phœbus, Sol, Helios, Cynthius, Pytheus), god of the sun, of medicine, music, poetry, and all fine arts.

> " Bright-hair'd Apollo !—thou who ever art
> A blessing to the world—whose mighty heart
> Forever pours out love, and light, and life ;
> Thou, at whose glance, all things of earth are rife
> With happiness ; to whom, in early spring,
> Bright flowers raise up their heads, where'er they cling
> On the steep mountain side, or in the vale
> Are nestled calmly. Thou at whom the pale
> And weary earth looks up, when winter flees,
> With patient gaze : thou for whom wind-stripped trees
> Put on fresh leaves, and drink deep of the light
> That glitters in thine eye : thou in whose bright
> And hottest rays the eagle fills his eye
> With quenchless fire, and far, far up on high
> Screams out his joy to thee, by all the names
> That thou dost bear—whether thy godhead claims
> Phœbus or Sol, or golden-hair'd Apollo,
> Cynthian or Pythian, if thou dost follow
> The fleeing night, oh, hear
> Our hymn to thee, and willingly draw near ! "

Pike.

The Story of Latona

Apollo was the son of Jupiter and Latona, or Leto, the goddess of dark nights. Juno's jealousy had been aroused by Jupiter's preference for her rival. To avenge herself, she banished Latona to earth, and declared that if any one, mortal or immortal, showed her any pity or gave her any assistance, he would incur her lasting resentment.

After long, painful wanderings on earth, poor Latona, weary and parched with thirst, drew near to a small pool

44

by the wayside to refresh herself; but, urged by Juno, some reapers bade her pass on, and then, seeing she paid no heed to their commands, they sprang into the shallow waters, and stirred up the mud at the bottom until it was quite unpalatable. With tear-dimmed eyes, Latona prayed these cruel men might never leave the spot whereon they now stood; and Jupiter, in answer to her prayer, immediately transformed them into huge green frogs, which creatures have since then showed great preference for muddy pools.

Driven on once more by Juno's unrelenting hatred, Latona finally came to the seashore, where she stretched out imploring hands to Neptune, who sent a dolphin to bear her in safety to the floating island of Delos, raised in her behalf from the depths of the sea. The rocking motion, however, proving disagreeable to the goddess, Neptune chained the island fast in the Ægean Sea; and there in that delightful climate, justly praised by poets, were born to Jupiter and Latona twin children, Apollo and Diana, the divinities of the sun and moon.

The Story of Coronis

Apollo, having attained manhood, could not avoid the usual lot of the gods, as well as of mortal men— the pangs of love. They were first inspired by Coronis, a fair maiden, who kindled within his breast an ardent flame. The sun-god wooed the girl warmly and persistently, and at length had the deep satisfaction of seeing his affections returned. His bliss, however, proved but fleeting; for Coronis, reasoning that if one lover were so delightful, two would be doubly so, secretly encouraged another suitor.

> " Flirted with another lover
> (So at least the story goes)
> And was wont to meet him slyly,
> Underneath the blushing rose."—*Saxe.*

Although so cleverly managed, these trysts could not escape the bright eyes of Apollo's favourite bird, the snowy raven,—for such was his hue in those early times,—so *he* flew off in haste to his master to report the discovery he had made. Desperate with love and jealousy, Apollo did not hesitate, but, seizing his bow and deadly arrows, shot Coronis through the heart.

The deed was no sooner accomplished, than all his love returned with tenfold power ; and, hastening to Coronis' side, he vainly tried all his remedies to recall her to life.

> " The god of Physic
> Had no antidote ; alack !
> He who took her off so deftly
> Couldn't bring the maiden back ! "
>
> *Saxe.*

Bending over the lifeless body of his beloved one, he bewailed his fatal haste, and cursed the bird which had brought him the unwelcome tidings of her faithlessness.

> " Then he turned upon the Raven,
> ' Wanton babbler ! see thy fate !
> Messenger of mine no longer,
> Go to Hades with thy prate !
>
> " ' Weary Pluto with thy tattle !
> Hither, monster, come not back ;
> And—to match thy disposition—
> Henceforth be thy plumage black ! ' "
>
> *Saxe.*

The only reminder of this unfortunate episode was a young son of Apollo and Coronis, Æsculapius (Asklepios), who was carefully instructed by Apollo in the healing art. The disciple's talent was so great, that he soon rivalled his master, and even, it is said, recalled the dead to life. Of course, these miracles did not long remain concealed from Jupiter's all-seeing eye ;

Apollo Citharædus

Apollo and Daphne

ADMETUS AND ALCESTIS

and he, fearing lest the people would forget him and worship their physician, seized one of his thunderbolts, hurled it at the clever youth, and thus brought to an untimely end his brilliant medical career.

> "Then Jove, incensed that man should rise
> From darkness to the upper skies,
> The leech that wrought such healing hurled
> With lightning down to Pluto's world."
>> *Virgil (Conington's tr.).*

Æsculapius' race was not entirely extinct, however, for he left two sons—Machaon and Podalirius, who inherited his medical skill—and a daughter, Hygeia, who watched over the health of man.

Admetus and Alcestis

Maddened with grief at the unexpected loss of his son, Apollo would fain have wreaked his vengeance upon the Cyclopes, the authors of the fatal thunderbolt ; but ere he could execute his purpose, Jupiter interfered, and, to punish him, banished him to earth, where he entered the service of Admetus, King of Thessaly. One consolation alone now remained to the exiled god,—his music. His dulcet tones soon won the admiration of his companions, and even that of the king, who listened to his songs with pleasure, and to reward him gave him the position of head shepherd.

> "Then King Admetus, one who had
> Pure taste by right divine,
> Decreed his singing not too bad
> To hear between the cups of wine :

> "And so, well pleased with being soothed
> Into a sweet half sleep,
> Three times his kingly beard he smoothed
> And made him viceroy o'er his sheep."
>> *Lowell.*

47

Time passed. Apollo, touched by his master's kindness, wished to bestow some favour in his turn, and asked the gods to grant Admetus eternal life. His request was complied with, but only on condition, that, when the time came which had previously been appointed for the good king's death, some one should be found willing to die in his stead. This divine decree was reported to Alcestis, Admetus' beautiful young wife, who in a passion of self-sacrifice offered herself as substitute, and cheerfully gave her life for her husband. But immortality was too dearly bought at such a price; and Admetus mourned until Hercules, pitying his grief, descended into Hades, and brought her back from the tomb.

> "Did not Hercules by force
> Wrest from the guardian Monster of the tomb
> Alcestis, a reanimated Corse,
> Given back to dwell on earth in vernal bloom?"
>
> *Wordsworth.*

Apollo, after endowing Admetus with immortality, left his service, and went to assist Neptune, who had also been banished to earth, to build the walls of Troy. Scorning to perform any menial tasks, the God of Music seated himself near by, and played such inspiring tunes that the stones moved into place of their own accord.

Then, his term of exile being ended, he returned to heaven, and there resumed his wonted duties. From his exalted position he often cast loving glances down upon men, whose life he had shared for a short time, whose every privation he had endured; and, in answer to their prayers, he graciously extended his protection over them, and delivered them from misfortunes too numerous to mention. Among other deeds done for men was the slaying of the monster serpent Python, born from the slime and stagnant waters which remained upon the surface of the earth after the Deluge. None had dared approach the monster; but Apollo fearlessly drew near, and slew him with his golden shafts The victory over the terrible Python won for Apollo the surname of Pytheus (the Slayer), by which appellation he was frequently invoked.

This annihilation of Python is, of course, nothing but an allegory, illustrating the sun's power to dry up marshes and stagnant pools, thus preventing the lurking fiend malaria from making further inroads.

Apollo has always been a favourite subject for painters and sculptors. The most beautiful statue of him is the Apollo Belvedere, which represents him at the moment of his conquest of the Python.

The Story of Hyacinthus

Although successful in war, Apollo was very unfortunate indeed in friendship. One day he came down to earth to enjoy the society of a youth of mortal birth, named Hyacinthus. To pass the time agreeably, the friends began a game of quoits, but had not played long, before Zephyrus, god of the south wind, passing by, saw them thus occupied. Jealous of Apollo, for he too loved Hyacinthus, Zephyrus blew Apollo's quoit aside so violently that it struck his playmate, and felled him to the ground. Vainly Apollo strove to check the stream of blood which flowed from the ghastly wound. Hyacinthus was already beyond aid, and in a few seconds breathed his last in his friend's arms. To keep some reminder of the departed, Apollo changed the fallen blood-drops into clusters of flowers, ever since called, from the youth's name, hyacinths; while Zephyrus, perceiving too late the fatal effect of his jealousy, hovered inconsolable over the sad spot, and

49

tenderly caressed the dainty flowers which had sprung from his friend's life-blood.

> " Zephyr penitent,
> Who now, ere Phœbus mounts the firmament,
> Fondles the flower."
>
> *Keats.*

The Story of Cyparissus

To divert his mind from the mournful fate of Hyacinthus, Apollo sought the company of Cyparissus, a clever young hunter; but this friendship was also doomed to a sad end, for Cyparissus, having accidentally killed Apollo's pet stag, grieved so sorely over this mischance, that he pined away and finally died. Apollo then changed his lifeless clay into a cypress tree, which he declared should henceforth be used to shade the graves of those who had been greatly beloved through life.

The Story of Daphne

Some time after this episode, Apollo encountered in the forest a beautiful nymph by the name of Daphne, daughter of the river god Peneus. Love at first sight was the immediate consequence on Apollo's part, and he longed to speak to the maid and win her affections. He first tried to approach her gently, so as not to frighten her; but, before he could reach her side, she fled, and he, forgetful of all else, pursued her flying footsteps. As he ran he called aloud to Daphne, entreating her to pause were it only for a moment, and promising to do her no harm.

> " Abate, fair fugitive, abate thy speed,
> Dismiss thy fears, and turn thy beauteous head ;
> With kind regard a panting lover view ;
> Less swiftly fly, less swiftly I'll pursue :
> Pathless, alas ! and rugged is the ground,
> Some stone may hurt thee, or some thorn may wound.

THE STORY OF DAPHNE

"You fly, alas! not knowing whom you fly;
No ill-bred swain, nor rustic clown, am I."

Prior.

The terrified girl paid no heed to promises or entreaties, but sped on until her strength began to fail, and she perceived, that, notwithstanding her utmost efforts, her pursuer was gaining upon her. Panting and trembling, she swerved aside, and rushed down to the edge of her father's stream, calling out loudly for his protection. No sooner had she reached the water's edge, than her feet seemed rooted to the ground. A rough bark rapidly enclosed her quivering limbs, while her trembling hands were filled with leaves. Her father had answered her prayer by changing her into a laurel tree.

Apollo, coming up just then with outstretched arms, clasped nothing but a rugged tree trunk. At first he could not realise that the fair maiden had vanished from his sight for ever; but, when the truth dawned upon him, he declared that from henceforth the laurel would be considered his favourite tree, and that prizes awarded to poets, musicians, &c.. should consist of a wreath of its glossy foliage.

"I espouse thee for my tree:
Be thou the prize of honour and renown;
The deathless poet, and the poem, crown;
Thou shalt the Roman festivals adorn,
And, after poets, be by victors worn."

Ovid (Dryden's tr.).

This story of Apollo and Daphne was an illustration of the effect produced by the sun (Apollo) upon the dew (Daphne). The sun is captivated by its beauty, and longs to view it more closely; the dew, afraid of its ardent lover, flies, and, when its fiery breath touches it, vanishes, leaving nothing but verdure in the self-same spot where but a moment before it sparkled in all its purity.

51

"Climbing Heaven's blue dome,
I walk over the mountains and the waves,
Leaving my robe upon the ocean foam;
My footsteps pave the clouds with fire; the caves
Are filled with my bright presence, and the air
Leaves the green earth to my embraces bare."

Shelley.

Cephalus and Procris

The ancients had many analogous stories, allegories of the sun and dew, amongst others the oft-quoted tale of Cephalus and Procris. Cephalus was a hunter, who fell in love with and married one of Diana's nymphs, Procris. She brought him as dowry a hunting dog, Lelaps, and a javelin warranted never to miss its mark. The newly-married pair were perfectly happy; but their content was viewed with great displeasure by Eos (Aurora), goddess of dawn, who had previously tried, but without success, to win Cephalus' affections, and who now resolved to put an end to the bliss she envied.

All day long Cephalus hunted in the forest, and, when the evening shadows began to fall, joined his loving wife in their cosy dwelling. Her marriage gifts proved invaluable, as Lelaps was swift of foot, and tireless in the chase. One day, to test his powers, the gods from Olympus watched him course a fox, a special creation of theirs; and so well were both animals matched in speed and endurance, that the chase bade fair to end only with the death of one or both of the participants. The gods, in their admiration for the fine run, declared the animals deserved to be remembered for ever, and changed them into statues, which retained all the spirited action of the living creatures.

In the warm season, when the sun became oppressive, Cephalus was wont to rest during the noon hour in some shady spot, and as he flung himself down upon the

Apollo and Daphne

Clytie

short grass he often called for a breeze, bidding it cool his heated brow.

> " A hunter once in that grove reclin'd,
>   To shun the noon's bright eye,
> And oft he woo'd the wandering wind,
>   To cool his brow with its sigh.
> While mute lay ev'n the wild bee's hum,
>   Nor breath could stir the aspen's hair,
> His song was still, ' Sweet air, oh come ! '
> While Echo answered, ' Come, sweet air ! ' "
>
> *Moore.*

Eos heard of this habit, and was fully aware that he merely addressed the passing wind ; nevertheless she sought Procris, and informed her that her husband was faithless, and paid court to a fair maid who daily met him at noonday in the forest solitudes. Procris, blinded by sudden jealousy, gave credit to the false story, and immediately resolved to follow her husband.

The morning had well-nigh passed, and the sun was darting its perpendicular rays upon the earth, when Cephalus came to his usual resort, near which Procris was concealed.

" Sweet air, oh come !" the hunter cried; and Procris, cut to the heart by what she considered an infallible proof of his infidelity, sank fainting to the ground. The rustle caused by her swoon attracted Cephalus' attention. Under the mistaken impression that some wild beast was lurking there ready to pounce upon him, he cast his unerring javelin into the very midst of the thicket, and pierced the faithful bosom of his wife. Her dying moan brought him with one bound to her side ; ere she breathed her last, an explanation was given and received ; and Procris died with the blissful conviction that her husband had not deserved her unjust suspicions, and that his heart was all her own.

There are, of course, many other versions of these

self-same myths; but one and all are intended to illustrate the same natural phenomena, and are subject to the same interpretation.

Apollo's principal duty was to drive the sun chariot. Day after day he rode across the azure sky, nor paused on his way till he reached the golden boat awaiting him at the end of his long day's journey, to bear him in safety back to his eastern palace.

> " Helios all day long his allotted labour pursues ;
> No rest to his passionate heart and his panting horses given,
> From the moment when roseate-fingered Eos kindles the dews
> And spurns the salt sea-floors, ascending silvery the heaven,
> Until from the hand of Eos Hesperos, trembling, receives
> His fragrant lamp, and faint in the twilight hangs it up."
> *Owen Meredith.*

The Story of Clytie

A fair young maiden, named Clytie, watched Apollo's daily journey with strange persistency ; and from the moment when he left his palace in the morning until he came to the far western sea in the evening, she followed his course with loving eyes, thought of the golden-haired god, and longed for his love.   But, in spite of all this fervour, she never won favour in Apollo's eyes, and languished until the gods, in pity, changed her into a sunflower.

Even in this altered guise Clytie could not forget the object of her love; and now, a fit emblem of constancy, she still follows with upturned face the glowing orb in its daily journey across the sky.

> " No, the heart that has truly lov'd never forgets,
> But as truly loves on to the close ;
> As the sunflower turns on her god when he sets
> The same look which she turn'd when he rose."
> *Moore.*

54

The Story of Marsyas

A young shepherd, lying in the cool grass one summer afternoon, became aware of a distant sound of music, so sweet, so thrilling, that he fairly held his breath to listen. These weird, delightful tones were produced by Minerva, who, seated by the banks of a small stream, was trying her skill on the flute. As she bent over the limpid waters, she suddenly beheld her puffed cheeks and distorted features, and impetuously threw the instrument into the water, vowing never to touch it again.

> " Hence, ye banes of beauty, hence !
> What ? shall I my charms disgrace
> By making such an odious face ? "
> *Melanippides.*

The sudden break in the entrancing music caused the youth, Marsyas, to start from his abstraction and look about him. He then perceived the rejected flute sailing gently down the stream past his feet. To seize the instrument and convey it to his lips was the work of an instant; and no sooner had he breathed into it than the magic strain was renewed. No recollection of his pastoral duties could avail to tear Marsyas away from his new-found treasure; and so rapidly did his skill increase, that he became insufferably conceited, and boasted he could rival Apollo, whom he actually challenged to a musical contest.

Intending to punish him for his presumption, Apollo, accompanied by the nine Muses, the patronesses of poetry and music, appeared before the musician and challenged him to make good his boastful words.

55

Marsyas was called upon first to exhibit his proficiency, and charmed all by his melodious strains.

> " So sweet that alone the south wind knew,
> By summer hid in green reeds' jointed cells
> To wait imprisoned for the south wind's spells,
> From out his reedy flute the player drew,
> And as the music clearer, louder grew,
> Wild creatures from their winter nooks and dells,
> Sweet furry things with eyes like starry wells,
> Crept wonderingly out ; they thought the south wind blew.
> With instant joyous trust, they flocked around
> His feet who such a sudden summer made,
> His eyes, more kind than men's, enthralled and bound
> Them there."

H. H.

The Muses bestowed much deserved praise, and then bade Apollo surpass his rival if he could. No second command was necessary. The god seized his golden lyre and poured forth impassioned strains. Before pronouncing their decision, the Muses resolved to give both musicians a second hearing, and again both strove ; but on this occasion Apollo joined the harmonious accents of his godlike voice to the tones of his instrument, causing all present, and the very Muses too, to hail him as conqueror.

> " And, when now the westering sun
> Touch'd the hills, the strife was done,
> And the attentive Muses said :
> 'Marsyas, thou art vanquished !'"

Matthew Arnold.

According to a previous arrangement—that the victor should have the privilege of flaying his opponent alive—Apollo bound Marsyas to a tree and slew him cruelly. When the mountain nymphs heard of their favourite's sad death, they began to weep and shed such torrents of tears that they formed a river, called Marsyas, in memory of the sweet musician.

56

Apollo and Midas

The mournful termination of this affair should have served as a warning to all rash mortals. Such was not the case, however; and shortly after Apollo found himself engaged in another musical contest with Pan, King Midas' favourite flute-player. Upon this occasion Midas himself retained the privilege of awarding the prize, and, blinded by partiality, gave it to Pan, in spite of the marked inferiority of his playing. Apollo was so incensed by this injustice, that he determined to show his opinion of the dishonest judge by causing generous-sized ass's ears to grow on either side of his head.

> "The god of wit, to show his grudge,
> Clapt asses' ears upon the judge;
> A goodly pair, erect and wide,
> Which he could neither gild nor hide."
>
> *Swift.*

Greatly dismayed by these new ornaments, Midas retreated into the privacy of his own apartment, and sent in hot haste for a barber, who, after having been sworn to secrecy, was admitted, and bidden to fashion a huge wig, which would hide the deformity from the eyes of the king's subjects. The barber acquitted himself deftly, and, before he was allowed to leave the palace, was again charged not to reveal the secret, under penalty of immediate death.

But a secret is difficult to keep; and this one, of the king's long ears, preyed upon the poor barber's spirits, so that, incapable of enduring silence longer, he sallied out into a field, dug a deep hole, and shouted down into the bosom of the earth,—

> "'King Midas wears
> (These eyes beheld them, these) such ass's ears!'"
>
> *Horace.*

57

Unspeakably relieved by this performance, the barber returned home. Time passed. Reeds grew over the hole, and, as they bent before the wind which rustled through their leaves, they were heard to murmur, "Midas, King Midas, has ass's ears!" and all who passed by caught the whisper, and noised it abroad, so that the secret became the general topic of all conversations.

Orpheus and Eurydice

As Apollo had frequent opportunities of meeting the Muses, it is not to be wondered at that he fell a victim to the charms of the fair Calliope, who, in her turn, loved him passionately, and even wrote verses in his honour. This being the state of her feelings, she readily consented to their union, and became the proud mother of Orpheus, who inherited his parents' musical and poetical gifts.

> "Orpheus with his lute made trees,
> And the mountain-tops, that freeze,
>   Bow themselves when he did sing:
> To his music plants and flowers
> Ever sprung; as sun and showers
>   There had made a lasting spring.
>
> "Everything that heard him play,
> Even the billows of the sea,
>   Hung their heads, and then lay by."
>
> *Shakespeare.*

This talent waxed greater as the years passed by, and became so remarkable, that the youth's fame was very widespread; and when he fell in love with Eurydice, he brought all his skill into play, and wooed her with voice and glance and with tender, passionate music. Eurydice was touched by his courtship, and ere long requited the love lavished upon her by conferring her hand upon Orpheus.

58

ORPHEUS AND EURYDICE

Shortly after their union, while walking alone in the fields, the bride encountered a youth named Aristæus, whose bold admiration proved so distasteful, that she fled from him as quickly as possible. In her haste she accidentally trod upon a venomous serpent lurking in the long grass, which immediately turned upon her, and bit her heel. A short period of agonised suffering ensued ; then Eurydice died, and her spirit was conducted down into the gloomy realms of Pluto, leaving Orpheus broken-hearted.

Plaintive, heartrending laments now replaced the joyous wedding strains ; but even the charms of music failed to make life endurable, and Orpheus wandered off to Olympus, where he so piteously implored Jupiter to restore his wife to his longing arms, that the great god's heart was moved to compassion. He gave him permission, therefore, to go down into the Infernal Regions to seek his wife, but warned him at the same time that the undertaking was perilous in the extreme.

Nothing daunted, Orpheus hastened to the entrance of Hades, and there saw the fierce three-headed dog, named Cerberus, who guarded the gate, and would allow no living being to enter, nor any spirit to pass out of Hades. As soon as this monster saw Orpheus, he began to growl and bark savagely, to frighten him away ; but Orpheus merely paused, and began to play such melting chords, that Cerberus' rage was appeased, and he finally allowed him to pass into Pluto's dark kingdom.

The magic sounds penetrated even into the remote depths of Tartarus, where the condemned shades suspended their toil for a moment, and hushed their sighs and groans to listen. Even Tantalus suspended his eternal effort to quaff the ever-receding stream, and

Ixion's wheel stayed for a moment in its ceaseless course.

> "Poor Sisyphus, doomed to tumble and toss
> The notable stone that gathers no moss,
> Let go his burden, and turned to hear
> The charming sounds that ravished his ear."
>
> *Saxe.*

No living being had ever before penetrated thus into the Infernal Regions, and Orpheus wandered on until he came to the throne of Pluto, king of these realms, whereon the stern ruler sat in silence, his wife Proserpina beside him, and the relentless Fates at his feet.

Orpheus made known his errand, and succeeded in moving the royal pair to tears, whereupon they graciously consented to restore Eurydice to life and to her fond husband's care.

> "Hell consented
> To hear the Poet's prayer:
> Stern Proserpine relented,
> And gave him back the fair.
> Thus song could prevail
> O'er death and o'er hell,
> A conquest how hard and how glorious!
> Tho' fate had fast bound her
> With Styx nine times round her,
> Yet music and love were victorious."
>
> *Pope.*

But one condition was imposed before he was allowed to depart; that is, that he should leave the Infernal Regions without turning once to look into his beloved wife's face.

Orpheus accepted the condition joyfully, and wended his way out of Hades, looking neither to the right nor to the left, but straight before him; and as he walked he wondered whether Eurydice were changed by her sojourn in these rayless depths. Forgetful of the condition imposed by Pluto, his longing to feast his eyes

Orpheus

The Farnese Bull

once more upon her loved features induced him to turn just before he reached the earth ; and as he did so the form of the wife he had so nearly snatched from the grave vanished from before his affrighted eyes.

> " No word of plaint even in that second Death
> Against her lord she uttered,—how could Love
> Too anxious be upbraided ?—but one last
> And sad ' Farewell ! ' scarce audible, she sighed,
> And vanisht to the Ghosts that late she left."
>
> *Ovid (H. King's tr.).*

All was now over. He had tried and failed. No hope remained. In despair, the lonely musician retreated to the forest solitudes, and there played his mournful laments,—

> " Such strains as would have won the ear
> Of Pluto, to have quite set free
> His half-regained Eurydice."
>
> *Milton.*

But there were none to hear except the trees, winds, and wild beasts in the forest, who strove in their dumb way to comfort him as he moved restlessly about, seeking a solace for his bursting heart. At times it seemed to his half-delirious fancy that he could discern Eurydice wandering about in the dim distance, with the self-same mournful expression of which he had caught a mere glimpse as she drifted reluctantly back into the dark shadows of Hades.

> " At that elm-vista's end I trace
> Dimly thy sad leave-taking face,
> Eurydice ! Eurydice !
> The tremulous leaves repeat to me
> Eurydice ! Eurydice ! "
>
> *Lowell.*

At last there dawned a day when some Bacchantes overtook him in the forest, and bade him play some gay music, so they might indulge in a dance. But poor

Orpheus, dazed with grief, could not comply with their demands; and the sad notes which alone he now could draw from his instrument so enraged the merrymakers, that they tore him limb from limb, and cast his mangled remains into the Hebrus River.

As the poet-musician's head floated down the stream, the pallid lips still murmured, " Eurydice ! " for even in death he could not forget his wife; and, as his spirit drifted on to join her, he incessantly called upon her name until the brooks, trees, and fountains he had loved so well caught up the longing cry, and repeated it again and again.

Nothing was now left to remind mortals of the sweet singer who had thus perished, except his lute, which the gods placed in the heavens as a bright constellation, Lyra, also called by Orpheus' name.

The Story of Amphion

Another musician celebrated in mythological annals is Amphion, whose skill was reported to be but little inferior to Orpheus'.

> " 'Tis said he had a tuneful tongue,
>   Such happy intonation,
> Wherever he sat down and sung
>   He left a small plantation ;
> Wherever in a lonely grove
>   He set up his forlorn pipes,
> The gouty oak began to move,
>   And flounder into hornpipes."
>
> *Tennyson*

This musician, a son of Jupiter and Antiope, had a twin brother Zethus, who, however, shared none of his artistic tastes. Hearing that their mother Antiope had been repudiated by her second husband, Lycus, so that he might marry another wife by the name of Dirce, these youths hastened off to Thebes, where they found the state of affairs even worse than represented; for poor Antiope was now imprisoned, and subject daily to her rival's cruel treatment.

Zethus and Amphion, after besieging and taking the city, put Lycus to death, and, binding Dirce to the tail of a wild bull, let him loose to drag her over briars and stones until she perished. This punishment inflicted upon Dirce is the subject of the famous group once belonging to the Farnese family, and now called by their name.

Amphion's musical talent was of great use to him when he subsequently became King of Thebes, and wished to fortify his capital by building a huge rampart all around it; for the stones moved in rhythmic time, and, of their own volition, marched into their places.

The Story of Arion

Next to him in musical fame was Arion, the musician who won untold wealth by his talent. On one occasion, having gone to Sicily to take part in a musical contest which had attracted thither the most famous musicians from all points of the compass, he resolved to return home by sea.

Unfortunately for him, the vessel upon which he had embarked was manned by an avaricious, piratical crew, who, having heard of his treasures, resolved to murder him to obtain possession of them. He was allowed but scant time to prepare for death; but, just as they were about to toss him overboard, he craved permission to play for the last time. The pirates consented. His clear notes floated over the sea, and allured a school of dolphins, which came and played about the ship. The pirates, terrified by the power of his music, and in dread lest their hearts should be moved, quickly laid hands upon him, and hurled him into the water, where he fell upon the broad back of a dolphin, who bore him in safety to the nearest shore.

> "Then was there heard a most celestiall sound
> Of dainty musicke, which did next ensew
> Before the spouse : that was Arion crownd ;
> Who, playing on his harpe, unto him drew
> The eares and hearts of all that goodly crew,
> That even yet the Dolphin, which him bore
> Through the Agean seas from Pirates vew,
> Stood still by him astonisht at his lore,
> And all the raging seas for joy forgot to rore."
>
> *Spenser.*

To commemorate this miracle, the gods placed Arion's harp, together with the dolphin, in the heavens, where they form a constellation.

The Story of Phaeton

In the sunny plains of Greece there once dwelt Clymene, a fair nymph. She was not alone, however, for her golden-haired little son Phaeton was there to gladden her heart with all his childish graces.

Early in the morning, when the sun's bright orb first appeared above the horizon, Clymene would point it out to her boy, and tell him that his father, Apollo, was setting out for his daily drive. Clymene so often entertained her child with stories of his father's beauty and power, that at last Phaeton became conceited, and acquired a habit of boasting rather loudly of his divine parentage. His playmates, after a time, wearied of his arrogance, and, to avoid the constant repetition of his vain speeches, bade him show some proof of his divine origin, or keep his peace.

Stung to the quick by some insolent taunts which they added, Phaeton hastened to his mother, and begged her to direct him to his father, that he might obtain

the desired proof. Clymene immediately gave him all
necessary information, and bade him make haste if he
would reach his father's palace in the far east before the
sun chariot passed out of its portals to accomplish its
daily round. Directly eastward Phaeton journeyed, nor
paused to rest until he came in view of the golden and
jewelled pinnacles and turrets of his father's abode.

> " The sun's bright palace, on high columns rais'd
> With burnish'd gold and flaming jewels blaz'd,
> The folding gates diffus'd a silver light,
> And with a milder gleam refresh'd the sight."
>
> *Addison.*

Quite undazzled by this splendour, the youth still
pressed on, straining his eyes to catch the first glimpse
of the godly father, whose stately bearing and radiant
air his mother had so enthusiastically described.

Apollo, from his golden throne, had watched the
boy's approach, and, as he drew nearer, recognised him
as his own offspring. Timidly now Phaeton advanced
to the steps of his father's throne, and humbly waited
for permission to make his errand known. Apollo
addressed him graciously, called him his son, and bade
him speak without fear. In a few minutes the youth
impetuously poured out the whole story, and watched
with pleasure the frown which gathered on Apollo's
brow when he repeated his companions' taunts. As
soon as he had finished his tale, Apollo exclaimed that
he would grant him any proof he wished, and confirmed
these words by a solemn oath.

> " ' By the terrible Styx ! ' said the angry sire,
> While his eyes flashed volumes of fury and fire,
> ' To prove your reviler an infamous liar,
> I swear I will grant you whate'er you desire ! ' "
>
> *Saxe.*

This oath was the most solemn any god could utter,

and in case of perjury he was obliged to drink the waters of this river, which would lull him into senseless stupidity for one whole year. During nine years following he was deprived of his office, banished from Olympus, and not allowed to taste of the life-giving nectar and ambrosia.

With a flash of triumph in his dark eyes, Phaeton, hearing this oath, begged permission to drive the sun chariot that very day, stating that all the world would be sure to notice his exalted position, and that none would ever dare doubt his veracity after such a signal mark of Apollo's favour.

When the god heard this presumptuous request, he started back in dismay, for he alone could control the four fiery steeds which drew the golden-wheeled sun-car. Patiently he then explained to Phaeton the great danger of such an undertaking, earnestly begging him to select some other, less fatal boon.

> " Choose out a gift from seas, or earth, or skies,
> For open to your wish all nature lies ;
> Only decline this one unequal task,
> For 'tis a mischief, not a gift, you ask."
>
> *Addison.*

But Phaeton, who, like many another conceited youth, fancied he knew better than his sire, would not give heed to the kindly warning, and persisted in his request, until Apollo, who had sworn the irrevocable oath, was obliged to fulfil his promise.

The hour had already come when the Sun usually began his daily journey. The pawing, champing steeds were ready ; rosy-fingered Aurora only awaited her master's signal to fling wide the gates of morn ; and the Hours were ready to escort him as usual.

Apollo, yielding to pressure, quickly anointed his son with a cooling essence to preserve him from the

Aurora

Niobe

burning sunbeams, gave him the necessary directions for his journey, and repeatedly and anxiously cautioned him to watch his steeds with the utmost care, and to use the whip but sparingly, as they were inclined to be very restive.

The youth, who had listened impatiently to cautions and directions, then sprang into the seat, gathered up the reins, signalled to Aurora to fling the gates wide, and dashed out of the eastern palace with a flourish.

For an hour or two Phaeton bore in mind his father's principal injunctions, and all went well ; but at length, elated by his exalted position, he became very reckless, drove faster and faster, and soon lost his way. In finding it again he drove so close to the earth, that all the plants shrivelled up, the fountains and rivers were dried in their mossy beds, the smoke began to rise from the parched and blackened earth, and even the people of the land over which he was passing were burned black, —a hue retained by their descendants to this day.

Terrified at what he had done, Phaeton whipped up his steeds, and drove so far away, that all the vegetation which had survived the intense heat came to an untimely end on account of the sudden cold.

The cries of mortals rose in chorus, and their clamours became so loud and importunate, that they roused Jupiter from a profound sleep, and caused him to look around to discover their origin. One glance of his all-seeing eye sufficed to reveal the devastated earth and the youthful charioteer. How had a beardless youth dared to mount the sun chariot ? Jupiter could scarcely credit what he saw. In his anger he vowed he would make the rash mortal expiate his presumption by immediate death. He therefore selected the deadliest thunderbolt in his arsenal, aimed it with special care, and hurled it at Phaeton, whose burned and blackened

corpse fell from his lofty seat down into the limpid
waves of the Eridanus River.

> " And Phaethon, caught in mid career,
> And hurled from the Sun to utter sunlessness,
> Like a flame-bearded comet, with ghastliest hiss,
> Fell headlong in the amazed Eridanus,
> Monarch of streams, who on the Italian fields
> Let loose, and far beyond his flowery lips
> Foam-white, ran ruinous to the Adrian deep."
>
> *Worsley.*

The tidings of his death soon reached poor Clymene,
who mourned her only son, and refused to be comforted ; while the Heliades, Phaeton's sisters, three in
number,—Phaetusa, Lampetia, and Ægle,—spent their
days by the riverside, shedding tears, wringing their white
hands, and bewailing their loss, until the gods, in pity,
transformed them into poplar trees, and their tears into
amber, which substance was supposed by the ancients
to flow from the poplar trees like tear-drops.   Phaeton's
intimate friend, Cycnus, piously collected his charred
remains, and gave them an honourable burial.   In his
grief he continually haunted the scene of his friend's
death, and repeatedly plunged into the river, in the
hope of finding some more scattered fragments, until
the gods changed him into a swan ; which bird is ever
sailing mournfully about, and frequently plunging his
head into the water to continue his sad search.

The Nine Muses

Apollo, as the dearly loved leader of the nine Muses,
—daughters of Jupiter and Mnemosyne, goddess of
memory,—was surnamed Musagetes.

> " Whom all the Muses loved, not one alone ;—
> Into his hands they put the lyre of gold,
> And, crowned with sacred laurel at their fount,
> Placed him as Musagetes on their throne."
>
> *Longfellow.*

THE NINE MUSES

Although the Muses united at times in one grand song, they had each separate duties assigned them.

Clio, the Muse of history, recorded all great deeds and heroic actions, with the names of their authors, and was therefore generally represented with a laurel wreath and a book and stylus, to indicate her readiness to note all that happened to mortal men or immortal gods.

Euterpe, the graceful " Mistress of Song," was represented with a flute, and garlands of fragrant flowers.

Thalia, Muse of pastoral poetry, held a shepherd's crook and mask, and wore a crown of wild flowers.

> " Mild pastoral Muse !
> That, to the sparkling crown Urania wears,
> And to her sister Clio's laurel wreath,
> Preferr'st a garland culled from purple heath ! "
> *Wordsworth.*

Her graver sister, Melpomene, who presided over tragedy, wore a crown of gold, and wielded a dagger and a sceptre; while Terpsichore, the light-footed Muse of dancing, was represented treading an airy measure.

Erato, who preferred lyric poetry to all other styles of composition, was pictured with a lyre ; and Polyhymnia, Muse of rhetoric, held a sceptre to show that eloquence rules with resistless sway.

Calliope, Muse of heroic poetry, also wore a laurel crown ; and Urania, Muse of astronomy, held mathematical instruments, indicative of her love of the exact sciences.

This glorious sisterhood was wont to assemble on Mount Parnassus or on Mount Helicon, to hold their learned debates on poetry, science, and music.

The Story of Comatas

A certain goatherd, named Comatas, used to feed his goats on the slopes of Mount Helicon, and when the nights were warm would stay out all night with them. On one occasion he had thus seen the Muses dancing round the fountain of Hippocrene in the moonlight, and from that moment he was their willing slave.

Not far from this spot was a small altar devoted to the Muses, and Comatas one day took a kid and offered it as a sacrifice.

When his master discovered that one was missing from his flock, in a fit of passion he took the goatherd and fastened him in a great chest, intending that he should die of starvation. The Muses, however, would not suffer their servant to die thus miserably, and they sent some bees with honey, which they carried to him daily through a chink in the chest.

Months passed, and one day the chest was opened; but, instead of a heap of mouldering bones, there was Comatas, live and well! His lord, knowing that honey-bees were the special servants of the Muses, believed that the latter had taken Comatas under their special care, and thereafter treated him with the utmost kindness.

Aurora and Tithonus

Apollo's favourite attendant was Eos (Aurora), the fair goddess of dawn, whose rose-tipped fingers opened wide the eastern gates of pearl, and who then flashed across the sky to announce her master's coming.

> " Hail, gentle Dawn ! mild blushing goddess, hail !
> Rejoiced I see thy purple mantle spread
> O'er half the skies ; gems pave thy radiant way,
> And orient pearls from every shrub depend."
>
> *Somerville.*

This dainty goddess loved and married Tithonus,

Prince of Troy, and won from the gods the boon of everlasting life to confer upon him. Alas! however, she forgot to ask at the same time for continued youth; and her husband grew older and older, and finally became so decrepit, that he was a burden to her.

> " Immortal age beside immortal youth."
>
> *Tennyson.*

Knowing he would never die, and wishing to rid herself of his burdensome presence, she changed him into a grasshopper.

At this time the goddess fell in love with Cephalus, the young hunter, and frequently visited him on Mount Hymettus.

> " ' Come,' Phœbus cries, ' Aurora, come—too late
> Thou linger'st slumbering with thy wither'd mate
> Leave him, and to Hymettus' top repair !
> Thy darling Cephalus expects thee there ! '
> The goddess, with a blush, her love betrays,
> But mounts, and, driving rapidly, obeys."
>
> *Keats.*

The principal temples dedicated to the worship of Apollo were at Delos, his birthplace, and at Delphi, where a priestess called Pythia gave out mysterious oracles purporting to have come from the god. The ancients everywhere could not fail to recognise the sun's kindly influence and beneficent power, and were therefore ever ready to worship Apollo.

> " I marvel not, O sun ! that unto thee
> In adoration man should bow the knee,
>   And pour his prayers of mingled awe and love ,
> For like a God thou art, and on thy way
> Of glory sheddest with benignant ray,
>   Beauty, and life, and joyance from above."
>
> *Southey.*

The most renowned among the numerous festivals held in honour of Apollo were, without exception,

71

the Pythian Games, celebrated at Delphi every three years.

A manly, beardless youth of great beauty, Apollo is generally crowned with laurels, and bears either a bow or a lyre.

> " The Lord of the unerring bow,
> The God of life, and poesy, and light—
> The Sun in human limbs array'd, and brow
> All radiant from his triumph in the fight ;
> The shaft hath just been shot—the arrow bright
> With an immortal's vengeance ; in his eye
> And nostril beautiful disdain, and might
> And majesty, flash their full lightnings by,
> Developing in that one glance the Deity."
>
> *Byron.*

One of the Seven Wonders of the ancient world, the famous Colossus of Rhodes, was a statue of Apollo, his head encircled with a halo of bright sunbeams, and his legs spread wide apart to allow vessels, with all their sails spread, to pass in and out of the harbour, whose entrance he guarded for many a year.

CHAPTER VI : DIANA

The Goddess of the Chase

DIANA (Cynthia, Phœbe, Selene, Artemis), the fair twin sister of Apollo, was not only goddess of the moon, but also of the chase.

> " 'Goddess serene, transcending every star !
> Queen of the sky, whose beams are seen afar !
> By night heaven owns thy sway, by day the grove,
> When, as chaste Dian, here thou deign'st to rove.' "
>
> *Byron.*

In works of art this goddess is generally represented as a beautiful maiden, clad in a short hunting dress, armed with a bow, a quiver full of arrows at her side, and a crescent on her well-poised head.

> " Near the Delian olive-tree
> Latonia gave thy life to thee,
> That thou shouldst be for ever queen
> Of mountains and of forests green ;
> Of every deep glen's mystery ;
> Of all streams and their melody."
>
> *Catullus (R. C. Jebb's tr.).*

Proud of her two children, Apollo and Diana, Latona boasted far and wide that such as hers had never been, for they excelled all others in beauty, intelligence, and power.

The Story of Niobe

The daughter of Tantalus, Niobe, heard this boast, and laughed in scorn ; for she was the mother of fourteen children,—seven manly sons and seven beautiful daughters. In her pride she called aloud to Latona, and taunted her because her offspring numbered but two.

Shortly after, Niobe even went so far as to forbid her people to worship Apollo and Diana, and gave orders that all the statues representing them in her kingdom should be torn down from their pedestals and destroyed. Enraged at this insult, Latona called her children to her side, and bade them go forth and slay all her luckless rival's offspring.

Provided with well-stocked quivers, the twins set out to do her bidding; and Apollo, meeting the seven lads out hunting, cut their existence short with his unfailing arrows.

> " Phœbus slew the sons
> With arrows from his silver bow, incensed
> At Niobe."
>
> Homer (*Bryant's tr.*).

With all proverbial speed the tidings reached Niobe, whose heart failed when she heard that her seven sons, her pride and delight, had fallen under Apollo's shafts, and that they now lay cold and stiff in the forest, where they had eagerly hastened a few hours before, to follow the deer to its cover.

As she mourned their untimely death, she thought her cup of sorrow was full; but long ere her first passion of grief was over, Diana began to slay her daughters.

> " But what is this ?   What means this oozing flood ?
> Her daughters, too, are weltering in their blood :
> One clasps her mother's knees, one clings around
> Her neck, and one lies prostrate on the ground ;
> One seeks her breast ; one eyes the coming woe
> And shudders ; one in terror crouches low."
>
> *Meleager.*

In vain the poor girls sought to escape the flying arrows. In vain Niobe sought to protect them, and called upon all the gods of Olympus. Her daughters fell one by one, never to rise again. The last clung convulsively to her mother's breast; but, even in that fond mother's passionate embrace, death found and claimed her. Then the gods, touched by the sight of woe so intense, changed Niobe into stone, just as she stood, with upturned face, streaming eyes, and quivering lips.

> "One prayer remains
> For me to offer yet.
> Thy quiver holds
> More than nine arrows : bend thy bow ; aim here !
> I see, I see it glimmering through a cloud.
> Artemis, thou at length art merciful :
> My children will not hear the fatal twang ! "
>
> *W. S. Landor.*

The statue was placed on Mount Sipylus, close to a stream of running water; and it was said that tears continually flowed down the marble cheeks, for, though changed, Niobe still felt, and wept for her great loss.

This story is an allegory, in which Niobe, the mother, represents winter, hard, cold, and proud; until Apollo's deadly arrows, the sunbeams, slay her children, the winter months. Her tears are emblems of the natural thaw which comes in spring, when winter's pride has melted.

As soon as the young Goddess of the Moon had been introduced into Olympus, all the gods expressed a wish to marry her ; but she refused to listen to their entreaties, begged her father's permission to remain single all her life, and pleaded her cause so ably, that Jupiter was forced to grant her request.

Every evening, as soon as the Sun had finished his course, Diana mounted her moon car, and drove her milk-white steeds across the heavens, watched over and loved by the countless stars, which shone their brightest to cheer her on her way; and as she drove she often bent down to view the sleeping earth, so shadowy and dreamlike, and to breathe the intoxicating perfume of the distant flowers. It always seemed to her then as if

THE CLASSICAL MYTHS

Nature, so beautiful during the day, borrowed additional charms from the witching hours of the night.

> " 'Twas now the time when Phœbus yields to night,
> And rising Cynthia sheds her silver light,
> Wide o'er the world in solemn pomp she drew
> Her airy chariot hung with pearly dew."

The Story of Endymion

One evening, as she was driving noiselessly along, she suddenly checked her steeds ; for there on the hillside she saw a handsome young shepherd fast asleep, his upturned face illumined by the moon's soft light. Diana wonderingly gazed upon his beauty, and before long felt her heart beat with more than admiration. Gliding gently from her chariot, she floated to his side, bent slowly, and dropped an airy kiss upon his slightly parted lips.

The youth Endymion, only partially awakened by this demonstration, half raised his fringed lids, and for a moment his sleep-dimmed eyes rested wonderingly upon the beautiful vision. That one glance, although it drove Diana away in great haste, kindled in his heart an inextinguishable passion. He rose with a start, and rubbed his sleepy eyes; but when he saw the moon, which he fancied close beside him, sailing away across the deep blue sky, he felt sure the whole occurrence had been but a dream, but so sweet a dream that he cast himself down upon the sward, hoping to woo it to visit him once more.

It did not come again that night, however; but the next night, as he lay on the self-same spot, it recurred in all its sweetness ; and night after night it was repeated when the pale moonbeams fell athwart his sleeping face.

> " Then, as the full orb poised upon the peak,
> There came a lovely vision of a maid,
> Who seemed to step as from a golden car
> Out of the low-hung moon."—*Lewis Morris.*

Endymion

Diana of Versailles

Diana, fully as enamoured as he, could not bear to pass him by without a caress, and invariably left her car for a moment, as it touched the mountain peak, to run to him and snatch a hasty kiss.

> " Chaste Artemis, who guides the lunar car,
> The pale nocturnal vigils ever keeping,
> Sped through the silent space from star to star,
> And, blushing, stooped to kiss Endymion sleeping."
> *Boyesen.*

But, even when asleep, Endymion watched for her coming, and enjoyed the bliss of her presence ; yet a spell seemed to prevent his giving any sign of consciousness.

Time passed thus. Diana, who could not bear to think of the youth's beauty being marred by want, toil, and exposure, finally caused an eternal sleep to fall upon him, and bore him off to Mount Latmus, where she concealed him in a cave held sacred to her, and never profaned by human gaze. There each night the goddess paused to gaze enraptured upon his beloved countenance, and to press a soft kiss upon his unconscious lips. Such is the tale of Diana and her lowly lover, which has inspired poets of all ages.

> " Queen of the wide air ; thou most lovely queen
> Of all the brightness that mine eyes have seen !
> As thou exceedest all things in thy shrine,
> So every tale, does this sweet tale of thine."
> *Keats.*

The Story of Orion

Endymion was not, however, the only mortal loved by Diana, for it is also related that her affections were bestowed upon a young hunter by the name of Orion. All day long this youth scoured the forest, his faithful dog Sirius at his heels.

One day, in the dense shade of the forest, he met a

group of Diana's nymphs, the seven Pleiades, daughters of Atlas. These fair maidens needed but to be seen to be passionately loved, and Orion's heart burned as he sought to approach them ; but they were very coy, and, as he drew near and addressed them, turned and fled.

Afraid lest he should never see them again were he now to lose sight of them, he pursued them hotly ; but the nymphs sped on, until, their strength failing, they called upon their patroness's aid. Their prayer was no sooner heard than answered, and Orion, panting and weary, came up just in time to see seven snow-white pigeons wing their way up into the azure sky.

There a second transformation overtook the Pleiades, who were changed into a constellation, composed of seven bright stars, and there they shone undimmed for ages; but when Troy fell into the enemy's hands, all grew pale with grief, and one, more timid and impressionable than the rest, withdrew from sight to hide her anguish from the curious eyes of men.

> " And is there glory from the heavens departed ?—
>   O void unmark'd—thy sisters of the sky
>   Still hold their place on high,
> Though from its rank thine orb so long hath started,
>   Thou, that no more art seen of mortal eye ! "
>
> *Hemans.*

Orion, like a fickle youth, was soon consoled for their disappearance, and loved Merope, daughter of Œnopion, King of Chios, who consented to their union on condition that his future son-in-law should win his bride by some heroic deed. Now, as Orion was anything but a patient man, the delay was very unwelcome indeed, and he made up his mind to abduct his bride instead of marrying her openly ; but the plan was frustrated by Œnopion's watchfulness, and Orion was

78

punished by the loss not only of his bride, but also of his eyesight.

Blind, helpless, and alone, he now wandered from place to place, hoping to find some one capable of restoring his sight. At last he reached the Cyclopes' cave, and one of them took pity on him, and led him to the Sun, from whose radiance he borrowed a store of light,—

> " When, blinded by Œnopion,
> He sought the blacksmith at his forge,
> And, climbing up the mountain gorge,
> Fixed his blank eyes upon the sun."
>
> *Longfellow.*

Happy once more, he resumed his favourite sport, and hunted from morn till eve. Diana met him in the forest, and, sharing his tastes, soon learned to love him ; but this affection was viewed with great displeasure by Apollo, from whose piercing glance nothing that occurred by day could be hidden, and he resolved to put an end to his sister's infatuation. He therefore summoned her to his side. To divert her suspicions, he began to talk of archery, and, under the pretext of testing her skill as a markswoman, bade her shoot at a dark speck rising and falling far out at sea.

Diana seized. her bow, feathered her arrow, and sent it with such force and accurate aim, that she touched the point, and saw it vanish beneath the waves, little suspecting that the dark head of Orion, who was refreshing himself by a sea bath, was given her as a target. When she discovered her error, she mourned his loss with many tears, vowed never to forget him, and placed him and his faithful dog Sirius as constellations in the sky.

The Story of Actæon

When Diana had finished her nightly journey in her moon car, she seized her bow and arrows, and, attended by her nymphs, was wont to sally forth to hunt the wild beasts in the forest.

One summer afternoon, after an unusually long and exciting pursuit, Diana and her followers came to one of the still mountain pools where they had often resorted to enjoy a plunge. The cool waters rippled so invitingly, that the goddess and her attendants hastened to divest themselves of their short hunting garments, and lave their heated limbs.

But unfortunately the goddess and her attendant nymphs had not been the only hunters out that day. Actæon, the huntsman, had risen at dawn to stalk the deer; and now, weary and parched with thirst, he too sought the well-known mountain spring.

As he drew near the accustomed spot, Actæon fancied he heard bursts of silvery laughter: so he crept on very cautiously, and soon, gently parting the thick branches of the underbrush, beheld the sporting group.

At the self-same moment Diana turned to ascertain the cause of the rustle which had caught her practised ear, and met the admiring gaze of the astonished young hunter. Speechless with indignation that a mortal had beheld her thus, she caught some water in her hollow palm, flung it in his face, and bade him go and declare, if he could, that he had seen Diana disrobed.

The glittering drops had no sooner touched the young man's face than he turned to obey her command, and found himself transformed into a stag, with slender, sinewy limbs, furry skin, and wide-branching antlers. Nothing remained of his former self except the woeful consciousness of his transformation; and as he stood there, motionless and dismayed, the distant baying of his hounds coming to join him fell upon his ear.

An electric thrill of fear shot through every vein, as, mindful of his new form, he bounded away through the

Diana's Hunt

Cupid Asleep

forest. Alas! too late; for the pack had caught one glimpse of his sleek sides, and were after him in full cry.

In vain poor Actæon strained every muscle. His limbs refused their support, and, as he sank exhausted to the ground, the hounds sprang at his quivering throat and tore him to death as he lay.

Diana was widely worshipped, and temples without number were dedicated to her service; among others the world-renowned sanctuary of Ephesus. The ancients also celebrated many festivals in honour of this fair goddess of the moon, who was ever ready to extend her protection over all deserving mortals.

> " Queen and huntress, chaste and fair,
>   Now the Sun is laid to sleep ;
> Seated in thy silver chair,
>   State in wonted manner keep :
> Hesperus entreats thy light,
> Goddess excellently bright.
>
> " Earth, let not thy curious shade
>   Dare itself to interpose ;
> Cynthia's shining orb was made
>   Heaven to clear, when day did close ;
> Bless us then with wishèd sight,
> Goddess excellently bright.
>
> " Lay thy bow of pearl apart,
>   And thy crystal-shining quiver ;
> Give unto the flying hart
>   Space to breathe, how short soever :
> Thou that mak'st a day of night,
> Goddess excellently bright."
>
> *Ben Jonson.*

CHAPTER VII : VENUS

The Birth of Venus

VENUS (Dione, Aphrodite, Cytherea), the goddess of beauty, love, laughter, and marriage, is by some said to be the daughter of Jupiter and Dione, goddess of moisture: others report that she sprang from the foam of the sea.

> " Look, look, why shine
> Those floating bubbles with such light divine ?
> They break, and from their mist a lily form
> Rises from out the wave, in beauty warm.
> The wave is by the blue-veined feet scarce press'd,
> Her silky ringlets float about her breast,
> Veiling its fairy loveliness ; while her eye
> Is soft and deep as the blue heaven is high.
> The Beautiful is born ; and sea and earth
> May well revere the hour of that mysterious birth."
>
> *Shelley.*

The ocean nymphs were the first to discover her, cradled on a great blue wave; and they carried her down into their coral caves, where they tenderly nursed her, and taught her with the utmost care. Then, her education being completed, the sea nymphs judged it time to introduce her to the other gods, and, with that purpose in view, carried her up to the surface of the sea, —where Tritons, Oceanides, and Nereides all crowded around her, loudly expressing their ardent admiration, —and offered her pearls and choice bits of coral from the deep, as a tribute to her charms.

Then they pillowed her softly on a great wave, and entrusted her to the care of Zephyrus, the soft south wind, who blew a gentle breath, and wafted her to the Island of Cyprus.

The four beautiful Horæ (the Seasons), daughters

82

THE BIRTH OF VENUS

of Jupiter and Themis, goddess of justice, stood there on the shore to welcome her.

> " An ethereal band
> Are visible above : the Seasons four,—
> Green-kirtled Spring, flush Summer, golden store
> In Autumn's sickle, Winter frosty hoar."
>
> *Keats.*

And they were not alone to watch for her coming, for the three Charities (Graces, or Gratiæ) were also present.

> " 'These three on men all gracious gifts bestow,
> Which decke the body or adorne the mynde,
> To make them lovely or well-favoured show ;
> As comely carriage, entertainement kynde,
> Sweete semblaunt, friendly offices that bynde,
> And all the complements of curtesie :
> They teach us how to each degree and kynde
> We should our selves demeane, to low, to hie,
> To friends, to foes ; which skill men call Civility.' "
>
> *Spenser.*

Daughters of Jupiter and Eurynome, these maidens, who bore the respective names of Aglaia, Euphrosyne, and Thalia, longed to show their love for their new mistress. When the wave upon which she reclined came nearer still, the "rosy-bosomed Hours, fair Venus' train," appeared. The wind finally brought the fair goddess in safety to the shore ; and, as soon as her foot touched the white sand, all bent in homage to her surpassing beauty, and reverentially watched her dry her hair.

> " Idalian Aphrodite beautiful,
> Fresh as the foam, new-bathed in Paphian wells,
> With rosy slender fingers backward drew
> From her warm brows and bosom her deep hair
> Ambrosial, golden round her lucid throat
> And shoulder : from the violets her light foot
> Shone rosy-white, and o'er her rounded form
> Between the shadows of the vine bunches
> Floated the glowing sunlights, as she moved."
>
> *Tennyson.*

This hasty and somewhat primitive toilet completed, Venus and her followers set out for Mount Olympus, and on their way thither were joined by Himerus, god of the desire of love; Pothos, god of the amities of love; Suadela, god of the soft speech of love; and Hymen, god of marriage.

A throne had been prepared for the expected goddess, and, when she suddenly appeared to take possession of it, the assembled gods could not restrain a rapturous murmur of admiration. Her beauty took them by storm, and her grace won their hearts; but, although they one and all expressed a desire to marry her, Venus scornfully rejected their proposals. Even the king of gods was slighted, and, to punish her for her pride, he decreed she should marry Vulcan, god of the forge, the most ill-favoured of all the heavenly council.

This compulsory union was anything but a happy one; for Venus never showed any affection for her deformed consort, and, instead of being a faithful wife, soon deserted him, and openly declared she would please herself.

The Story of Alectryon

Her first fancy was for Mars, the handsome god of war, who was not slow in reciprocating the fair goddess's affections, and many and sweet were the secret interviews they enjoyed. Yet, fearful lest some of the gods passing by should discover them together, Mars always placed his attendant Alectryon on guard, bidding him give due warning of any one's approach, and especially to call him before the sun rose, as the lovers were particularly anxious that Apollo should not witness their parting caresses.

All prospered according to their desires, until one night the unfortunate Alectryon fell asleep; and so

profound were his slumbers, that he did not even stir
when Aurora flung open the gates of the east, and Apollo
flashed forth to receive the melodious greetings of the
feathered denizens of the forest.

The sun god drove rapidly on, glancing right and
left, and taking note of all he saw. Nothing escaped
his bright and piercing eye, as it flashed its beams hither
and thither, and he was soon aware of the sleeping
watchman and of the guilty lovers. As fast as his
fleet-footed steeds could carry him, Apollo hastened to
Vulcan, to whom he vividly described the sight which
had greeted his eyes.

The irate husband lost no time, but, seizing a net
of linked steel, went in search of his runaway wife.
Stealthily he approached the lovers' bower, and deftly
flung the net over both sleepers, who were caught in
its fine meshes, and could not escape ; and there he
kept them imprisoned, in spite of their entreaties, until
all the gods had seen their humiliating plight, and
turned them into ridicule. But when he at last set
them free, Mars darted away, vowing vengeance upon
the negligent sentinel, who was still blissfully sleeping.
Pouncing upon him, Mars awakened him roughly,
administered a sharp reproof, changed him into a cock,
banished him into the barnyard, and condemned him to
give daily warning of the sun's approach.

> " And, from out a neighbouring farmyard,
>   Loud the cock Alectryon crowed."
>
> *Longfellow.*

Several beautiful children were born to Mars and
Venus. Hermione, or Harmonia, their daughter,
married Cadmus, King of Thebes ; and Cupid (Cupido,
Eros, Amor), their little son, was appointed god of love.
Although nursed with tender solicitude, this second-

born child did not grow as other children do, but remained a small, rosy, chubby child, with gauzy wings and roguish, dimpled face. Alarmed for his health, Venus consulted Themis, who oracularly replied, "Love cannot grow without Passion."

In vain the goddess strove to catch the concealed meaning of this answer. It was only revealed to her when Anteros, god of passion, was born. When with his brother, Cupid grew and flourished, until he became a handsome, slender youth; but when separated from him, he invariably resumed his childish form and mischievous habits.

The Story of Adonis

Venus, however, did not lavish all her love upon Mars, for she is said to have felt a tender passion for a young man named Adonis, a bold young hunter, whose rash pursuit of dangerous game caused Venus many anxious alarms. In vain she besought him to forego the pleasures of the chase and remain with her. He laughingly escaped, and continued to join the other hunters in his favourite sport. But, alas, one day, after an exciting pursuit, he boldly attacked a wild boar, which, goaded to madness, turned upon him, buried his strong tusk in the youth's unprotected side, and trampled him to death.

" The white tusk of a boar has transpierced his white thigh.

.   .   .   .

" The youth lieth dead while his dogs howl around,
And the nymphs weep aloud from the mists of the hill."
Bion (Mrs. Browning's tr.).

Venus ran straight to the scene of his tragic death, rushing through underbrush and briars, tearing her delicate skin, and her blood tingeing all the white roses along her way with a faint pink. When she

Dying Adonis

Venus

arrived, she found her beloved Adonis cold in death, and her passionate caresses met with no response. Then she burst into such a passion of tears, that the wood and water nymphs, the gods, men, and all nature in fact, joined with her to mourn the beloved youth.

> " Her loss the Loves deplore :
> Woe, Venus, woe ! Adonis is no more."
> *Bion (Elton's tr.).*

Very reluctantly Mercury at last appeared to lead the soul of the departed down into the Infernal Regions, where it was welcomed by Proserpina, queen of the realm, and led to the place where pure and virtuous mortals enjoyed an eternity of bliss. Venus, still inconsolable, shed countless tears, which, as they dropped upon the ground, were changed to anemones, while the red drops which had fallen from Adonis' side were transformed into red roses.

> " As many drops as from Adonis bled,
> So many tears the sorrowing Venus shed :
> For every drop on earth a flower there grows :
> Anemones for tears ; for blood the rose."
> *Bion (Elton's tr.).*

As time did not soften Venus' grief, but, on the contrary, made it more and more unendurable, she went to Olympus, where she fell at Jupiter's feet, imploring him to release Adonis from death's embrace, or allow her to share his lot in Hades.

To allow Beauty to desert the earth was not possible, nor could he resist her pleading : so he finally decreed that Adonis should be restored to her longing arms. But Pluto, whose subject he had now become, refused to yield up Adonis ; and after much dispute a compromise was agreed upon, by virtue of which Adonis was allowed to spend one-half of the year on earth, providing he spent the remaining six months in the Elysian Fields.

In early spring, therefore, Adonis left the Lower World, and came with bounding tread to join his beloved. On his path the flowers bloomed and the birds sang, to show their joy at his coming. An emblem of vegetation, which rises from the ground in early spring to deck the earth with beautiful foliage and flowers, and cause the birds to sing for gladness, Adonis reluctantly returned to Hades, when Winter, the cruel boar, slew him again with his white tusk, and made nature again droop, and mourn his departure.

> " But even in death, so strong is Love,
> I could not wholly die ; and year by year,
> When the bright springtime comes, and the earth lives,
> Love opens these dread gates, and calls me forth
> Across the gulf."
>
> *Lewis Morris.*

Venus and Anchises

The Goddess of Beauty also loved Anchises, Prince of Troy, but, ashamed of lavishing favours upon a mere mortal, extorted from him a promise that he would never reveal their secret marriage. Unfortunately, however, Anchises was of a boastful disposition, and ere long yielded to temptation and revealed the secret, incurring her wrath to such an extent, that some mythologists accuse her of borrowing one of Jupiter's thunderbolts and slaying him. Others, however, report that Anchises lived to a ripe old age, and escaped from burning Troy on his son Æneas' back. Venus' love was, however, all transferred to her son Æneas, whom she signally protected throughout his checkered career.

Venus' most ardent admirers and faithful worshippers were the young people, for she delighted in their youthful sentiments, and was ever ready to lend a helping hand to all true lovers when apparently insurmountable obstacles appeared in their path.

Hero and Leander

This was the case with a lovely maiden by the name of Hero, who was dedicated by her parents to Venus' service, and, as soon as old enough, spent all her time in the temple, ministering to the goddess, or in a lonely tower by the sea, where she dwelt alone with her aged nurse.

> " Honey-sweet Hero, of a princely race,
> Was priestess to Queen Venus in that place ;
> And at her father's tower, by the sea set—
> Herself a Queen of Love, though maiden yet—
> Dwelt."
>
> *Edwin Arnold.*

The maiden's beauty increased with her years, until the fame of her loveliness spread throughout her native city Sestus, and even passed over the Hellespont and reached Abydus, where Leander, the bravest and handsomest youth of the town, was fired with a desire to view the charming young priestess.

Just at the time a solemn festival in honour of Venus was to be celebrated at Sestus, to which all the youths and maidens were cordially invited. Under pretext of paying homage to the goddess, Leander entered her temple, and saw the young priestess, whose charms far surpassed all descriptions.

Venus, as has already been stated, was always deeply interested in young lovers; and when she saw these two, so well matched in beauty and grace, she bade Cupid pierce them with his love darts, which behest the mischief-loving god immediately obeyed.

An undying passion was thus simultaneously kindled in both young hearts ; and, thanks to Venus' assistance, Leander managed to exchange a few words with Hero, declared his love, implored her to view his suit kindly, and, above all, to grant him an interview, or he would surely die.

> "God Eros, setting notch to string,
> Wounded two bosoms with one shaft-shooting,
> A maiden's and a youth's—Leander he,
> And lovely Hero, Sestos' sweetest, she;
> She of her town, and he of his, the boast;
> A noble pair!"

Edwin Arnold.

The maiden listened to his pleading with mingled joy and terror, for she knew her parents would never consent to their union Then, afraid lest one should notice that she was talking to a stranger, she bade him depart; but he refused to go until he had learned where she lived, and proposed to swim across the Hellespont when the shades of night had fallen, and none could see his goal, and pay her a visit in her lonely tower.

> "'Sweet! for thy love,' he cried, 'the sea I'd cleave,
> Though foam were fire, and waves with flame did heave;
> I fear not billows if they bear to thee;
> Nor tremble at the hissing of the sea."

Edwin Arnold.

At last his prayers overcame the maiden's scruples, and she arranged to receive him in her sea-girt tower, promising at a given hour to light a torch and hold it aloft to guide him safely across the sea. Then only he departed.

Night came on; darkness stole over the earth; and Leander impatiently paced the sandy shore, and watched for the promised signal, which no sooner appeared than he exultantly plunged into the dark waves, and parted them with lusty strokes, as he hastened across the deep to join his beloved. At times the huge billows towered above his head; but when he had escaped their threatening depths, and rose up on their foamy crests, he could catch a glimpse of the torch burning brightly, and pictured to himself the shy, sweet blushes which would dye Hero's cheek as he clasped her to his passionate heart.

> " Leander had no fear—he cleft the wave—
> What is the peril fond hearts will not brave !"
>
> *Landon.*

Venus, from the top of " many-peaked Olympus," smilingly viewed the success of her scheme, and nerved Leander's arm to cleave the rapid current. At last he reached the tower steps, and was lovingly greeted by Hero, whose heart had throbbed with anxiety at the thought of the perils her lover was braving for the sake of seeing her once more.

It was only when the dawn began to whiten the east that the lovers finished their interview and parted, he to return to Abydus, and she to prepare for the daily duties which would soon claim her attention But separation by day was all these fond lovers could endure, and night after night, as soon as the first stars appeared, Hero lighted her torch, and Leander hastened to her, to linger by her side till dawn.

> " Thus pass'd the summer shadows in delight :
> Leander came as surely as the night,
> And when the morning woke upon the sea,
> It saw him not, for back at home was he."
>
> *Leigh Hunt.*

No one suspected their meetings; and all went well until the first fierce storms of winter swept down over the Hellespont. Hero, in the grey dawn of a winter's morning, besought her lover not to leave her to battle against the waves, which beat so violently against the stone tower; but he gently laughed at her fears, and departed, promising to return at night as usual.

The storm, which had raged so fiercely already in the early morning, increased in violence as the day wore on, until the waves were lashed into foam, while the wind howled more and more ominously as the darkness came on again ; but none of these signs could deter Leander from visiting Hero.

> "There came one night, the wildest of the year,
> When the wind smote like edge of hissing spear,
> And the pale breakers thundered on the beach."
>
> *Edwin Arnold.*

All day long Hero had hoped that her lover would renounce his nightly journey; but still, when evening came, she lighted her torch to serve as beacon, should he risk all to keep his word. The wind blew so fiercely that the torch wavered and flickered, and nearly went out, although Hero protected its feeble flame by standing over it with outstretched robes.

At sight of the wonted signal, Leander, who had already once been beaten back by the waves, made a second attempt to cross the strait, calling upon the gods to lend him their aid. But this time his prayers were unheard, drowned in the fury of the storm ; yet he struggled on a while longer, with Hero's name on his lips.

At last, exhausted and ready to sink, he lifted his eyes once more to view the cheering light. It was gone, extinguished by a passing gust of wind. Like a stone Leander sank, once, twice, thrice, and the billows closed for ever over his head.

Hero in the meanwhile had relighted her torch, and, quite unconscious of the tragedy which had taken place, stood on the tower, straining her eyes to pierce the darkness. All night long she waited and watched for the lover who did not come; and, when the first sunbeams shone over the tossing sea, she cast an anxious glance over the waters to Abydus. No one was in sight as far as she could see. She was about to descend to pursue her daily tasks, when, glancing at the foot of the tower, she saw her lover's corpse heaving up and down on the waves.

> " As shaken on his restless pillow,
> His head heaves with the heaving billow ;
> That hand, whose motion is not life,
> Yet feebly seems to menace strife,
> Flung by the tossing tide on high,
> Then levell'd with the wave."
>
> *Byron.*

Hero's heart broke at this sad sight, and she longed to die, too, that she might not be parted from Leander. To hasten their meeting, she threw herself into the sea, and perished in the waves, close by his side. Thus lived and died the faithful lovers, whose attachment has passed into a proverb.

> " Come hither all sweet maidens soberly,
> Down looking aye, and with a chasten'd light,
> Hid in the fringes of your eyelids white,
> And meekly let your fair hands joinèd be,
> As if so gentle that ye could not see,
> Untouch'd, a victim of your beauty bright,
> Sinking away to his young spirit's night."
>
> *Keats.*

The poet Byron attempted and achieved Leander's feat of swimming across the Hellespont, and, on his return from that dangerous venture, wrote the following lines, which are so familiar to English-speaking people :

> " The winds are high on Helle's wave,
> As on that night of stormy water
> When Love, who sent, forgot to save
> The young, the beautiful, the brave,
> The lonely hope of Sestos' daughter.

93

Oh ! when alone along the sky
Her turret-torch was blazing high,
Though rising gale, and breaking foam,
And shrieking sea-birds warn'd him home »
And clouds aloft and tides below,
With signs and sounds, forbade to go,
He could not see, he would not hear,
Or sound or sign foreboding fear ;
His eye but saw that light of love,
The only star it hail'd above ;
His ear but rang with Hero's song,
' Ye waves, divide not lovers long ! '
That tale is old, but love anew
May nerve young hearts to prove as true."

Pyramus and Thisbe

Equally loving and unfortunate were Pyramus and Thisbe. Although no waves divided them, and they had the good fortune to occupy adjoining houses in Babylon, their parents having quarrelled, they were forbidden to see or speak to each other. This decree wrung their tender hearts ; and their continuous sighs finally touched Venus, who prepared to give them her aid. Thanks to this goddess's kind offices, a crack was discovered in the party wall, through which the lovers could peep at each other, converse, and even, it is said, exchange a kiss or two.

Sundry stolen interviews through this crack made them long for uninterrupted and unrestrained meetings; so they made an appointment to meet on a certain day and hour, under a white mulberry tree, just without the city gates.

Thisbe, anxious to see her lover, was the first to reach the trysting-place, and, as she slowly paced back and forth to while away the time of waiting, she wondered what had happened to delay Pyramus. Her meditation was suddenly broken by a rustling sound in some neighbouring bushes; and, thinking Pyramus was concealed there, she was about to call to him that he was discovered, when, instead of her lover, she saw a lion emerge from the thicket and come towards her, slowly lashing his sides with his tail, and licking his bloody jaws. With one terrified shriek the girl ran away, dropping her veil, which the lion caught in his bloody mouth and tore to shreds, before beating a retreat into the forest.

Shortly after, Pyramus came rushing up, out of breath, and full of loving excuses for Thisbe, who was not there, however, to receive them. Wondering at her absence, Pyramus looked around, and after a short investigation discerned the lion's footprints and the mangled veil. These signs sufficed to convince him that Thisbe had perished, and in a fit of despair he drew his dagger from its sheath and thrust it into his heart.

A few minutes later, Thisbe cautiously drew near, peering anxiously about to discover whether the lion were still lurking there. The first glance showed her Pyramus stretched dead beneath the mulberry tree, with her bloody veil pressed convulsively to his lips. With a cry of terror she flew to his side, and tried to revive him; but, when assured that all her efforts were in vain, she drew the dagger from his breast, and, plunging it into her own bosom, fell beside him lifeless.

> " In her bosom plunged the sword,
> All warm and reeking from its slaughtered lord."
> *Ovid (Eusden's tr.).*

Since that ominous day the fruit of the mulberry tree, which had been white, assumed a blood-like hue, dyed by the blood which flowed from the death wounds of Pyramus and Thisbe.

Echo and Narcissus

The lovely and talkative nymph Echo lived free from care and whole of heart until she met Narcissus, hunting in the forest. This frivolous girl no sooner beheld the youth, than she fell deeply in love with him, and was proportionately grieved when she saw that he did not return her affection.

All her blandishments were unavailing, and in her despair at his hard-heartedness, she implored Venus to punish him by making him suffer the pangs of unrequited love; then, melancholy and longing to die, she wandered off into the mountains, far from the haunts of her former companions, and there, brooding continually over her sorrow, pined away until there remained naught of her but her melodious voice.

The gods, displeased at her lack of proper pride, condemned her to haunt rocks and solitary places, and, as a warning to other impulsive maidens, to repeat the last sounds which fell upon her ear

> " But her voice is still living immortal,—
> The same you have frequently heard
> In your rambles in valleys and forests,
> Repeating your ultimate word."
>
> *Saxe.*

Venus alone had not forgotten poor Echo's last passionate prayer, and was biding her time to punish the disdainful Narcissus. One day, after a prolonged chase, he hurried to a lonely pool to slake his thirst.

> " In some delicious ramble, he had found
> A little space, with boughs all woven round;
> And in the midst of all, a clearer pool
> Than e'er reflected in its pleasant cool
> The blue sky here, and there, serenely peeping
> Through tendril wreaths fantastically creeping."
>
> *Keats.*

Echo and Narcissus

Pygmalion

Quickly he knelt upon the grass, and bent over the pellucid waters to take a draught; but he suddenly paused, surprised. Down near the pebbly bottom he saw a face so passing fair, that he immediately lost his heart, for he thought it belonged to some water nymph gazing up at him through the transparent flood.

With sudden passion he caught at the beautiful apparition; but, the moment his arms touched the water, the nymph vanished. Astonished and dismayed, he slowly withdrew to a short distance, and breathlessly awaited the nymph's return.

The agitated waters soon resumed their mirror-like smoothness; and Narcissus, approaching noiselessly on tiptoe, and cautiously peeping into the pool, became aware first of curly, tumbled locks, and then a pair of beautiful, watchful, anxious eyes. It seemed to him that the nymph was about to emerge from her hiding place to reconnoitre.

More prudent this time, the youth gradually bent further over the pool; and, reassured by his kindly glances, the nymph's whole head appeared. In gentle tones the youth now addressed her; and her ruby lips parted and moved as if she were answering, though not a sound came to his ear. In his excitement he began to gesticulate, whereupon two snowy arms repeated his every gesture; but when, encouraged by her loving glances and actions, he tried once more to clasp her in his arms, she vanished as rapidly as the first time.

Time and again the same pantomime was enacted, and time and again the nymph eluded his touch; but the enamoured youth could not tear himself away from the spot haunted by this sweet image, whose sensitive face reflected his every emotion, and who grew as pale and wan as he,—evidently, like him, a victim to love and despair.

97

Even the shades of night could not drive Narcissus away from his post, and, when the pale moonbeams illumined his retreat, he bent over the pool to ascertain whether she too were anxious and sleepless, and saw her gazing longingly up at him.

There Narcissus lingered day and night, without eating or drinking, until he died, little suspecting that the fancied nymph was but his own image reflected in the clear waters. Echo was avenged; but the gods of Olympus gazed compassionately down upon the beautiful corpse, and changed it into a flower bearing the youth's name, which has ever since flourished beside quiet pools, wherein its pale image is clearly reflected.

> " A lonely flower he spied,
> A meek and forlorn flower, with naught of pride,
> Drooping its beauty o'er the watery clearness,
> To woo its own sad image into nearness :
> Deaf to light Zephyrus it would not move ;
> But still would seem to droop, to pine, to love."
>
> *Keats.*

Pygmalion and Galatea

Pygmalion, King of Cyprus, was a very celebrated sculptor. All his leisure moments were spent in the faithful portrayal of the gods and goddesses, but one day he determined to fashion the image of a lovely woman. The statue became so beautiful under his practised hand that even before it was entirely finished its author loved it. When completed, Pygmalion gave it the name of Galatea, and, deeming it too beautiful to remain inanimate, he besought Venus to give it life, stating that he wished a wife just like it.

> " O Aphrodite, kind and fair,
> That what thou wilt canst give,
> Oh, listen to a sculptor's prayer,
> And bid mine image live ! "
>
> *Andrew Lang.*

CUPID AND PSYCHE

As Pygmalion had always been an obdurate bachelor, and had frequently declared he would never marry, Venus was delighted to see him at last a victim of the tender passion, and resolved to grant his request. A suitable opportunity soon arrived. One day as Pygmalion clasped the exquisite image to his breast some of his own warmth was infused into the icy bosom, and as he pressed kiss after kiss upon the chiselled lips they grew at last soft and warm to his touch, and a faint colour flushed the pale cheeks, while a breath dilated her lungs, and sent her blood coursing through her veins,—

> " As once with prayers in passion flowing,
> Pygmalion embraced the stone,
> Till, from the frozen marble glowing,
> The light of feeling o'er him shone."
>
> *Schiller.*

Pygmalion's delight at seeing his fair image a living and breathing maiden was unbounded, and after a short but passionate wooing the object of his affections became his happy wife.

Cupid and Psyche

In those same remote ages of "sweet mythology" there lived a king whose three daughters were world-renowned on account of their matchless beauty. Psyche, the youngest of the sisters, was so lovely that her father's subjects declared her worthy to be called the Goddess of Beauty, and offered to pay homage to her instead of to Venus. Offended by this proposal, which Psyche had good sense enough to refuse, Venus resolved to demonstrate forcibly to that benighted race that the maiden was mortal. She therefore bade her son Cupid slay her.

Armed with his bow and arrows, and provided with a deadly poison, Cupid set out to do her bidding, and

99

at nightfall reached the palace, crept noiselessly past the sleeping guards, along the deserted halls, and came to Psyche's apartment, into which he glided unseen. Stealthily he approached the couch upon which the fair maiden was sleeping, and bent over her to administer the poisoned dose.

A moonbeam falling athwart her face revealed her unequalled loveliness, and made Cupid start back in surprise; but, as he did so, one of his own love arrows came into contact with his rosy flesh, and inflicted a wound, from which he was to suffer for many a weary day.

All unconscious of the gravity of his hurt, he hung enraptured over the sleeping maiden, and let her fair image sink into his heart; then, noiselessly as he had entered, he stole out again, vowing he would never harm such innocence and beauty.

Morning dawned. Venus, who had expected to see the sun illumine her rival's corpse, saw her sporting as usual in the palace gardens, and realised that her first plan had completely failed. She therefore began to devise various torments of a petty kind, and persecuted the poor girl so remorselessly, that she fled from home with the firm intention of putting an end to the life she could no longer enjoy in peace.

To achieve this purpose, Psyche painfully toiled up a rugged mountain, and, creeping to the very edge of a great precipice, cast herself down, expecting to be dashed to pieces on the jagged rocks below; but Cupid who had indignantly though helplessly seen all his mother's persecutions, had followed Psyche unseen, and, when he perceived her intention to commit suicide, he called to Zephyrus (the South Wind), and entreated him to catch the maiden in his strong yet gentle arms, and bear her off to a distant isle.

Psyche and Zephyrus

Psyche

Consequently, instead of a swift, sharp fall and painful death, Psyche felt herself gently wafted over hill and dale, across sparkling waters; and, long before she wearied of this new mode of travel, she was gently laid on a flowery bank, in the midst of an exquisite garden.

Bewildered, she slowly rose to her feet, rubbed her pretty eyes to make sure she was not dreaming, and wonderingly strolled about the beautiful grounds. Ere long she came to an enchanted palace, whose portals opened wide to receive her, while gentle voices bade her enter, and invisible hands drew her over the threshold and waited upon her.

When night came, and darkness again covered the earth, Cupid appeared in search of his beloved Psyche. In the perfumed dusk he confessed his love, and tenderly begged for some return.

Now, although the fading light would not permit her to discern the form or features of her unknown lover, Psyche listened to his soft tones with unconcealed pleasure, and soon consented to their union. Cupid then entreated her to make no attempt to discover his name, or to catch a glimpse of his face, warning her that if she did so he would be forced to leave her, never to return.

> " ' Dear, I am with thee only while I keep
> My visage hidden; and if thou once shouldst see
> My face, I must forsake thee : the high gods
> Link Love with Faith, and he withdraws himself
> From the full gaze of Knowledge.' "
>
> *Lewis Morris.*

Psyche solemnly promised to respect her mysterious lover's wishes, and gave herself up entirely to the enjoyment of his company. All night long they talked; and when the first faint streak of light appeared above the horizon, Cupid bade Psyche farewell, promising to return with the welcome shades of night. All day long Psyche thought of him, longed for him, and, as soon as the sun had set, sped to the bower where the birds were sleepily trilling forth their evening song, and breathlessly waited until he came to join her.

> " Now on broad pinions from the realms above
> Descending Cupid seeks the Cyprian grove ;
> To his wide arms enamour'd Psyche springs,
> And clasps her lover with aurelian wings.
> A purple sash across his shoulder bends,
> And fringed with gold the quiver'd shafts suspends."
>
> *Darwin.*

Although the hours of day seemed interminable, spent as they were in complete solitude, Psyche found the hours of night all too short in the sweet society of Love. Her every wish was gratified almost as soon as expressed ; and at last, encouraged by her lover's evident anxiety to please her, she gave utterance to her longing to see and converse with her sisters once more. The ardent lover could not refuse to grant this request, yet Psyche noticed that his consent seemed somewhat hesitating and reluctant.

The next morning, while enjoying a solitary stroll, Psyche suddenly encountered her two sisters. After rapturous embraces and an incoherent volley of questions and answers, they settled down to enjoy a long talk. Psyche related her desperate attempt at suicide, her miraculous preservation from certain death, her aerial journey, her entrance into the enchanted palace, her love for her mysterious nightly visitor,—all, in short, that had happened since she had left her father's home.

Now, the elder sisters had always been jealous of Psyche's superior beauty ; and when they saw her luxurious surroundings, and heard her raptures about

102

her lover, they were envious, and resolved to mar the happiness which they could not enjoy. They therefore did all in their power to convince poor Psyche that her lover must be some monster, so hideous that he dare not brave the broad light of day, lest he should make her loathe him, and further added that, if she were not very careful, he would probably end by devouring her.

They thereupon advised poor troubled Psyche to conceal a lamp and dagger in her lover's apartment, and to gaze upon him in secret, when his eyes were closed in sleep. If the light of the lamp revealed, as they felt sure it would, the hideous countenance and distorted form of a monster, they bade her use the dagger to kill him. Then, satisfied with their work, the sisters departed, leaving Psyche alone to carry out their evil suggestions.

When safe at home once more, the sisters constantly brooded over the tale Psyche had poured into their ears, and, hoping to secure as luxurious a home and as fascinating a lover, they each hurried off in secret to the mountain gorge, cast themselves over the precipice, and—perished.

And now night was come, bringing Cupid, usually so welcome, and Psyche, tortured with doubt, could with difficulty conceal her agitation. After repeated efforts to charm her from her silent mood, Cupid fell asleep; and, as soon as his regular breathing proclaimed him lost in slumber, Psyche noiselessly lighted her lamp, seized her dagger, and, approaching the couch with great caution, bent over her sleeping lover. The lamp, which she held high above her head, cast its light full upon the face and form of a handsome youth.

Psyche's heart beat loudly with joy and pride as she beheld, instead of the monster, this graceful youth; and as she hung over him, enraptured, she forgot all caution. An inadvertent motion tipped her lamp, and one drop of burning oil, running over the narrow brim, fell upon Cupid's naked shoulder.

> "Now trembling, now distracted; bold,
> And now irresolute she seems;
> The blue lamp glimmers in her hold,
> And in her hand the dagger gleams.
> Prepared to strike, she verges near,
> Then, the blue light glimmering from above,
> The hideous sight expects with fear—
> And gazes on the god of Love."
>
> *Apollonius.*

The sudden pain made him open his eyes with a start. The lighted lamp, the glittering dagger, the trembling Psyche, told the whole story. Cupid sprang from the couch, seized his bow and arrows, and, with a last sorrowful, reproachful glance at Psyche, flew away through the open window, exclaiming,—

> "'Farewell! There is no Love except with Faith,
> And thine is dead! Farewell! I come no more!'"
>
> *Lewis Morris.*

When he had vanished into the dusky air without, the balmy night winds ceased to blow; and suddenly a tempest began to rage with such fury, that poor frightened Psyche dared not remain alone in the palace, but hastened out into the gardens, where she soon lost consciousness of her misery in a deep swoon. When she opened her eyes once more, the storm had ceased, the sun was high in the heavens, and palace and gardens had vanished.

Poor Psyche lingered there the following and many succeeding nights, vainly hoping for Cupid's return, and shedding many bitter tears of repentance. Finally she resolved once more to commit suicide, and, with that purpose in view, plunged into a neighbouring river; but the god of the stream caught and carried

Pan and Psyche

Cupid and Psyche

her ashore, where his daughters, the water nymphs, restored her to life. Thus forced to live, Psyche wandered about disconsolate, seeking Cupid, and questioning all she met, the nymphs, Pan, and Ceres, who compassionately listened to her confession of love for her husband.

Ceres had often seen Cupid, and had heard that very morning that he was having a wound in his shoulder dressed by Venus: so she advised Psyche to go to the Goddess of Beauty, to enter her service, and to perform every task with cheerful alacrity, knowing that such a course would ultimately bring about a meeting and reconciliation between the lovers.

Psyche gratefully accepted and followed Ceres' advice, and having succeeded in her endeavour to enter the service of Venus, she laboured early and late to satisfy her exacting mistress, who appointed such difficult tasks, that the poor girl would never have been able to accomplish them had she not been aided by all the beasts and insects, who loved her dearly.

Venus repeatedly tested her fidelity and endurance, and finally resolved, as a crucial experiment, to send her to Hades to fetch a box of ointment which had wonderful power to render beautiful whomsoever might be anointed with it, for which Proserpina alone had the recipe. Directed by Zephyrus, her old friend, Psyche encountered the terrors of Hades in safety, delivered her message, and in return received a small box. The gates of Hades were closed behind her, and she had nearly finished her last task, when she suddenly fancied that it would be wise to appropriate a little of the magic preparation to efface the traces of sleepless nights and many tears.

The box, however, contained naught but the spirit of Sleep, who, pouncing upon Psyche, laid her low by the roadside. Cupid, passing by, saw her there, marked the ravages of grief, remembered his love and her suffering, and, wrestling with the spirit, forced him to re-enter the narrow bounds of his prison, and woke Psyche with a loving kiss.

> "'Dear, unclose thine eyes.
> Thou mayst look on me now. I go no more,
> But am thine own for ever.'"
>
> *Lewis Morris.*

Then, hand in hand, they winged their flight to Olympus, entered the council hall, and there Cupid presented Psyche, his chosen bride, to the assembled deities, who all promised to be present at the nuptial ceremony. Venus even, forgetting all her former envy, welcomed the blushing bride, who was happy ever after.

The ancients, for whom Cupid was an emblem of the heart, considered Psyche the personification of the soul, and represented her with butterfly wings; that little insect being another symbol of the soul, which cannot die.

> "O latest born and loveliest vision far
>   Of all Olympus' faded hierarchy!
> Fairer than Phœbe's sapphire-region'd star,
>   Or Vesper, amorous glow-worm of the sky;
> Fairer than these, though temple thou hast none,
>   Nor altar heap'd with flowers;
> Nor virgin-choir to make delicious moan
>   Upon the midnight hours;
> No voice, no lute, no pipe, no incense sweet
>   From chain-swung censer teeming;
> No shrine, no grove, no oracle, no heat
>   Of pale-mouth'd prophet dreaming.
>
> "O brightest! though too late for antique vows,
>   Too, too late for the fond believing lyre,
> When holy were the haunted forest boughs,
>   Holy the air, the water, and the fire;

CUPID AND PSYCHE

Yet even in these days so far retir'd
   From happy pieties, thy lucent fans,
   Fluttering among the faint Olympians,
I see, and sing, by my own eyes inspired.
So let me be thy choir, and make a moan
     Upon the midnight hours;
Thy voice, thy lute, thy pipe, thy incense sweet
   From swingèd censer teeming;
Thy shrine, thy grove, thy oracle, thy heat
   Of pale-mouth'd prophet dreaming."

Keats.

One of the latest myths concerning Venus is that of
Berenice, who, fearing for her beloved husband's life,
implored the goddess to protect him in battle, vowing
to sacrifice her luxuriant hair if he returned home in
safety. The prayer was granted, and Berenice's beautiful locks laid upon Venus' shrine, whence they, however, very mysteriously disappeared. An astrologer,
consulted concerning the supposed theft, solemnly
pointed to a comet rapidly coming into view, and
declared that the gods had placed Berenice's hair
among the stars, there to shine for ever in memory of
her wifely sacrifice.

Venus, goddess of beauty, is represented either
entirely nude, or with some scanty drapery called a
" cestus." Seated in her chariot, formed of a single
pearl shell, and drawn by snow-white doves, her
favourite birds, she journeyed from shrine to shrine,
complacently admiring the lavish decorations of jewels
and flowers her worshippers provided. The offerings
of young lovers were ever those which found most
favour in her sight.

" Venus loves the whispers
   Of plighted youth and maid,
In April's ivory moonlight
   Beneath the chestnut shade."

Macaulay.

THE CLASSICAL MYTHS

Numerous ancient and some modern statues of this goddess grace the various art galleries, but among them all the most perfect is the world-renowned Venus de Milo.

Venus' festivals were always scenes of graceful amusements ; and her votaries wore wreaths of fresh, fragrant flowers, the emblem of all natural beauty.

CHAPTER VIII : MERCURY

The Childhood of Mercury

AS already repeatedly stated in the course of this work, Jupiter was never a strictly faithful spouse, and, in spite of his wife's remonstrances, could not refrain from indulging his caprice for every pretty face he met along his way. It is thus, therefore, that he yielded to the charms of Maia, goddess of the plains, and spent some blissful hours in her society. This divine couple's happiness culminated when they first beheld their little son, Mercury (Hermes, Psychopompus, Oneicopompus), who was born in a grotto on Mount Cyllene, in Arcadia,—

> " Mercury whom Maia bore,
> Sweet Maia, on Cyllene's hoary top."
> *Virgil (Cowper's tr.).*

This infant god was quite unlike mortal children, as will readily be perceived by the numerous pranks he played immediately after his birth. First he sprang from his mother's knee, grasped a tortoise shell lying on the ground, bored holes in its sides, stretched strings across its concavity, and, sweeping his hands over them, produced strains of sweetest music, thus inventing the first lyre.

> " There went
> Up from beneath his hand a tumult sweet
> Of mighty sounds, and from his lips he sent
> A strain of unpremeditated wit,
> Joyous and wild and wanton—such you may
> Hear among revellers on a holiday."
> *Shelley.*

Being very hungry towards evening, young Mercury escaped from his sleeping mother, and sallied out in search of food. He had not gone very far, before he came to a wide meadow, where Apollo's herds were at pasture. The oxen were fat and sleek ; and the mischievous little god, after satisfying himself that they were young, and therefore promised to be tender and juicy, drove fifty of them off to a secluded spot, taking good care to envelop their feet in leafy branches, so that they would leave no traces. Then, his hiding-place being reached in safety, Mercury coolly killed two of the oxen, which he proceeded to eat.

Apollo soon missed his cattle, and began to search for some clue to their hiding-place or to the thief. He could, however, discover nothing but some broken twigs and scattered leaves. Suddenly he remembered that the babe whose birth had been announced early that morning in high Olympus had been appointed god of thieves. He therefore lost no time in useless search and conjecture, but strode off to Mount Cyllene, where he found Mercury peacefully sleeping in his cradle. With a rude shake, the sun god roused him from his slumbers, and bade him restore the stolen cattle. Mercury pretended innocence, until Apollo, exasperated, dragged him off to Olympus, where he was convicted of the theft, and condemned to restore the stolen property. Mercury yielded to the decree, produced the remaining oxen, and, in exchange for the two missing, gave Apollo the lyre he had just fashioned.

This, like most other myths, admits of a natural explanation. Apollo (the Sun) was supposed by the ancients to possess great herds of cattle and sheep,—the clouds ; and Mercury, the personification of the wind, born in the night, after a few hours' existence waxes sufficiently strong to drive away the clouds and conceal them, leaving no trace of his passage except a few broken branches and scattered leaves.

The gift of the lyre pleased Apollo so well, that he in return wished to make a present to Mercury, and gave

Flying Mercury

The Forge of Vulcan

him a magic wand, called Caduceus, which had the power of reconciling all conflicting elements. Mercury, anxious to test it, thrust it between two quarrelling snakes, who immediately wound themselves in amity around it. This so pleased him, that he bade them remain there for ever, and used the wand on all occasions.

> " A snake-encircl'd wand ;
> By classic authors term'd Caduceus
> And highly fam'd for several uses."
>
> *Goldsmith.*

Mercury was in due time appointed messenger of the gods, who, to make him fleet of foot, presented him with winged sandals, the Talaria, which endowed him with marvellous rapidity of motion. As these sandals did not seem quite sufficient, however, the gods added the winged cap, Petasus, to the winged shoes.

> " Foot-feather'd Mercury appear'd sublime
> Beyond the tall tree tops ; and in less time
> Than shoots the slanted hail-storm, down he dropt
> Towards the ground ; but rested not, nor stopt
> One moment from his home ; only the sward
> He with his wand light touch'd, and heavenward
> Swifter than sight was gone."
>
> *Keats.*

Mercury was not only the messenger of the gods, but was also appointed god of eloquence, commerce, rain, wind, and the special patron of travellers, shepherds, cheats, and thieves.

The Story of Io

Jupiter often entrusted to Mercury messages of a delicate nature, and always found him an invaluable ally ; but the faithful messenger was never so much needed or so deeply appreciated as during Jupiter's courtship of Io, the peerless daughter of the river god Inachus.

To avoid Juno's recriminations, Jupiter had carried on this affair with even more than his usual secrecy visiting his beloved only when quite certain that his wife was asleep, and taking the further precaution of spreading a cloud over the spot where he generally met her, to shield her from all chance of being seen from Olympus.

One fine afternoon, all conditions being favourable, Jupiter hastened down to earth to see Io, and began to stroll with her up and down the river edge. They heeded not the noonday heat, for the cloud over their heads screened them from the sun's too ardent rays.

From some cause Juno's slumbers were less protracted than usual, and she soon arose from her couch to look about her realm, the atmosphere, and convince herself that all was well. Her attention was soon attracted by an opaque, immovable cloud near the earth,—a cloud which had no business there, for had she not bidden them all lie still on the blue sea until she awoke ? Her suspicions being aroused by the presence of this cloud, she sought her husband in Olympus, and, not finding him, flew down to earth, brushing the cloud aside in her haste.

Jupiter, thus warned of her coming, had but time to change the maiden beside him into a heifer, ere his wife alighted and inquired what he was doing there. Carelessly the god pointed to the heifer, and declared he had been whiling away the time by creating it ; but the explanation failed to satisfy Juno, who, seeing no other living creature near, suspected that her spouse had been engaged in a clandestine flirtation, and had screened its fair object from her wrath only by a sudden transformation.

Dissimulating these suspicions with care, Juno begged her husband to give her his new creation, which request he could not refuse, but granted most reluctantly, thus adding further confirmation to her jealous fears. The Queen of Heaven then departed, taking Io with her, and placed her under the surveillance of Argus, one of her servants, who possessed a myriad eyes, only one half of which he closed at a time.

> " The eyes of Argus, sentinel of Heaven :
> Those thousand eyes that watch alternate kept,
> Nor all o'er all his body waked or slept."
>
> *Statius (Elton's tr.).*

She bade him watch the heifer closely, and report anything unusual in its actions. One day, therefore, as he was watching his charge pasture by the river, Argus heard her relate to her father, Inachus, the story of her transformation, and immediately imparted his discovery to Juno, who, advising still closer watchfulness, sent him back to his post.

Mercury and Argus

Jupiter, in the meanwhile, was in despair; for days had passed without his being able to exchange a word with Io, or deliver her from her imprisonment. Finally he called Mercury to his aid, and bade him devise some plan to rescue her. Armed with a handful of poppies, Mercury approached Argus, and offered to while away the time by telling him tales.

As Mercury was the prince of story-tellers, this offer was not to be despised, and Argus joyfully accepted ; but, instead of exerting himself to be entertaining, Mercury droned out such lengthy, uninteresting stories, that Argus soon closed half his eyes in profound sleep Still talking in the same monotonous way, Mercury softly shook the poppies over the giant's head, until one by one the remaining eyelids closed, and Argus was wrapped in complete slumber.

Then Mercury seized the giant's sword, and with

one well-directed blow severed his head from the huge trunk. Only one half of the task was successfully accomplished : and while Mercury was driving the heifer away, Juno discovered his attempt, and promptly sent an enormous gadfly to torment the poor beast, who, goaded to madness by its cruel stings, fled wildly from one country to another, forded streams, and finally plunged into the sea, since called Ionian. After swimming across it, she took refuge in Egypt, where Jupiter restored her to all her girlish loveliness, and where her son Epaphus was born, to be the first king and the founder of Memphis.

> " In coming time that hollow of the sea
> Shall bear the name Ionian, and present
> A monument of Io's passage through,
> Unto all mortals."
>
> *E. B. Browning.*

Juno mourned the loss of her faithful Argus most bitterly, and, gathering up his myriad eyes, scattered them over the tail of her favourite bird, the peacock, in order to have some memento of her faithful servant ever near her.

> " From Argus slain a painted peacock grew,
> Fluttering his feathers stain'd with various hue."
>
> *Moschus.*

This story also is an allegory. Io personifies the moon, restlessly wandering from place to place ; Argus, the heavens, whose starry eyes keep ceaseless watch over the moon's every movement ; Mercury is the rain, whose advent blots out the stars one by one, thus killing Argus, who else was never known to close all his eyes at once.

To Mercury was entrusted the charge of conducting the souls of the departed to Hades, and when occupied in this way he bore the name of Psychopompus,

while, when addressed as conductor of Dreams, he was
Oneicopompus.

> " Gently as a kiss came Death to sever
> From spirit flesh, and to the realm of gloom
> The pallid shades with fearless brow descended
> To Hades, by the winged god attended."
>
> *Boyesen.*

He was one of the twelve principal gods of Olympus, and was widely worshipped. Temples, altars, and
shrines were dedicated to his service throughout the
ancient world. His statues were considered sacred
boundary marks, and their removal punished by death.
Solemn annual festivals were held in Rome in Mercury's
honour in the month of May, and from him received
their name of Mercuralia.

CHAPTER IX : MARS

The Character of Mars

MARS (Ares), son of Jupiter and Juno, was the god of war, the personification of the angry clouded sky, and, although but little worshipped in Greece, was one of the principal Roman divinities. He is said to have first seen the light in Thrace, a country noted for its fierce storms and war-loving people.

> " Infant Mars, where Thracia's mountains rose,
> Press'd with his hardy limbs th' encrusted snows."
> *Statius (Elton's tr.).*

Never sated with strife and bloodshed, this god preferred the din of battle to all other music, and found no occupation so congenial as the toils and dangers of war. No gentle deeds of kindness were ever expected from him ; no loving prayers were ever addressed to him ; and the ancients felt no love for him, but, on the contrary, shuddered with terror when his name was mentioned.

Mars was generally represented in a brilliant suit of armour, a plumed helmet on his proud young head, a poised spear in one muscular hand, and a finely wrought shield in the other, showing him ever ready to cope with a foe.

His attendants, or some say his children, sympathised heartily with his quarrelsome tastes, and delighted in following his lead. They were Eris (Discord), Phobos (Alarm), Metus (Fear), Demios (Dread), and Pallor (Terror).

Bellona, or Enyo, goddess of war, also accompanied him, drove his chariot, parried dangerous thrusts, and watched over his general safety. Mars and Bellona were therefore worshipped together in the self-same temple, and their altars were the only ones ever polluted by human sacrifices.

> " And to the fire-ey'd maid of smoky war,
>   All hot and bleeding, will we offer them :
>   The mailèd Mars shall on his altar sit,
>   Up to the ears in blood."

Shakespeare.

Otus and Ephialtes

As strife was his favourite element, Mars was very active indeed during the war between the gods and giants, but in his martial ardour he frequently forgot all caution. On one occasion he was obliged to surrender to Otus and Ephialtes,—two giants, who, though but nine years of age, were already of immense stature, since they increased in height at the rate of nine inches each month.

Proud of their victory over the God of War, these giants bore him off in triumph, and bound him fast with iron chains slipped through iron rings. Day and night they kept watch over him ; and even when they slept, the rattle of the chains, whenever any one of the gods attempted to set him free, woke them up, and frustrated all efforts to deliver him. During fifteen weary months poor Mars lingered there in durance vile, until Mercury, the prince of thieves, noiselessly and deftly slipped the chains out of the rings, and restored him to freedom.

In revenge for the cruel treatment inflicted by Otus and Ephialtes, Mars prevailed upon Apollo and Diana to use their poisoned arrows, and thus rid the world of these two ugly and useless giants.

Of a fiery disposition, Mars was never inclined to forgive an injury ; and when Halirrhothius, Neptune's son, dared to carry off his daughter Alcippe, Mars hotly pursued the abductor, and promptly slew him. Neptune, angry at this act of summary justice, cited the God of War to appear before a tribunal held in the open air, on a hill near the newly founded city of Athens.

It was then customary for such cases to be tried at night, in utter darkness, so that the judges might not be influenced by the personal appearance of either plaintiff or defendant; and no rhetoric of any kind was allowed, that their minds might remain quite unbiassed. Mars appeared before the judges, simply stated his case, and was acquitted. Since then the hill upon which his trial took place has been called the Areopagus (Ares' Hill) or Mars' Hill, and the judges of the principal court of justice at Athens received the name of Areopagitæ.

Although such a partisan of strife, Mars was not impervious to softer emotions, and passionately returned the devotion of Venus, who bore him three beautiful children,—Harmonia, Cupid, and Anteros. Mars also fell in love with a beautiful young Vestal named Ilia, a descendant of Æneas, who, in spite of the solemn pledge not to listen to a lover's pleadings until her time of service at the goddess Vesta's altar was accomplished, yielded to Mars' impetuous wooing, and consented to a clandestine union.

Romulus and Remus

Although secretly married, Ilia continued to dwell in the temple until the birth of her twin sons Romulus and Remus. Her parents, hearing she had broken her vows, commanded that she should suffer the prescribed punishment of being buried alive, and that the children should be exposed to the teeth and claws of the wild beasts of the forest. The double sentence was ruthlessly carried out, and the young mother perished; but, contrary to all previsions, the babes survived, and, after having been suckled for a time by a she-wolf, were found and adopted by a shepherd.

Romulus and Remus throve under this man's kind care, and grew up strong and fearless. When they reached manhood, they longed for a wider sphere for their youthful activity, and, leaving the mountain where they had grown up, journeyed out into the world to seek their fortunes. After some time they came to a beautiful hilly country, where they decided to found a great city, the capital of their future realm. Accordingly the brothers began to trace the outline of their city limits, and, in doing so, quarrelled over the name of the prospective town.

Blinded by anger, Romulus suddenly raised the tool he held, and struck Remus such a savage blow that he fell to the ground, slain by his brother in a fit of passion. Alone now, Romulus at first vainly tried to pursue his undertaking, but, being soon joined by a number of adventurers as wicked and unscrupulous as he, they combined their forces, and built the celebrated city of Rome.

> " Then, with his nurse's wolf-skin girt,
> Shall Romulus the line assert,
> Invite them to his new raised home,
> And call the martial city Rome."
>
> *Virgil (Conington's tr.).*

As founder of this city, Romulus was its first king, and ruled the people with such an iron hand that his tyranny eventually became unbearable. The senators, weary of his exactions and arbitrary measures, finally resolved to free themselves of his presence. Taking advantage of an eclipse, which plunged the city in sudden darkness at noonday, and which occurred while all were assembled on the Forum, the magistrates slew

Romulus, cut his body into pieces, and hid them under their wide togas.

When the light returned, and the terrified and awe-struck people, somewhat reassured, looked about them for their king, they were told he had gone, never to return, carried off by the immortal gods, who wished him to share their abode and dignity. The senators further informed the credulous population that Romulus was to be henceforth worshipped as a god under the name of Quirinus, and gave orders for the erection of a temple on one of the seven hills, which since then has been known as Mount Quirinal. Yearly festivals in Romulus' honour were ever after held in Rome, under the name of Quirinalia.

Well pleased with the new city of Rome and its turbulent, lawless citizens, Mars took it under his special protection ; and once, when a plague was raging which threatened to destroy all the people, the Romans rushed in a body to his temple, and clamoured for a sign of his favour and protection.

Even while they prayed, it is said, a shield, Ancile, fell from heaven, and a voice was distinctly heard to declare that Rome would endure as long as this token of the god's goodwill was preserved. The very same day the plague ceased its frightful ravages, and the Romans, delighted with the result of their petitions, placed the heavenly shield in one of their principal temples.

Then, in constant dread lest some of their enemies should succeed in stealing it, they caused eleven other shields to be made, so exactly like the heaven-sent Ancile, that none but the guardian priests, the Salii, who kept continual watch over them, could detect the original from the facsimiles. During the month of March, which, owing to its blustery weather, was dedicated to Mars and bore his name, the ancilæ were carried in a procession all through the city, the Salii chanting their rude war-songs, and executing intricate war dances.

A Roman general, ere setting out on any warlike expedition, always entered the sanctuary of Mars, touched the sacred shield with the point of his lance, shook the spear in the hand of the god's effigy, and called aloud, " Mars, watch over us ! "

A common superstition among the Roman soldiery was, that Mars, under the name of Gradivus, marched in person at the head of their army, and led them on to victory. Mars' principal votaries were therefore the Roman soldiers and youths, whose exercising ground was called, in his honour, the Campus Martius, or Field of Mars. All the laurel crowns bestowed upon victorious generals were deposited at the foot of his statues, and a bull was the customary thank-offering after a successful campaign.

> " The soldier, from successful camps returning
> With laurel wreath'd, and rich with hostile spoil,
> Severs the bull to Mars."
>
> *Prior.*

CHAPTER X : VULCAN

The Fall of Vulcan

VULCAN, or Hephæstus, son of Jupiter and Juno, god of fire and the forge, seldom joined the general council of the gods. His aversion to Olympus was of old standing. He had once been tenderly attached to his mother, had lavished upon her every proof of his affection, and had even tried to console her when she mourned Jupiter's neglect. On one occasion, intending to punish Juno for one of her usual fits of jealousy, Jupiter hung her out of heaven, fast bound by a golden chain ; and Vulcan, perceiving her in this plight, tugged at the chain with all his might, drew her up, and was about to set her free, when Jupiter returned, and, in anger at his son's interference in his matrimonial concerns, hurled him out of heaven.

The intervening space between heaven and earth was so great, that Vulcan's fall lasted during one whole day and night, ere he finally touched the summit of Mount Mosychlus, in the Island of Lemnos.

> " From morn
> To noon he fell, from noon to dewy eve,
> A summer's day ; and with the setting sun
> Dropt from the zenith like a falling star,
> On Lemnos th' Ægean isle."
>
> *Milton.*

Of course, to any one but a god such a terrible fall would have proved fatal ; and even Vulcan did not escape entirely unharmed, for he injured one of his legs, which accident left him lame and somewhat deformed for the remainder of his life.

Now, although Vulcan had risked so much and suffered so greatly in taking his mother's part, she never even made the slightest attempt to ascertain whether he had reached the earth in safety. Hurt by her indifference and ingratitude, Vulcan vowed never again to return to Olympus, and withdrew to the solitudes of Mount Ætna, where he established a great forge in the heart of the mountain, in partnership with the Cyclopes, who helped him manufacture many cunning and useful objects from the metals found in great profusion in the bosom of the earth.

Among these ingenious contrivances were two golden handmaidens gifted with motion, who attended the god wherever he went, and supported his halting footsteps.

> " Two golden statues, like in form and look
> To living maidens, aided with firm gait
> The monarch's steps."
>
> *Homer (Bryant's tr.).*

Vulcan also devised a golden throne with countless hidden springs, which, when unoccupied, did not present an extraordinary appearance ; but as soon as any one ventured to make use of it, the springs moved, and, the chair closing around the person seated upon it, frustrated all attempts to rise and escape from its treacherous embrace.

Vulcan despatched this throne, when completed, to his mother, who, delighted with its beauty and delicate workmanship, proudly seated herself upon it, and found herself a prisoner. In vain she strove to escape, in vain the gods all gallantly came to her assistance. Their united strength and skill proved useless against the cunning springs.

Finally Mercury was sent to Vulcan, primed with a most diplomatic request to honour high Olympus with his presence ; but all Mercury's eloquence and persuasions failed to induce the god of the forge to leave his sooty abode, and the messenger god was forced to return alone and report the failure of his attempt. Then the gods deliberated anew, and decided to send Bacchus, god of wine, hoping his powers of persuasion would prove more effective

Armed with a flask of his choicest vintage, Bacchus presented himself before Vulcan, and offered him a refreshing draught. Vulcan, predisposed to thirst, and incited to drink by the very nature of his labour, accepted the offered cup, and allowed himself to be beguiled into renewing his potations, until he was quite intoxicated. In this condition, Bacchus led him passive to Olympus, made him release the Queen of Heaven, and urged him to embrace his father and crave forgiveness.

Although restored to favour, Vulcan would not remain permanently in Olympus, but preferred to return to his forge and continue his labours. He undertook, however, the construction of magnificent golden palaces for each of the gods upon the Olympian heights, fashioned their sumptuous furniture from precious metals, and further embellished his work by a rich ornamentation of precious stones.

> " Then to their starry domes the gods depart,
> The shining monuments of Vulcan's art :
> Jove on his couch reclin'd his awful head,
> And Juno slumber'd on the golden bed."
>
> *Homer (Pope's tr.).*

Aided by the Cyclopes, Vulcan manufactured Jupiter's weapons, the dread thunderbolts, whose frightful power none could withstand, and Cupid's love-inspiring darts.

Vulcan, in spite of his deformity, extreme ugliness, and well-known aversion to any home but his sooty forge, was none the less prone to fall in love with the various goddesses. He first wooed Minerva, who, having sworn never to marry, contemptuously dismissed his suit. To console Vulcan for this rebuff, and at the same time punish the Goddess of Beauty, who, according to some mythologists, had refused even his addresses, Jupiter bestowed upon him the fair hand of Venus and sent her and her mischievous train of Loves and Graces to reside in the dark caves of Mount Ætna.

Amused by all the strange sights and sounds, the goddess at first seemed quite contented; but after a time Vulcan's gloomy abode lost all its attractions: so she forsook her ill-favoured husband, and went in search of another more congenial mate.

Some time after, Vulcan married one of the Graces, who, however, seems to have also soon wearied of his society, for she deserted him.

Vulcan's children were mostly monsters, such as Cacus, Periphetes, Cercyon, &c., all of whom play an important part in heroic mythology. He is also the reputed father of Servius Tullius, sixth king of Rome, by a slave Ocrisia, whom he was wont to visit in the guise of a bright flame, which played harmlessly about her.

Vulcan was worshipped by all blacksmiths and artisans, who recognised him as their special patron, and venerated him accordingly.

> "Those who labour
> The sweaty forge, who edge the crooked scythe,
> Bend stubborn steel, and harden gleaming armour,
> Acknowledge Vulcan's aid."
>
> *Prior*.

Great festivals, the Vulcanalia and the Hephæstia, were celebrated in honour of this god, who is generally represented as a short, muscular man, with one leg shorter than the other, a workman's cap on his curly locks, a short upper garment, and a smith's tools in his hand.

CHAPTER XI : NEPTUNE

The Realm of Neptune

WHEN Jupiter assigned to each of his brothers a separate portion of the universe, he decreed that Neptune, or Poseidon, should govern all the waters upon the face of the earth, and be sole monarch of the ocean.

> " Neptune, the mighty marine god, I sing ;
> Earth's mover, and the fruitless ocean's king,
> That Helicon and th' Ægean deeps dost hold.
> O thou earth-shaker ; thy command, twofold
> The gods have sorted ; making thee of horses
> The awful tamer, and of naval forces
> The sure preserver.   Hail, O Saturn's birth !
> Whose graceful green hair circles all the earth.
> Bear a benign mind ; and thy helpful hand
> Lend all, submitted to thy dread command."
>
> Homer (Chapman's tr.).

Before this new ruler made his appearance, the Titan Oceanus had wielded the sceptre of the sea ; and regretfully he now resigned it to his youthful supplanter, whom he nevertheless admired sincerely, and described in glowing colours to his brothers.

> " Have ye beheld the young God of the Seas,
> My dispossessor ?   Have ye seen his face ?
> Have ye beheld his chariot, foam'd along
> By noble winged creatures he hath made ?
> I saw him on the calmed waters scud,
> With such a glow of beauty in his eyes,
> That it enforc'd me to bid sad farewell
> To all my empire."
>
> Keats.

Laomedon and Hesione

Neptune, the personification as well as the god of the sea, was of an exceedingly encroaching disposition. Dissatisfied with the portion allotted him, he once conspired

126

to dethrone Jupiter ; but, unfortunately for the success of his undertaking, his plot was discovered before he could put it into execution, and Jupiter, in punishment for his temerity, exiled him to earth. There he was condemned to build the walls of Troy for Laomedon, king of that city, who, in return, promised a handsome compensation.

Apollo, also banished from heaven at that time, volunteered to aid Neptune by playing on his lyre, and moving the stones by the power of sweet sounds. The task satisfactorily ended, Laomedon, an avaricious and dishonest king, refused the promised guerdon, whereupon Neptune created a terrible monster, which came upon the shore, devoured the inhabitants, devastated everything within his reach, and inspired all with great terror.

To save themselves from the awful death which threatened them all, the Trojans consulted an oracle, who advised the sacrifice of a beautiful virgin, and promised the monster would disappear as soon as he had devoured the appointed victim.

A young girl was therefore chosen by lot, led down to the seashore, and chained by the priest's own hands to a slimy rock. As soon as her mourning friends had forsaken her, the hideous serpent came out of his lair in the waves, and devoured her ; then he vanished, and nothing more was heard of him for a whole year, at the end of which time he reappeared, and resumed his former depredations, which were only checked by the sacrifice of a second virgin.

Year after year, however, he returned, and year after year a fair girl was doomed to perish, until finally the lot fell upon Hesione, the king's only daughter. He could not bear the thought of the terrible fate awaiting her, and tried every means in his power to save her.

127

As a last resort he sent heralds to publish far and wide that the king would give a great reward to any man who would dare attack and succeed in slaying the monster.

Hercules, on his return from the scene of one of his stupendous labours, heard the proclamation, and, with no other weapon than the oaken club he generally carried, slew the monster just as he was about to drag poor Hesione down into his slimy cave. Laomedon was, of course, overjoyed at the monster's death, but, true to his nature, again refused the promised reward, and by his dishonesty incurred the hatred and contempt of this hero also. Some time after, having finished his time of servitude with Eurystheus, Hercules, aided by a chosen band of adventurers, came to Troy to punish him for his perfidy. The city was stormed and taken, the king slain, and his wife and children carried to Greece as captives. There Hesione became the bride of Telamon; while her brother Podarces, later known as Priam, was redeemed by his people and made King of Troy.

Laomedon's failure to pay his just debts was the primary cause of the enmity which Apollo and Neptune displayed towards the Trojans during their famous war with the Greeks.

Their term of exile ended, the gods were reinstated in their exalted positions, and hastened to resume their former occupations; but, in spite of the severe lesson just received, Neptune was not yet cured of his grasping tendencies. Not long after his return from Troy, he quarrelled with Minerva for the possession of the recently founded city of Athens, then nameless, and entered into the memorable contest in which he was signally defeated. He also disputed the sovereignty of Trœzene with Minerva, and that of Corinth with

Neptune

The Fates

LAOMEDON AND HESIONE

Apollo. In the latter instance, the disputants having chosen Briareus as umpire, the prize was awarded to him as the most powerful of all the gods except Jupiter.

As god of the sea, Neptune did not generally remain in Olympus, but dwelt in the coral caves of his kingdom, over which he ruled with resistless sway. By one word he could stir up or calm the wildest storm, and cause the billows to roar with fury or subside into peaceful ripples.

> " He spake, and round about him called the clouds
> And roused the ocean,—wielding in his hand
> The trident,—summoned all the hurricanes
> Of all the winds, and covered earth and sky
> At once with mists, while from above the night
> Fell suddenly."
>
> *Homer (Bryant's tr.).*

The rivers, fountains, lakes, and seas were not only subject to his rule, but he could also cause terrible earthquakes at will, and, when he pleased, raise islands from the deep, as he did when Latona entreated him to shelter her from Juno's persecutions.

Neptune is said to have loved the goddess Ceres, and to have followed her during her prolonged search for her daughter, Proserpina. Annoyed by his persistent wooing, the goddess, to escape him, assumed the form of a mare; but the God of the Sea, not at all deceived by this stratagem, straightway assumed the form of a horse, in which guise he contentedly trotted after her and renewed his attentions.

The offspring of this equine pair was Arion, a wonderful winged steed, gifted with the power of speech, whose early education was entrusted to the Nereides. They trained him to draw his father's chariot over the waves with incredible rapidity, and parted with him regretfully when he was given to Copreus, Pelops' son. This marvellous horse passed successively into Hercules' and Adrastus' hands; and the latter won all the chariot races, thanks to his fleetness.

On another occasion, Neptune, having fallen deeply in love with a maiden named Theophane, and fearful lest some one of her numerous suitors should find favour in her eyes before he had time to urge his wooing, suddenly changed her into a sheep, and conveyed her to the Island of Crumissa, where he assumed the guise of a ram, and in this metamorphosed condition carried on his courtship, which eventually proved successful. The offspring of this union was the golden-fleeced ram which bore Phryxus in safety to the Colchian shores, and whose pelt was the goal of the Argonautic expedition.

Neptune also loved and married Medusa in the days of her youth and beauty, and when some drops of blood fell from her severed head into the salt sea foam, he produced from them the graceful winged steed Pegasus.

Neptune is also said to be the father of the giants Otus and Ephialtes, of Neleus Pelias, and Polyphemus.

Amphitrite

The Queen of the Ocean, Neptune's own true and lawful wife, was a Nereid, one of the fifty daughters of Doris and Nereus,—the personification of the calm and sunlit aspect of the sea. Her name was Amphitrite, or Salacia. At first she was in great awe of her distinguished suitor, and in her fear fled at his approach, leaving him no chance to admire any of her charms, except the grace and celerity with which she managed to flit, or rather glide, out of his sight.

> "Along the deep
> With beauteous ankles, Amphitrite glides."
>
> *Hesiod* (*Elton's tr.*).

IDAS AND MARPESSA

This conduct grieved Neptune so sorely, that he sent a dolphin to plead his cause, and persuade the fair nymph to share his throne. The messenger, carefully instructed beforehand, carried out the directions with such skill, that Amphitrite formally consented to become Neptune's wife.

The King of the Deep was so overjoyed at these good tidings, that he transferred the dolphin to the sky, where he forms a well-known constellation. Neptune and Amphitrite in due time became the happy parents of several children, among whom the most celebrated is Triton, whose body was half man and half fish, and who gave his name to all his male descendants.

Idas and Marpessa

Like all other gods, Neptune took a lively interest in men's affairs, and sometimes interfered in their behalf. On one occasion, for instance, he even lent his beautiful chariot to a youth by the name of Idas, who, loving a maiden dearly, and unable to win her father's consent to their union, had resolved to abduct her. Marpessa, for such was the girl's name, allowed herself to be carried off without protest; and the lovers were blissfully speeding along in Neptune's chariot, when her father, Evenus, perceiving their escape, started in pursuit of them. In spite of the most strenuous efforts, he could not overtake the fleeing pair, and in his anger plunged into a river, where he was drowned, and which from him received the name of Evenus.

Idas and Marpessa were just congratulating themselves upon their narrow escape, when suddenly Apollo appeared before them, and, checking their steeds, declared he loved the maiden too, and would not tamely yield her up to a rival.

This was quite equivalent to a challenge; and Idas,

131

stepping down from the chariot, was about to engage in the fight, when suddenly out of a clear sky a thunderbolt came crashing down to earth, and an imperious voice was heard to declare that the quarrel could be settled by Marpessa only, and that she should freely choose the suitor she preferred as husband.

The maiden glanced at both her lovers, and quickly reviewed their respective attractions. Remembering that Apollo, being immortal, would retain all his youthful bloom when her more ephemeral beauty had vanished, and that he would probably cease to love her, she held out her hand to Idas, declaring she preferred to link her fate to that of a mortal, who would grow old when she did, and love her as long as they both lived. This choice was approved by Jupiter; and the lovers, after reaching a place of safety, returned the wondrous chariot to Neptune, with many thanks for his timely aid.

All the Nereides, Tritons, and lesser sea divinities formed a part of Neptune and Amphitrite's train, and followed closely when they rode forth to survey their kingdom.

Neptune had, besides this, many subordinates, whose duty it was to look after various seas, lakes, rivers, fountains, &c., confided to their special care. In harmony with their occupations, these divinities were either hoary river gods (such as Father Nile), slender youths, beautiful maidens, or little babbling children. They seldom left the cool waves of their appointed dwellings, and strove to win Neptune's approbation mostly by the zeal they showed in the discharge of their various duties.

Proteus

Proteus, too, another inferior deity, had the care of the flocks of the deep, and he always attended Neptune

when it was safe to leave his great herds of sea calves
to bask on the sunny shores.

> " In ages past old Proteus, with his droves
> Of sea calves sought the mountains and the groves."
>
> *Cowper.*

In common with all the other gods, Proteus enjoyed
the gift of prophecy, and had the power to assume any
shape he pleased. The former gift he was wont to
exercise very reluctantly ; and when mortals wished
to consult him, he would change his form with be-
wildering rapidity, and, unless they clung to him
through all his changes, they could obtain no answer
to their questions.

> " Shouting [we] seize the god : our force t'evade,
> His various arts he soon resumes in aid :
> A lion now, he curls a surgy mane ;
> Sudden, our hands a spotted pard restrain ;
> Then, arm'd with tusks, and lightning in his eyes,
> A boar's obscener shape the god belies :
> On spiry volumes, there, a dragon rides ;
> Here, from our strict embrace a stream he glides ·
> And last, sublime, his stately growth he rears,
> A tree, and well-dissembled foliage wears."
>
> *Homer (Pope's tr.).*

But if these manifestations proved unavailing to
drive his would-be hearers away, the god answered
every question circumstantially.

Amphitrite, Neptune's wife,—generally represented
as a beautiful nude nymph, crowned with seaweed, and
reclining in a pearl-shell chariot drawn by dolphins, or
sea-horses,—was worshipped with her husband.

Neptune, majestic and middle-aged, with long,
flowing hair and beard, wearing a seaweed crown, and
brandishing a trident, or three-pronged fork, was
widely worshipped throughout Greece and Italy, and

133

had countless shrines. His principal votaries were the
seamen and horse trainers, who often bespoke his aid.

> " Hail, Neptune, greatest of the gods !
> Thou ruler of the salt sea floods;
> Thou with the deep and dark-green hair,
> That dost the golden trident bear;
> Thou that, with either arm outspread,
> Embosomest the earth we tread :
> Thine are the beasts with fin and scales,
> That round thy chariot, as it sails,
> Plunging and tumbling, fast and free,
> All reckless follow o'er the sea."
>
> *Arion.*

Many large temples were dedicated exclusively to the
worship of Neptune, and games were frequently celebrated in his honour. The most noted of all were
undoubtedly the Isthmian Games,—a national festival,
held every four years at Corinth, on the isthmus of the
same name. Hither people came from all points of
the compass, and all parts of the then known world,
either to witness or to take part in the noted wrestling,
boxing, and racing matches, or in the musical and
poetical contests.

> " King of the stormy sea !
> Brother of Jove, and co-inheritor
> Of elements ! Eternally before
> Thee the waves awful bow. Fast, stubborn rock,
> At thy fear'd trident shrinking, doth unlock
> Its deep foundations, hissing into foam.
> All mountain-rivers, lost in the wide home
> Of thy capacious bosom, ever flow.
> Thou frownest, and old Æolus thy foe
> Skulks to his cavern, 'mid the gruff complaint
> Of all his rebel tempests. Dark clouds faint
> When, from thy diadem, a silver gleam
> Slants over blue dominion. Thy bright team
> Gulphs in the morning light, and scuds along
> To bring thee nearer to that golden song

PROTEUS

Apollo singeth, while his chariot
Waits at the doors of heaven.   Thou art not
For scenes like this : an empire stern hast thou ;
And it hath furrow'd that large front : yet now,
As newly come of heaven, dost thou sit
To blend and interknit
Subduèd majesty with this glad time.
O shell-borne king sublime !
We lay our hearts before thee evermore—
We sing, and we adore ! "

Keats.

CHAPTER XII : PLUTO

The Realm of Pluto

PLUTO [1] (Dis, Hades, Orcus, Aïdoneus), son of Cronus and Rhea, received as his share of the world the supervision of the Infernal Regions, situated beneath the earth, and was also appointed god of the dead and of riches, for all precious metals are buried deep in the bosom of the earth.

This god inspired all men with a great fear. They never spoke of him without trembling, and fervently prayed that they might never see his face ; for, when he appeared on the surface of the earth, it was only in search of some victim to drag down into his dismal abode, or to make sure there was no crevice through which a sunbeam might glide to brighten its gloom and dispel its shadows. Whenever the stern god set out on one of these expeditions, he rode in a chariot drawn by four coal-black steeds ; and, if any obstacle presented itself to impede his progress, he struck it with his two-pronged fork, the emblem of his power, and the obstacle was immediately removed. It was on one of these occasions that Pluto abducted Proserpina, the fair goddess of vegetation, daughter of Ceres, whom he set on his throne in Hades, and crowned as his queen.

Pluto is always represented as a stern, dark, bearded man, with tightly closed lips, a crown on his head, a sceptre and a key in hand, to show how carefully he

---

[1] Besides this Pluto, god of the Infernal Regions, the Greeks also worshipped Plutus, a son of Ceres and Jason, who was known exclusively as the god of wealth. Abandoned in infancy, he was brought up by Pax, the goddess of peace, who is often represented holding him in her lap. Because Plutus insisted upon bestowing his favours upon good and noble mortals only, Jupiter soon deprived him of his sight. Since then the blind god's gifts have been distributed indiscriminately.

guards those who enter his domains, and how vain are their hopes to effect their escape. No temples were dedicated to him, and statues of this god are very rare. Human sacrifices were sometimes offered on his altars; and at his festivals, held every hundred years, and thence called Secular Games, none but black animals were slain.

His kingdom, generally called Hades, was very difficult of access. According to Roman traditions, it could only be entered at Avernus, but the Greeks asserted that there was another entrance near the Promontory of Tænarum. Both nations agreed, however, in saying that it was an almost impossible feat to get out again if one were rash enough to venture in.

> " To the shades you go a down-hill, easy way ;
> But to return and re-enjoy the day,
> This is a work, a labour ! "
>
> *Virgil.*

To prevent all mortals from entering, and all spirits from escaping, Pluto placed a huge three-headed dog, called Cerberus, to guard the gate.

> " There in state old Cerberus sate,
> A three-headed dog, as cruel as Fate,
> Guarding the entrance early and late."
>
> *Saxe.*

From thence a long subterranean passage, through which shadowy spirits glided incessantly, led to the throne room, where Pluto and Proserpina sat in state, clad in their sable robes. From the foot of this throne flowed the rivers which channelled the Lower World. One, the Cocytus, rolled salt waves, composed of naught but the tears flowing continually from the eyes of the criminals condemned to hard labour in Tartarus, the

137

portion of Hades reserved for the exclusive use of the wicked.

> " Cocytus, named of lamentation loud
> Heard on the rueful stream."
>
> *Homer.*

To separate this section from the remainder of his realm, Pluto surrounded it with the Phlegethon, a river of fire ; while the Acheron, a black and deep stream, had to be passed by all souls ere they reached Pluto's throne and heard his decree. The current of this river was so swift that even the boldest swimmer could not pass over ; and, as there was no bridge, all the spirits were obliged to rely upon the aid of Charon, an aged boatman, who plied the only available skiff—a leaky, worm-eaten craft—from shore to shore. Neither would he allow any soul to enter his bark, unless he was first given a small coin, called an obolus, the ferryman's fare, which the ancients carefully laid under the tongue of the dead, that they might pass on to Pluto without delay. Charon's leaky boat no sooner touched the shore than a host of eager spirits pressed forward to claim a place The cruel boatman repulsed them roughly, and brandished his oars, while he leisurely selected those he would next ferry across the stream

> " The shiv'ring army stands,
> And press for passage with extended hands.
> Now these, now those, the surly boatman bore ;
> The rest he drove to distance from the shore."
>
> *Virgil (Dryden's tr.).*

All those who could not produce the required obolus were obliged to wait one hundred years, at the end of which time Charon reluctantly ferried them over free of charge.

There was also in Hades the sacred river Styx, by whose waters the gods swore their most irrevocable oaths; and the blessed Lethe, whose waters had the power to make one forget all unpleasant things, thus preparing the good for a state of endless bliss in the Elysian Fields.

> " Lethe, the river of oblivion, rolls
>   Her wat'ry labyrinth, whereof who drinks,
>   Forthwith his former state and being forgets,
>   Forgets both joy and grief, pleasure and pain."
>
> *Milton.*

Near Pluto's throne were seated the three judges of Hades, Minos, Rhadamanthus, and Æacus, whose duty it was to question all newly arrived souls, to sort out the confused mass of good and bad thoughts and actions, and place them in the scales of Themis, the blindfolded, impartial goddess of justice, who bore a trenchant sword to indicate that her decrees would be mercilessly enforced. If the good outweighed the evil, the spirit was led to the Elysian Fields; but if, on the contrary, the evil prevailed, the spirit was condemned to suffer in the fires of Tartarus.

> " Where his decrees
>   The guilty soul within the burning gates
>   Of Tartarus compel, or send the good
>   To inhabit, with eternal health and peace,
>   The valley of Elysium."
>
> *Akenside.*

The guilty souls were always entrusted to the three snake-locked Furies (Diræ, Erinnyes, or Eumenides), who drove them with their stinging lashes to the gates of Tartarus. These deities, who were sisters, and children of Acheron and Nyx, were distinguished by the individual names of Alecto, Tisiphone, and Megæra, and with Nemesis, goddess of revenge, were noted for their hard hearts and the merciless manner in which they hurried the ghosts entrusted to their care over the fiery flood of the Phlegethon, and through the brazen gates of their future place of incessant torment.

> " There rolls swift Phlegethon, with thund'ring sound,
> His broken rocks, and whirls his surges round.
> On mighty columns rais'd sublime are hung
> The massy gates, impenetrably strong.
> In vain would men, in vain would gods essay,
> To hew the beams of adamant away.
> Here rose an iron tow'r : before the gate,
> By night and day, a wakeful Fury sate,
> The pale Tisiphone ; a robe she wore,
> With all the pomp of horror, dy'd in gore."
>
> *Virgil* (*C. Pitt's tr*).

The Story of Ibycus

The Furies also had an important part to play upon earth, as the avengers of unfilial deeds, irreverence to age, inhospitality, murder, perjury, and some other minor crimes. They secured the punishment of those who had incurred their wrath in various ways, and the following story is told of the murder of Ibycus, a poet dear to Apollo.

While on his way to a musical contest at Corinth this poet was attacked and slain by two robbers, and in his extremity he called upon a flock of cranes, which was passing overhead at the time, to bear witness of the foul deed. When his body was discovered, there was great grief throughout Greece, and all men demanded vengeance upon the murderer.

Shortly after, a play was being enacted in the great amphitheatre, in which the Furies were very graphically represented, and the multitude of spectators sat in deep silence listening with tense interest to the awful denunciations of the Furies upon the murderer in secret.

Suddenly a flock of cranes was seen winging its flight above the arena, and a voice from the audience was heard : "See, friend, the cranes of Ibycus !" Quick to grasp the meaning of this strange exclamation, the spectators shouted with one accord : " 'Tis the murderer of Ibycus ! " This was true, and the two murderers forthwith confessed, and were shortly afterwards executed for their crime.

The three Fates (Mœræ, Parcæ), sisters, also sat near Pluto's throne. Clotho, the youngest, spun the thread of life, in which the bright and dark lines were intermingled. Lachesis, the second, twisted it ; and under her fingers it was now strong, now weak.

> " Twist ye, twine ye ! even so,
> Mingle shades of joy and woe,
> Hope, and fear, and peace, and strife,
> In the thread of human life."
>
> *Scott.*

Atropos, the third sister, armed with a huge pair of shears, remorselessly cut short the thread of life,—an intimation that another soul would ere long find its way down into the dark kingdom of Hades.

When the gates of Tartarus turned on their hinges to receive the newcomer, a chorus of cries, groans, and imprecations from within fell upon his ear, mingled with the whistling of the whips incessantly plied by retributive deities.

> " What sounds were heard,
> What scenes appeared,
> O'er the dreary coasts !
> Dreadful gleams,
> Dismal screams,
> Fires that glow,
> Shrieks of woe,
> Sullen moans,
> Hollow groans,
> And cries of tortured ghosts."
>
> *Pope.*

THE CLASSICAL MYTHS

The Story of the Danaïdes

Many victims renowned while on earth for their cruelty found here the just punishment of their sins. Attention was first attracted by a group of beautiful maidens who carried water to fill a bottomless cask. Down to the stream they hastened, a long procession, filled their urns with water, painfully clambered up the steep and slippery bank, and poured their water into the cask; but when, exhausted and ready to faint from fatigue, they paused to rest for a moment, the cutting lash fell upon their bare shoulders, and spurred them on to renewed efforts to complete a task so hopeless that it has become proverbial.

These fair maidens were the Danaïdes, daughters of Danaus, who had pledged his fifty daughters to the fifty sons of his brother Ægyptus. The marriage preparations were all completed, when Danaus suddenly remembered an ancient prophecy which had quite escaped his memory, and which foretold that he would perish by the hand of his son-in-law.

It was now too late to prevent the marriages, so calling his daughters aside, he told them what the oracle had said, and, giving them each a sharp dagger, bade them slay their husbands on their wedding night. The marriages were celebrated, as was customary, with mirth, dance, and song; and the revelry continued until late at night, when, the guests having departed, the newly married couples retired. But as soon as Danaus' daughters were quite certain their husbands were fast asleep, they produced their daggers and slwe their mates.

> " Danaus arm'd each daughter's hana
> To stain with blood the bridal bed."
>
> *Euripides* (*Potter's tr.*).

THE STORY OF TANTALUS

One of the brides only, Hypermnestra, loved her husband too dearly to obey her father's command, and, when morning broke, only forty-nine of Ægyptus' sons were found lifeless. The sole survivor, Lynceus, to avenge his brothers' death, slew Danaus, thus fulfilling the ominous prophecy; while the gods, incensed by the Danaides' heartlessness, sent them to Hades, where they were compelled to fill the bottomless cask.

The Story of Tantalus

Tartarus also detained within its brazen portals a cruel king named Tantalus (the father of Niobe), who, while on earth, had starved and ill-treated his subjects, insulted the immortal gods, and on one occasion had even dared to cook and serve up to them his own son Pelops. Most of the gods were immediately aware of the deception practised upon them, and refused the new dish; but Ceres, who was very melancholy on account of the recent loss of her daughter, paid no heed to what was offered her, and in a fit of absent-mindedness ate part of the lad's shoulder.

The gods in pity restored the youth to life, and Ceres replaced the missing shoulder with one of ivory or of gold. Driven away from his kingdom, which was seized by the King of Troy, Pelops took refuge in Greece, where he ruled the extensive peninsula, the Peloponnesus, which still bears his name.

To punish the inhuman Tantalus, the gods then sent him to Tartarus, where he stood up to his chin in a stream of pure water, tormented with thirst; for, whenever he stooped to drink, the waters fled from his parched lips. Over his head hung a branch of luscious fruit. His hunger was as intolerable as his thirst; but, whenever he clutched at the fruit, the branch swung upward, and eluded his eager grasp.

> "Above, beneath, around his hapless head,
> Trees of all kinds delicious fruitage spread.
> The fruit he strives to seize; but blasts arise,
> Toss it on high, and whirl it to the skies."
>
> *Homer (Pope's tr.).*

This singular punishment inflicted upon Tantalus gave rise to the expression "to tantalise."

Sisyphus

Another criminal was Sisyphus, who, while king of Corinth, had misused his power, had robbed and killed travellers, and even deceived the gods. His reprehensible conduct was punished in Tartarus, where he was condemned to roll a huge stone to the top of a very steep hill; and just as he reached the summit, and fancied his task done, the rock would slip from his grasp and roll to the foot of the hill, thus obliging him to renew all his exertions.

> "With many a weary step, and many a groan,
> Up the high hill he heaves a huge round stone;
> The huge round stone, resulting with a bound,
> Thunders impetuous down, and smokes along the ground.
> Again the restless orb his toil renews,
> Dust mounts in clouds, and sweat descends in dews."
>
> *Homer (Pope's tr.).*

Salmoneus

Salmoneus, another king, had vainly tried to make his subjects believe he was Jupiter. With that object, he had once driven over a brazen bridge to imitate the roll of thunder, and, to simulate the thunderbolts, had thrown lighted torches down upon the multitude, purposely assembled below.

> "Th' audacious wretch four fiery coursers drew;
> He wav'd a torch aloft, and, madly vain,
> Sought godlike worship from a servile train,

The Wheel of Ixion

Bacchus and Ariadne

THE STORY OF IXION

Ambitious fool, with horny hoofs to pass
O'er hollow arches of resounding brass,
To rival thunder in its rapid course,
And imitate inimitable force ! "

Virgil (Dryden's tr.).

This insolent parody so incensed Jupiter, that he grasped one of his deadliest thunderbolts, brandished it aloft for a moment, and then hurled it with vindictive force at the arrogant king. In Tartarus, Salmoneus was placed beneath an overhanging rock, which momentarily threatened to fall and crush him under its mass.

" He was doomed to sit under a huge stone,
Which the father of the gods
Kept over his head suspended.
Thus he sat
In continual dread of its downfall,
And lost to every comfort."

Pindar.

Tityus

Still farther on was the recumbent form of Tityus, a giant whose body covered nine acres of ground. He had dared offer an insult to Juno, and in punishment was chained like Prometheus, while a vulture feasted on his liver.

" There Tityus was to see, who took his birth
From heav'n, his nursing from the foodful earth :
Here his gigantic limbs, with large embrace,
Infold nine acres of infernal space.
A rav'nous vulture in his open side
Her crooked beak and cruel talons try'd :
Still for the growing liver digg'd his breast,
The growing liver still supply'd the feast."

Virgil (Dryden's tr.).

The Story of Ixion

Here in Tartarus, too, was Ixion, king of the Lapithæ, who had been given the hand of Dia in marriage on condition that he would give her father a stipulated sum of

145

money in exchange, but who, as soon as the maiden was his, refused to keep his promise. The father-in-law was an avaricious man, and clamoured so loudly for his money, that Ixion, to be rid of his importunities, slew him. Such an act of violence could not be overlooked by the gods : so Jupiter summoned Ixion to appear before him and state his case.

Ixion pleaded so skilfully, that Jupiter was about to declare him acquitted, when he suddenly caught him making love to Juno, which offence seemed so unpardonable, that he sent him to Tartarus, where he was bound to a constantly revolving wheel of fire.

> " Proud Ixion (doom'd to feel
> The tortures of the eternal wheel,
> Bound by the hand of angry Jove)
> Received the due rewards of impious love."
>
> *Sophocles (Francklin's tr.).*

The Elysian Fields

Far out of sight and hearing of the pitiful sounds which so constantly rose out of Tartarus, were the Elysian Fields, lighted by a sun and moon of their own, decked with the most fragrant and beautiful of flowers, and provided with every charm that nature or art could supply. No storms or wintry winds ever came to rob these fields of their spring-like beauty ; and here the blessed spent eternity, in pleasant communion with the friends they had loved on earth.

> " Patriots who perished for their country's rights
> Or nobly triumphed in the fields of fight :
> There holy priest and sacred poets stood,
> Who sang with all the raptures of a god :
> Worthies whose lives by useful arts refined ;
> With those who leave a deathless name behind,
> Friends of the world, and fathers of mankind."

CHAPTER XIII : BACCHUS

The Story of Semele

AMONG all the mortal maidens honoured by the love of Jupiter, king of the gods, none was more attractive than Semele, daughter of Cadmus and Harmonia.

> " For Semele was moulded in the form
> Of elegance ; the beauty of her race
> Shone in her forehead."
>
> *Nonnus (Elton's tr.).*

Although conscious of these superior attractions, Semele was excessively coy, and it was only with the greatest difficulty that Jupiter, disguised as a mortal, could urge his love suit. When he had at last obtained a hearing, he told her who he was, calculating upon the effect which such a revelation must necessarily produce.

He was not mistaken in his previsions, for Semele, proud of having attracted the greatest among the gods, no longer offered any resistance, and consented to their union. Their love grew and prospered, and Jupiter came down from Olympus as often as possible to enjoy the society of his beloved. His frequent absences finally aroused Juno's suspicions, and, as usual, she spared no pains to discover what powerful charm could draw him from her side. After a few days she knew all, and straightway determined to have her revenge, and punish her fickle spouse. To accomplish this successfully, she assumed the face and form of Beroë, Semele's old nurse, and thus entered the young princess's apartment quite unsuspected.

> " Old Beroë's decrepit shape she wears,
> Her wrinkled visage, and her hoary hairs ;
> Whilst in her trembling gait she totters on,
> And learns to tattle in the nurse's tone."
>
> *Ovid (Addison's tr.).*

147

There she immediately entered into conversation with her supposed nursling, artfully extracted a complete confession, heard with suppressed rage how long Jupiter had wooed ere he had finally won the maiden's consent, and received a rapturous and minute catalogue of all his personal charms and a synopsis of all they had both said.

The false nurse listened with apparent sympathy; but in reality she was furious, and, to put an end to it all, asked Semele if she was quite sure he was king of the gods, as he asserted, and whether he visited her in all the pomp of his regal apparel. The maiden shame-facedly replied that he was wont to visit her in the guise of a mortal only; whereupon Beroë, with feigned indignation, told her nursling he must either be a vile impostor, or else that he did not love her as dearly as he loved Juno, in whose presence he seldom appeared except in godlike array.

With artful words she so worked upon the guileless nature of her rival, that, when Jupiter next came, the maiden used all her blandishments to extort from him a solemn oath to grant any request she chose to make. A lover is not very likely to weigh his words under such circumstances, and Jupiter took the most solemn of all the oaths to gratify her whim.

> " ' Bear me witness, Earth, and ye, broad Heavens
> Above us, and ye, waters of the Styx,
> That flow beneath us, mightiest oath of all,
> And most reverèd by the blessèd gods ! ' "
>
> *Homer (Bryant's tr.).*

The promise won, the delighted Semele bade her lover speedily return to Olympus, don his own majestic form and apparel, and hasten back to her side, sur-rounded by all his heavenly pomp, and armed with his dreaded thunderbolts. Jupiter, horrified at this im-prudent request, implored her to ask something else, and release him from a promise fraught with such danger to her; but all in vain. Semele, like many another fair lady, enjoyed having her own way, and would not be denied.

Jupiter, therefore, returned to Olympus, modified his costume as much as possible, dimmed his glory wherever he could, and chose the feeblest of all his bolts, for well he knew no mere mortal could endure the shock of his full glory. Then, mounted on a pale flash of lightning, he darted back to Semele.

> " To keep his promise he ascends, and shrouds
> His awful brow in whirlwinds and in clouds;
> Whilst all around, in terrible array,
> His thunders rattle, and his lightnings play.
> And yet, the dazzling lustre to abate,
> He set not out in all his pomp and state,
> Clad in the mildest lightning of the skies,
> And arm'd with thunder of the smallest size:
> Not those huge bolts, by which the giants slain,
> Lay overthrown on the Phlegrean plain.
> 'Twas of a lesser mould, and lighter weight;
> They call it thunder of a second-rate.
> For the rough Cyclops, who by Jove's command
> Temper'd the bolt and turn'd it to his hand,
> Work'd up less flame and fury in its make,
> And quench'd it sooner in the standing lake.
> Thus dreadfully adorn'd, with horror bright,
> Th' illustrious god, descending from his height,
> Came rushing on her in a storm of light."
>
> _Ovid_ (_Addison's tr._).

But, although so much milder than usual, this apparition was more than poor Semele's human nerves could bear, and she dropped to the floor in a swoon at the first glimpse of her lover. Oblivious of all but her alarming condition, Jupiter sprang to her side; but the lightning which played about his head set fire to the whole palace, which was reduced to ashes.

THE CLASSICAL MYTHS

Advent of Bacchus

Semele herself perished, burned to death; and the only person in all the building who escaped uninjured was Bacchus (Liber, Dionysus), the infant son of Jupiter and Semele, who was saved by his father's powerful hand. Jupiter was at first inconsolable at the death of Semele; and, to testify to all mortals how fondly he had loved her, he brought her spirit up to heaven, where he raised her to the rank of a deity.

> "'Died?'—so the Theban maidens think, and laugh,
> Saying, 'She had her wish, that Semele!'
> But sitting here upon Olympus' height,
> I look down, through that oval ring of stars,
> And see the far-off Earth, a twinkling speck—
> Dust-mote whirled up from the Sun's chariot wheel—
> And pity their small hearts that hold a man
> As if he were a god; or know the god—
> Or dare to know him—only as a man!
> O human love! art thou for ever blind?"
>
> *E. R. Sill.*

The infant Bacchus was first entrusted to the care of his aunt Ino, the second wife of Athamas, King of Thebes, who nursed him as tenderly as if he had been her own child. But all her love could not avail to screen him from the effects of Juno's persistent hatred: so Jupiter, fearing lest some harm might befall his precious son, bade Mercury convey him to the distant home of the Nysiades,—nymphs who guarded him most faithfully.

Juno, not daring to continue her persecutions, wreaked all her anger upon poor Ino and her unhappy household by sending the Fury Tisiphone to goad Athamas to madness. In a fit of deluded frenzy, he pursued his wife and children as if they were wild beasts. One of his sons, Learchus, fell beneath his

arrows ; and, to escape his murderous fury, Ino plunged
headlong into the sea with her second child in her arms.
The gods, in pity for her sufferings, changed her into
the goddess Leucothea, and her son into a sea deity by
the name of Palæmon.

When still but a youth, Bacchus was appointed god
of wine and revelry, and entrusted to the guidance of
Silenus, a satyr, half man and half goat, who educated
him, and accompanied him on all his travels ; for he
delighted in roaming all over the world, borne by his
followers, or riding in his chariot drawn by wild beasts,
while his tutor followed him, mounted on an ass, supported on either side by an attendant.

> " And near him rode Silenus on his ass,
>   Pelted with flowers as he on did pass."
>   *Keats.*

Bacchus' train was very large indeed, and composed
of men and women, nymphs, fauns, and satyrs, all
crowned with ivy leaves, who drank wine,—a drink
compounded for their express use out of water and
sunshine,—ate grapes, danced and sang, and loudly
proclaimed him their chosen leader.

> " ' We follow Bacchus ! Bacchus on the wing,
>   A-conquering !
>   Bacchus, young Bacchus ! good or ill betide,
>   We dance before him thorough kingdoms wide.' "
>   *Keats.*

The most unruly among his female followers were
the Bacchantes, who delighted in revelry, and were in
a perpetual state of intoxication as they went with him
from land to land, where he taught the people the
cultivation of the vine and the art of making wine.
He travelled thus, it is said, throughout Greece and
Asia Minor, and even ventured as far as India and
Ethiopia.

Bacchus and the Pirates

During these long journeys, Bacchus, as was inevitable, met with many adventures, which have been
fertile themes for poetry and art. On one occasion,
having strayed away from his followers and lost his
way, Bacchus laid himself down upon the sand on the
sea-shore to rest. Some pirates, sailing by, saw the
handsome young sleeper, and noiselessly bore him off
to their vessel, intending to sell him as a slave in Egypt.

They were already quite far out at sea when the god
awoke, and gazed around him in mute wonder at his
surroundings. When fully roused, he bade the seamen
take him back to land, but they merely replied by
laughter and mockery. Their amusement was cut
short, however, for the ship came to a sudden stand-
still; and, when they leaned over the sides to ascertain
why their oars could no longer propel it onward, they
saw a vine grow out of the sea, and twine its branches
and tendrils with lightning-like velocity around oars,
mast, and rigging, thus transforming the vessel into a
floating arbour. Then a sound of music and revelry
greeted their astonished ears, and Bacchus' followers
came thronging over the ship's sides, riding on wild
beasts, and chanting the praises of their god and of his
favourite beverage.

> " In chorus we sing of wine, sweet wine,
> Its power benign, and its flavour divine."
>
> *Martinez de la Rosa.*

These extraordinary sights and sounds so bewildered
the poor sailors, that they lost all presence of mind,
and jumped overboard into the sea, where they were
drowned and changed into dolphins.

On another occasion, Silenus, after a great carousal,
lost his way in the forest, and helplessly wandered from

place to place in search of his companions, until he finally came to the court of Midas, King of Lydia.

Bacchus and Midas

Midas no sooner beheld the red nose and bloated appearance of the wanderer, than he recognised him as Bacchus' tutor, and volunteered to lead him back to his divine pupil. Delighted to see Silenus again, Bacchus promised Midas any reward he wished; whereupon Midas, who was an avaricious old king, fell upon his knees, and humbly besought the god to grant that all he touched might be changed into gold.

> " ' Give me,' says he (nor thought he ask'd too much),
> 'That with my body whatsoe'er I touch,
> Changed from the nature which it held of old,
> May be converted into yellow gold.' "
>
> *Ovid (Croxall's tr.).*

Bacchus immediately signified that his prayer was granted ; and Midas, overjoyed at the success of his bold venture, wandered back to his palace, testing his new-won power, which changed all to gold at a mere touch of one of his fingers.

> " Down from a lowly branch a twig he drew,
> The twig straight glitter'd with a golden hue.
> He takes a stone, the stone was turn'd to gold :
> A clod he touches, and the crumbling mould
> Acknowledged soon the great transforming power,
> In weight and substance like a mass of ore.
> He pluck'd the corn, and straight his grasp appears
> Fill'd with a bending tuft of golden ears.
> An apple next he takes, and seems to hold
> The bright Hesperian vegetable gold :
> His hand he careless on a pillar lays,
> With shining gold the fluted pillars blaze."
>
> *Ovid (Croxall's tr.).*

The sight of these and many other wonders, wrought by a mere touch, filled his heart with joy ; and in his elation he bade his servants prepare a sumptuous feast, and invite all his courtiers to share his merriment. His commands were obeyed with the utmost celerity, and Midas beamed with satisfaction as he took his place at the head of the board, and viewed the choice dishes and wines prepared for his delectation.

Here, too, however, a new revelation awaited him; for cloth, plate, and cup turned to gold, as did the food and drink as soon as they met his eager lips.

> " Whose powerful hands the bread no sooner hold,
> But all its substance is transform'd to gold:
> Up to his mouth he lifts the savoury meat,
> Which turns to gold as he attempts to eat:
> His patron's noble juice of purple hue,
> Touch'd by his lips, a gilded cordial grew,
> Unfit for drink ; and, wondrous to behold,
> It trickles from his jaws a fluid gold.
> The rich poor fool, confounded with surprise,
> Starving in all his various plenty lies."
>
> Ovid (Croxall's tr.).

In the midst of plenty, the gnawing pangs of hunger now made themselves felt ; and the precious gift, which prevented his allaying them, soon lost all its attractions. With weary feet, Midas now retraced the road he had travelled in his pride a few hours before, again cast himself at Bacchus' feet, and this time implored him to take back the inconvenient gift, which prevented him from satisfying his natural appetites.

His distress seemed so real, that Bacchus bade him go and wash in the Pactolus River, if he would be rid of the power which had so soon turned into a curse. Midas hastened off to the river and plunged in its tide, noting that even its sands all turned to gold beneath his tread ; since when,

> " Pactolus singeth over golden sands."
>
> Gray.

Bacchus and Ariadne

Bacchus' favourite place of resort was the island of Naxos, which he visited after every journey. During one of his sojourns there, he discovered a fair maiden lying alone on the sandy shore. Ariadne, for such was the girl's name, had been forsaken there by her lover, Theseus, who had sailed away while she slept. As soon as she awoke, she called her faithless lover; but no answering sound fell upon her ear except the mocking tones of Echo. Her tears flowed freely as she beat her breast in despair; but suddenly her lamentations ceased, as she caught the faint sound of music floating toward her on the summer breeze. Eagerly turning toward the pleasant music, she caught sight of a merry procession, headed by the God of Wine.

> " 'And as I sat, over the light blue hills
> There came a noise of revellers : the rills
> Into the wide stream came of purple hue—
>   'Twas Bacchus and his crew !
> The earnest trumpet spake, and silver thrills
> From kissing cymbals made a merry din—
>   'Twas Bacchus and his kin !
> Like to a moving vintage down they came,
> Crown'd with green leaves, and faces all on flame;
> All madly dancing through the pleasant valley.' "
>
> *Keats.*

Bacchus, the first to perceive the fair mourner, hastened to her side, and brought all his powers of persuasion into play to console her. His devotion at last induced her to forget her recreant lover, and, after a short courtship, Bacchus won her as a bride.

Their wedding was the gayest ever seen, and the feasting lasted for several days. The bridegroom presented the bride with a crown adorned with seven glittering stars,—an ornament which fitly enhanced her peerless beauty. Shortly after her marriage, however, poor Ariadne sickened and died, leaving a disconsolate widower, who took the crown she had so often worn and flung it up into the air. It rose higher and higher, until the gods fixed it in the sky, where it still forms a brilliant constellation, known as Ariadne's Crown, or Corona.

> " And still her sign is seen in heaven,
> And, 'midst the glittering symbols of the sky,
> The starry crown of Ariadne glides."
>
> *Apollonius Rhodius.*

Bacchus' lightheartedness had all vanished, and he no longer took any pleasure in music, dance, or revelry, until Jupiter, in pity for his bereavement, restored Ariadne to his longing arms, and, to prevent her being again claimed by Death, gave her immortal life.

The Story of Pentheus

When but a short distance from Thebes, Bacchus once sent a herald to Pentheus, the king, to announce his approach, and bespeak a suitable reception and sumptuous entertainment. Rumours of the noise and disorder, which seem to have been the invariable accompaniment of the god's presence, had already reached Pentheus, who therefore dismissed the herald with an insolent message, purporting that Bacchus had better remain outside of the city gates.

To avenge this insult, Bacchus inspired the Theban women with a species of dementia, which made them rush simultaneously out of the city and join his followers. Then they all clamoured for permission to witness the religious rites in his honour, generally called Mysteries, which permission was graciously granted.

The king's spies reported all that had occurred, and

their accounts made Pentheus long to view the ceremonies in secret. He therefore disguised himself, and
hid in a bush near the consecrated place, hoping to see
all without being seen ; but an inadvertent movement
attracted the attention of the already excited Bacchantes,
who, led by Agave, the king's own mother, dragged
him from his hiding-place and tore him limb from
limb.

Bacchus, god of wine, was worshipped throughout
the ancient world, and festivals without number were
held in his honour. The most noted were the Greater
and Lesser Dionysia, the Liberalia, and the Bacchanalia,
where the wildest merrymaking and licence were freely
indulged in by all participants.

> " Bacchus, on thee they call, in hymns divine,
> And hang thy statues on the lofty pine :
> Hence plenty every laughing vineyard fills,
> Thro' the deep valleys and the sloping hills ;
> Where'er the god inclines his lovely face,
> More luscious fruits the rich plantations grace.
> Then let us Bacchus' praises duly sing,
> And consecrated cakes, and chargers bring,
> Dragg'd by their horns let victim goats expire,
> And roast on hazel spits before the sacred fire."

> " Come, sacred sire, with luscious clusters crown'd,
> Here all the riches of thy reign abound ;
> Each field replete with blushing autumn glows,
> And in deep tides for thee the foaming vintage flows."
>
> *Virgil (Warton's tr.).*

Bacchus is generally represented as a handsome
youth, crowned with ivy or grape leaves and clusters,
bearing the thyrsus, an ivy-circled wand, as sceptre,
and riding in a chariot drawn by panthers or leopards.

CHAPTER XIV : CERES AND PROSERPINA

Pluto and Proserpina

CERES (Demeter), daughter of Cronus and Rhea, and one of Jupiter's numerous consorts, was goddess of agriculture and civilisation. Her manifold cares were shared by her daughter, Proserpina (Cora, Pherephatta, Persephone), the goddess of vegetation. Whenever her duties permitted, this fair young goddess hastened off to the Island of Sicily, her favourite place of resort, where she wandered about all day long, attended by a merry girlish train, gathering flowers, on the green slopes of Mount Ætna, and danced with the nymphs in the beautiful plain of Enna.

> " Sacred Goddess, Mother Earth,
>   Thou from whose immortal bosom,
> Gods, and men, and beasts have birth,
>   Leaf and blade, and bud and blossom,
> Breathe thine influence most divine
> On thine own child, Proserpine.

> " If with mists of evening dew
>   Thou dost nourish these young flowers
> Till they grow, in scent and hue,
>   Fairest children of the hours,
> Breathe thine influence most divine
> On thine own child, Proserpine."
>
> *Shelley.*

One day, weary of labour, Proserpina called these fair playmates to join her and spend a merry day gathering flowers. The maidens sang merry lays as they wound their long garlands ; and the joyous song of Proserpina, mingled with ripples of silvery laughter, attracted the attention of Pluto, who happened to be driving past in his dark chariot drawn by four fiery coal-black steeds.

158

Pluto and Proserpina

The Return of Persephone

PLUTO AND PROSERPINA

To ascertain whence these sounds proceeded, the god stepped out of his car, and cautiously peeped through the thick foliage.

He saw Proserpina sitting on a mossy bank, almost buried in many-hued blossoms, her laughing companions picturesquely grouped around her. One glance sufficed to convince Pluto of her loveliness and grace, and to make him feel that his happiness depended on the possession of this bright young creature.

Long ere this he had tried to persuade one after another of the goddesses to share his gloomy throne; but one and all had refused the honour, and declined to accompany him to a land where the sun never shone, the birds never sang, and the flowers never bloomed. Hurt and disappointed by these rebuffs, Pluto had finally registered a solemn vow never to go wooing again; and so, instead of gently inviting Proserpina to become his queen, he resolved to abduct her.

Straight through the bushes he strode, direct to the spot where she was seated. The noise of crackling branches and hasty footsteps made the assembled maidens swiftly turn. One glance sufficed to identify the intruder, for none but he could boast of such a dark, lowering countenance; and all exclaimed in mingled wonder and terror at his unwonted presence in those sunlit regions :

> " 'Tis he, 'tis he : he comes to us
> From the depths of Tartarus.
> For what of evil doth he roam
> From his red and gloomy home,
> In the centre of the world,
> Where the sinful dead are hurled ?
> Mark him as he moves along,
> Drawn by horses black and strong,
> Such as may belong to Night
> Ere she takes her morning flight.

Now the chariot stops : the god
On our grassy world hath trod :
Like a Titan steppeth he,
Yet full of his divinity.
On his mighty shoulders lie
Raven locks, and in his eye
A cruel beauty, such as none
Of us may wisely look upon."

Barry Cornwall.

Frightened by his impetuous approach, the trembling nymphs first crowded around Proserpina, who, in her astonishment and trepidation, dropped all her pretty flowers and stood motionless among them. Her uncertainty as to his purpose was only momentary, for, catching her in his brawny arms ere she could make an attempt to escape, he bore her off to his chariot, in spite of prayers and struggles, and drove away as fast as his fleet steeds could carry him.

He was soon out of hearing of the wild cries and lamentations of the nymphs, who vainly pursued him, and tried to overtake their beloved mistress. Afraid lest Ceres should come and force him to relinquish his new-won treasure, Pluto drove faster and faster, nor paused for an instant until he reached the banks of the Cyane River, whose waters, at his approach, began to seethe and roar in a menacing fashion, and spread themselves as much as possible, to check him in his flight.

Pluto quickly perceived that to attempt to cross the river in his chariot would be madness, while by retracing his footsteps he ran the risk of meeting Ceres, and being forced to relinquish his prize. He therefore decided to have recourse to other means, and, seizing his terrible two-pronged fork, struck the earth such a mighty blow that a crevice opened under his feet, through which horses and chariot plunged down into the darkness of the Lower World.

PLUTO AND PROSERPINA

Proserpina turned her weeping eyes to catch a parting glimpse of the fair earth she was leaving, and then, with a fond thought of her anxious mother, who, when evening came, would vainly seek her child in all her favourite haunts, she quickly flung her girdle into the Cyane, and called to the water nymph to carry it to Ceres.

Elated by the complete success of his bold venture, and no longer fearful of immediate pursuit, the happy god strained his fair captive to his breast, pressed kisses on her fresh young cheeks, and tried to calm her terrors, as the black steeds rushed faster and faster along the dark passage, nor paused until they reached the foot of their master's throne.

> "Pleased as he grasps her in his iron arms,
> Frights with soft sighs, with tender words alarms."
>
> *Darwin.*

Meanwhile the sun had sunk below the Sicilian horizon; and Ceres, returning from the fields of fast-ripening grain to her own dwelling, sought for the missing Proserpina, of whom no trace could be found except the scattered flowers. Hither and thither the mother wandered, calling her daughter, and wondering where she could be, and why she did not come bounding to meet her. As time passed, and still Proserpina did not appear, Ceres' heart beat fast with apprehension, and the tears coursed down her cheeks as she rushed about from place to place, calling her daughter.

> "What ails her that she comes not home ?
> Demeter seeks her far and wide,
> And gloomy-browed doth ceaseless roam
> From many a morn till eventide.
> 'My life, immortal though it be,
> Is naught !' she cries, 'for want of thee,
> Persephone—Persephone !'"
>
> *Ingelow.*

Night came, and Ceres, kindling a torch at the volcanic fires of Mount Ætna, continued her search. Day dawned, and still the mother called, awakening the morning echoes with her longing cries for her child. Her daily duties were all neglected. The rain no longer refreshed the drooping flowers, the grain was parched by the ardent rays of the sun, and the grass all perished, while Ceres roamed over hill and dale in search of Proserpina.

Weary at last of her hopeless quest, the goddess seated herself by the wayside, near the city of Eleusis, and gave way to her overwhelming grief.

> " Long was thine anxious search
> For lovely Proserpine, nor didst thou break
> Thy mournful fast, till the far-fam'd Eleusis
> Received thee wandering."

Orphic Hymn.

Ceres and Triptolemus

To avoid recognition, she had assumed the appearance of an aged crone; and as she sat there by the wayside, in tears, she attracted the compassionate inquiries of the daughters of Celeus, king of the country. Having heard her bewail the loss of her child, they entreated her to come to the palace, and, knowing nothing could so well soothe a breaking heart, offered her the charge of their infant brother Triptolemus.

Ceres, touched by their ready sympathy, accepted the offer; and when she arrived at the palace, the royal heir was entrusted to her care. Tenderly the goddess kissed the puny child's little pinched face; and at her touch the child became rosy and well, to the unbounded astonishment of the royal family and all the court.

In the night, while Ceres sat alone with her charge, it occurred to her that she might confer a still greater blessing upon him, that of immortality: so she anointed

162

his limbs with nectar, murmured a powerful charm, and placed him upon the red-hot coals, to consume all the perishable elements left in his body.

The queen, Metaneira, who had thought it somewhat imprudent to leave the child thus alone with a stranger, now stole noiselessly into the apartment, and with a wild shriek rushed to the fire and snatched her child out of the flames, pressed him anxiously to her breast, and, after ascertaining that he was quite unharmed, turned to vent her indignation upon the careless nurse; but the aged beggar woman had vanished, and in her stead she confronted the radiant Goddess of Agriculture.

> "From her fragrant robes
> A lovely scent was scattered, and afar
> Shone light emitted from her skin divine,
> And yellow locks upon her shoulders waved;
> White as from lightning, all the house was filled
> With splendour."
>
> *Homeric Hymn.*

With a gentle reproof to the queen for her untimely interference, Ceres explained what she fain would have done, and vanished, to continue her wanderings in other lands. She finally returned to Italy; and, while wandering along the river banks one day, the waters suddenly cast a glittering object at her feet. Stooping hastily to ascertain what it might be, she recognised the girdle her daughter had worn when she had parted from her in Sicily.

Joyfully she embraced the token, and, thinking she must now be upon Proserpina's track, hastened on until she came to a crystal fountain, by whose side she sat down to rest. Her eyes were heavy with the combined effect of tears, fatigue, and oppressive heat, and she was about to lose all consciousness of her trouble in sleep, when the murmur of the fountain increased, until she fancied it was talking; not as mortals do, but in its own silvery accents.

Arethusa and Alpheus

The goddess was not mistaken; for a few minutes later she could distinguish words, and heard the fountain entreat her to listen, if she would hear what had befallen her child. The fountain then went on to tell how she had not always been a mere stream, but was once a nymph, called Arethusa, in Diana's train, and how, overcome by the heat, she had once sought a cool stream wherein she might bathe her heated limbs.

She soon found one, the Alpheus River, and selected a spot where the trees hung over the limpid waters, where the sand on the bottom was fine and even, and where no mortal eyes could see her as she threw aside her sandals and outer garments. She was enjoying the refreshing sensation of the water rippling around her hot limbs, and was revelling in the complete solitude, when suddenly the river, until now as smooth as a mirror, was ruffled by waves, which crept nearer and nearer to the startled nymph, until in affright she sprang out of the water.

Then a voice—the voice of the river god Alpheus— was heard, calling to her in pleading accents to stay her flight and lend an ear to his wooing; but when the impetuous god, instead of waiting for an answer to his suit, rose up out of the water and rushed to clasp her in his arms, she turned and fled in great terror. She fled, but he pursued. Over hill and dale, through forest and field, Arethusa ran, still closely followed by her too ardent lover, until, exhausted, she paused for breath, crying aloud to Diana to come to her rescue.

Her prayer was answered. A moment later she was enveloped in a thick mist and transformed into a fountain. Alpheus could no longer see her, but wandered about, bewailing her disappearance, and calling her in passionate accents.

> " 'O Arethusa, peerless nymph ! why fear
> Such tenderness as mine ?   Great Dian, why,
> Why didst thou hear her prayer ?   Oh that I
> Were rippling round her dainty fairness now,
> Circling about her waist, and striving how
> To entice her to a dive !   then stealing in
> Between her luscious lips and eyelids thin.' "
>
> *Keats.*

The misty cloud in which Arethusa had been enveloped by Diana's protecting care was soon blown away by a mischievous breath from Zephyrus; and Alpheus, who was still hovering near there, suddenly beholding a fountain where none had ever existed before, surmised what had happened.   Changing himself into an impetuous torrent, he rushed to join his beloved, who sprang out of her mossy bed, and hurried on over sticks and stones, until Diana, seeing her new plight, opened a crevice, through which she glided away from the bright sunlight she loved so well into the depths of Pluto's realm.

While gliding there in the gloom, Arethusa had caught a glimpse of Proserpina on her sable throne, beside the stern-browed Pluto.   She could not, however, pause to inquire how she came there, but hurried on breathlessly, until another crevice offered her the means of returning to the upper world, and seeing once more the blue sky and sun on the Sicilian plains.

The monotonous murmur of the fountain now subsided again into its usual undertone; and Ceres, knowing where to seek her daughter, was about to depart, when she heard the sudden rush and roar of a large body of water.   She immediately turned, and beheld the torrent Alpheus, who, after a disconsolate search under-

THE CLASSICAL MYTHS

ground for the lost Arethusa, had found a crevice
through which he passed to join his beloved on the
Sicilian plains.

> "Alpheus, Elis' stream, they say,
> Beneath the seas here found his way,
> And now his waters interfuse
> With thine, O fountain Arethuse,
> Beneath Sicilian skies."
>
> *Virgil (Conington's tr.).*

In spite of her previous efforts to escape him, Arethusa must still have been very glad to see him once
more, for Ceres heard her murmur contentedly as she
sank into his arms and listened to his louder tones of
rapturous love.

> "And now from their fountains
> In Edna's mountains
> Down one vale where the morning basks,
> Like friends once parted
> Grown single-hearted,
> They ply their watery tasks."
>
> *Shelley.*

Maidens in Greece were wont to throw fresh garlands
into the Alpheus River; and it was said the self-same
flowers, carried away by his current, soon reappeared in
the Sicilian fountain, carried there as love offerings by
the enamoured river.

> "O my beloved, how divinely sweet
> Is the pure joy when kindred spirits meet!
> Like him, the river god, whose waters flow,
> With love their only light, through caves below,
> Wafting in triumph all the flowery braids
> And festal rings, with which Olympic maids
> Have decked his current, an offering meet
> To lay at Arethusa's shining feet.
> Think when at last he meets his fountain bride
> What perfect love must thrill the blended tide!
> And lost in each, till mingling into one,
> Their lot the same for shadow or for sun,
> A type of true love, to the deep they run."
>
> *Moore.*

The Return of Proserpina

Now, although poor Ceres had ascertained where to find her missing daughter, her grief was not at all diminished, for she felt convinced that Pluto would never willingly relinquish her. She therefore withdrew into a dark cave to mourn unseen, and still further neglected her wonted duties.

Famine threatened to visit the people, and they prayed and clamoured for her aid; but, absorbed in grief, she paid no heed to their distress, and vowed that nothing on earth should grow, with her permission, as long as her daughter was detained in Hades. In despair at this frightful state of affairs, the people then besought Jupiter to pity the sufferings they endured, and to allow Proserpina to revisit the upper world once more.

> " Arise, and set the maiden free ;
> Why should the world such sorrow dree
> By reason of Persephone ? "
> *Ingelow.*

As soon as she became aware of this petition, Ceres hastened to Olympus, to join her supplications to the cries which rose from all parts of the earth; until Jupiter, wearied by these importunities, consented to Proserpina's return, upon condition, however, that she had not touched any food during the whole time of her sojourn in the Infernal Regions.

Ceres in person hastened to her daughter's new abode, and was about to lead her away in spite of Pluto, when a spirit, Ascalaphus, suddenly declared that the queen had partaken of some pomegranate seeds that very day. Proserpina could not refute the charge, and Jupiter decreed that for every seed she had eaten she should spend one month of every year in her husband's gloomy kingdom.

Thus it came about that Proserpina was condemned to spend one half the year in Hades, and could linger on the bright earth only for six months at a time.

Mercury was chosen to lead her to and from Hades; and, whenever he brought her out of her gloomy prison, the skies became blue and sunny, the grass sprang fresh and green beneath her elastic tread, the flowers bloomed along her way, the birds trilled forth their merry lays, and all was joy and brightness.

> " And when, in springtime, with sweet-smelling flowers
> Of various kinds the earth doth bloom, thou'lt come
> From gloomy darkness back—a mighty joy
> To gods and mortal men."
>
> *Homeric Hymn.*

Ceres, happy once more in the possession of her beloved daughter, cheerfully and diligently attended to all her duties, and blessed the earth with plenty; but when the six months were over, and the skies wept and all nature mourned Proserpina's departure, she again returned to her cave, whence no entreaties could draw her.

As for the merry, happy-natured Proserpina, the moment Hades' portals closed behind her, she became pale and melancholy; and none would have dreamed the playful, flower-crowned Goddess of Vegetation was identical with the sad-faced, sable-vested Queen of Hades (now called Hecate), who held a pomegranate in one hand, and a torch in the other. Prosperina, like Adonis, was the personification of vegetation, visibly prosperous during the six favourable months of the year, and lurking hidden under the cold ground during the remainder of the time.

Many beautiful temples were dedicated to Ceres and Proserpina in Greece and Italy, where yearly festivals, the Thesmophoria and the Cerealia, were celebrated with great pomp.

> " To Ceres chief her annual rites be paid,
> On the green turf, beneath a fragrant shade,
> When winter ends, and spring serenely shines,
> Then fat the lambs, then mellow are the wines,

THE STORY OF ERISICHTHON

Then sweet are slumbers on the flowery ground,
Then with thick shades are lofty mountains crown'd.
Let all the hinds bend low at Ceres' shrine;
Mix honey sweet, for her, with milk and mellow wine;
Thrice lead the victim the new fruits around,
And Ceres call, and choral hymns resound:
Presume not, swains, the ripen'd grain to reap,
Till crown'd with oak in antic dance ye leap,
Invoking Ceres, and in solemn lays,
Exalt your rural queen's immortal praise."

Virgil (C. Pitt's tr.).

To commemorate her long search for her daughter, Ceres returned to Eleusis, taught her former nursling, Triptolemus, the various secrets of agriculture, and gave him her chariot, bidding him travel everywhere, and teach the people how to plough, sow, and reap; and then she instituted the Eleusinia, festivals held in honour of her daughter and herself at Eleusis.

Triptolemus did not fail to carry out the goddess's instructions, and journeyed far and wide until he finally reached the court of Lyncus, King of Scythia, where the false monarch would have treacherously slain him had not Ceres by timely interference prevented the execution of his base purpose by changing the traitor into a lynx, the emblem of perfidy.

Ceres was generally represented as a fair, matronly woman, clad in flowing draperies, sometimes crowned with wheat ears, and bearing a sheaf of grain and a sickle, or with a plough and a horn of plenty disgorging its wealth of fruit and flowers at her feet. Groves were frequently dedicated to her; and any mortal rash enough to lay the axe on one of those sacred trees was sure to incur the goddess's wrath, as is proved by the story of Erisichthon.

The Story of Erisichthon

This man was evidently a freethinker, and, to show his contempt for the superstitious veneration paid to

169

Ceres' trees, took his axe and cut down one of her sacred oaks. At his first blow, blood began to flow from the tree; but, undeterred by the phenomenon or the entreaties of the bystanders, Erisichthon continued. Finally, annoyed by the importunities of the spectators, he turned and slew one or two, and then completed his sacrilege.

Ceres, incensed by his insolence and cruelty, devised a terrible chastisement for the unfortunate man, and sent Famine to gnaw his vitals, and torment him night and day. The wretch, tortured by a hunger which no amount of food could allay, disposed of all his property to obtain the means of procuring nourishment; but his monstrous appetite continued, and, as he had but one daughter left, he sold her as a slave to obtain food.

The girl's master left her alone for a moment upon the sea-shore, and, in answer to her prayer, Neptune delivered her from servitude by changing her into a fisherman. When the master returned and found his slave gone, he questioned the fisherman, and, not obtaining any satisfactory information, departed. Neptune then restored the maiden to her own form, and let her return home; but, as her father sold her again, the god was obliged to interfere once more in her behalf, until at last Erisichthon, deprived of means to procure food, devoured himself.

Ceres and Stellio

Another anecdote illustrating Ceres' power is told about a lad, Stellio, who made fun of the goddess when she was journeying, on account of the haste with which she disposed of a bowl of gruel offered by some charitable person. To punish the boy for his rudeness, Ceres flung the remainder of the gruel into his face, and changed him into a lizard.

CHAPTER XV : VESTA

The Worship of Vesta

VESTA, or Hestia, daughter of Cronus and Rhea goddess of fire and of the family hearth, and guardian angel of mankind, was worshipped principally throughout Italy, although she also had shrines in Greece and Asia Minor.

The family hearth in ancient times possessed a far different signification from what it does now, and was considered the family altar, for there the father of the family was wont to offer up his daily prayers and sacrifices. "As, according to the old heathen custom, all men were regarded as enemies unless by a special compact they had been made friends, so Vesta presided especially over true and faithful dealing"; and she was therefore generally represented as pure and undefiled.

A beautiful circular temple in Rome was dedicated to Vesta's service ; and here the Palladium of Troy was supposed to be preserved, together with the goddess's sacred fire, originally kindled by the rays of the sun.

This fire—an emblem of the flame of life, which the ancients fancied was kept burning within each human breast by Vesta, the life-giver—was kept constantly burning, and never allowed to go out for want of fuel or timely care. Its flames were also intended to represent the purity of the goddess, who, although wooed by many lovers,—among whom Apollo and Neptune can justly claim the precedence,—remained always a virgin.

The Romans fancied that her worship had been introduced into Italy by Æneas, their famous ancestor, who brought thither his home gods, and who, according to tradition, selected the first Vestal Virgins.

The second king of Rome, Numa Pompilius, built a beautiful temple, and instituted various religious ceremonies, in honour of Vesta. The loveliest and noblest among the Roman maidens were chosen to serve this goddess, and were known as Vestals, or Vestal Virgins. Admitted into the temple at the early age of six, they were compelled to serve ten years in fitting themselves to fulfil the duties they would be called upon to perform during the next decade as priestesses and guardians of the sacred fire. The last ten years were spent in instructing the novices; and, when their thirty years' service was ended, they were at liberty either to continue in the temple, where they were treated with the greatest respect, or to leave it, and even marry, if such were their pleasure.

During their time of servitude, they were expected to keep their vows of chastity and fidelity to their patroness, and to maintain her sacred fire, under penalty of being buried alive in a vaulted chamber, fashioned for this express purpose by Numa Pompilius's order. In turn, each of the priestesses watched the fire, renewed the fuel, and fanned the flame, nor lost sight of it night or day; for the Romans considered the extinction of this sacred flame the precursor of some great public calamity.

The Vestals were, however, so pure and vigilant, that during one thousand years only eighteen failed to keep their vows satisfactorily, and suffered punishment. The Vestal Tuccia was accused of breach of faith, but, as proof of her purity, was given power to carry water in a sieve from the Tiber to the temple.

In return for the signal services the Vestals rendered to the State by maintaining this sacred fire, they enjoyed many privileges: among others, that of being preceded by a lictor with fasces when they walked abroad; of occupying the seats of honour in public ceremonies and festivities; of being buried within the city limits (a privilege granted to but very few); and of obtaining the pardon of criminals whom they met by accident on their way to the place of execution. Loved and greatly honoured by all, the Vestals have become types of all things pure and lovely in woman.

> " By these her trembling fires,
> Like Vesta's, ever burning ; and, like hers,
> Sacred to thoughts immaculate and pure."
>
> *Young.*

The Vestal Virgins were further distinguished by a vesture of pure white linen, with a purple border and a wide purple mantle. In time of war or danger they were answerable for the preservation of the sacred fire, which they were allowed to remove to any place of safety ; and on several occasions they therefore carried it out of Rome and down the Tiber, lest it should fall into the enemy's hands.

The Vestals continued their office until the reign of Theodosius the Great, who, being converted to Christianity A.D. 380, abolished the worship of Vesta, dispersed the Vestals, and extinguished the sacred fire.

Vesta's services were held with great pomp ; and her festivals, the Vestalia, were among the most beautiful and popular in Rome. Statues of this goddess— generally representing a woman of majestic beauty, clad in long robes, holding a lighted torch or lamp in one hand and a votive bowl in the other—were carried through the main streets of the city on all solemn occasions.

> And from the temple brings
> Dread Vesta, with her holy things,
> Her awful fillets, and the fire
> Whose sacred embers ne'er expire."
>
> *Virgil (Conington's tr.).*

In public processions the Vestals had the privilege of

carrying their sacred fire; while the Roman matrons, glad to swell their ranks, followed them, barefooted, chanting the praises of the good goddess Vesta.

On these occasions great banquets were prepared before each house, all daily toil was suspended, the millstones were decked with flowers, and the very asses used to turn them were covered with garlands and led in the processions.

Lares, Manes, and Penates

Among the Romans, Vesta was not the only goddess invoked on the family hearth, for she shared that place of honour with the Lares, Manes, and Penates, who all enjoyed special veneration and sacrifices.

The Lares, quite unknown to the Greeks, were two in number, the children of Mercury and Lara, a naiad famous for her beauty as well as for her extreme loquacity, which no one could check. Tradition relates that this fair maiden talked from morning till night, and told all she knew. Upon one occasion she incurred Jupiter's wrath by relating to Juno a conversation she had overheard between him and one of his numerous mistresses.

To punish her, and at the same time prevent further tale-bearing, the king of the gods cut off Lara's tongue, and, summoning Mercury, bade him lead her down to Hades to linger there for ever. But on the way to the dismal abode of the dead, the messenger god fell in love with his fair charge, who, being now effectually cured of her sole fault, was irresistibly charming ; and, instead of obeying Jupiter, he made love to her, and by pantomime obtained her consent to their union. She bore him two children, who from her were called Lares, and to whom the Romans always paid divine honours, reserving special places for them on the family hearth, for they were supposed to preside over houses and families. Their statues resembled monkeys covered with the skins of dogs ; while at their feet a barking dog, the symbol of their care and vigilance, was always represented.

The Manes—a name generally applied to souls when separated from the body—were also reckoned among the Roman divinities, and the illustrious ancestors of different families were often worshipped under this name.

As for the Penates, they presided over the houses and domestic affairs. Each head of a household was wont to choose his own Penates, whom he then invoked as his special patrons. The statues of the Penates were of clay, wax, ivory, silver, or gold, according to the wealth of the family whose hearth they graced, and the offerings generally made to them were a small part of each meal.

Upon removing from one house to another or from one place to another, it was customary for the head of the family to remove his household gods also, and establish them suitably before he thought of his own or his family's comfort, and in return for this kindly care the Penates blessed him with peace and prosperity.

CHAPTER XVI : JANUS

Janus' Two Faces

JANUS, god of the past, present, and future, of gates, entrances, war, and peace, and patron of all beginnings, although one of the most important of all the Roman divinities, was entirely unknown to the Greeks.

According to some mythologists, he was the son of Apollo; and, although born in Thessaly, he early in life came to Italy, where he founded a city on the Tiber, to which he gave the name Janiculum. Here he was joined by the exiled Saturn, with whom he generously shared his throne. Together they civilised the wild inhabitants of Italy, and blessed them with such prosperity that their reign has often been called the Age of Gold

> "Saturn fled before victorious Jove,
> Driven down and banish'd from the realms above.
> He, by just laws, embodied all the train,
> Who roam'd the hills, and drew them to the plain;
> There fixed, and Latium called the new abode,
> Whose friendly shores concealed the latent god.
> These realms, in peace, the monarch long controlled,
> And blessed the nations with an age of gold."
>
> *Virgil (C. Pitt's tr.).*

Janus is generally represented with two faces, turned in opposite directions, because he was acquainted with the past and future as well as with the present, and because he is considered an emblem of the sun, which opens the day at its rising, and closes the day at its setting.

In some statues he is represented with one white-haired and bearded face, and the other quite youthful in appearance, while others represent him with three and even four heads.

176

JANUS' TWO FACES

" Janus am I; oldest of potentates;
    Forward I look, and backward, and below
I count, as god of avenues and gates,
    The years that through my portals come and go.

I block the roads and drift the fields with snow;
    I chase the wild-fowl from the frozen fen;
My frosts congeal the rivers in their flow;
    My fires light up the hearths and hearts of men."

Longfellow.

The commencement of every new year, month, and day was held sacred to Janus, and at that time special sacrifices and prayers were offered up at his shrines. He also presided over all gates and avenues, and through him alone prayers were supposed to reach the immortal gods: therefore in all religious ceremonies his name was always the first invoked. From this circumstance he often appears with a key in his right hand, and a rod in his left; or, when he presides over the year, he holds the number 300 in one hand, and 65 in the other.

He was also supposed to watch over peace and war, and had numerous temples throughout all Italy. One very celebrated temple was called Janus Quadrifrons, because it was perfectly square. On each side of the building there was one door and three windows. These apertures were all symbolical,—the doors of the four seasons, and the windows of the twelve months, of the year.

In times of war the temple gates were opened wide, for the people, being in need of aid and comfort, were all anxious to enter and present their offerings; but when peace reigned, the doors were immediately closed, for the god's intercession was no longer necessary. The Romans, however, were such a belligerent people, that the temple gates were closed but thrice in more than seven centuries, and then only for a very short period.

Festivals in honour of Janus were celebrated on the

177

first day of the new year ; and one month bore the god's name, and was considered sacred to him. It was customary for friends and relatives to exchange calls, good wishes, and gifts on the first day of this month —a Roman custom in force to this day.

Janus is not the only one among the Greek and Latin divinities whose name has been given to a part of the year or week ; for in Latin the names of the days are *dies Solis* (Sun day), *dies Lunæ* (Moon day), *dies Martis* (Mars' day), *dies Mercurii* (Mercury's day), *dies Jovis* (Jove's day), *dies Veneris* (Venus' day), *dies Saturni* (Saturn's day) ; Latin names which are still in use in legislative and judiciary acts, while in English the common nomenclature is derived from the names of the corresponding Saxon divinities.

CHAPTER XVII : SOMNUS AND MORS

The Cave of Sleep

AFTER leaving the joyless regions of Pluto's realm, and following the even course of the Lethe River, the ancients fancied one reached a large cave in a remote and quiet valley. This cave was the dwelling of Somnus (or Hupnos), god of sleep, and of his twin brother Mors (or Thanatos), god of death ; and both were sons of the Goddess of Night, who had once ruled the whole universe. Near the entrance of the cave, shadowy forms kept constant watch, gently shaking great bunches of poppies, and, with finger to lips, enjoining silence on all who ventured near. These forms were the genii of sleep and death, represented in art as crowned with poppies or amaranths, and sometimes holding a funeral urn or a reversed torch.

The cave was divided into chambers, each one darker and more silent than the one which preceded it. In one of the inner rooms, which was all draped with sable curtains, stood a downy couch, upon which reclined the monarch of sleep. His garments were also black, but all strewn with golden stars. He wore a crown of poppies on his head, and held a goblet full of poppy juice in his languid hand. His drowsy head was supported by Morpheus, his prime minister, who watched incessantly over his prolonged slumbers, and hindered any one from troubling his repose.

> " Deep in a cavern dwells the drowsy god :
> Whose gloomy mansion nor the rising sun,
> Nor setting, visits, nor the lightsome noon :
> But lazy vapours round the region fly,
> Perpetual twilight, and a doubtful sky ;
> No crowing cock does there his wings display,
> Nor with his horny bill provoke the day :

Nor watchful dogs, nor the more wakeful geese,
Disturb with nightly noise the sacred peace:
Nor beast of nature, nor the tame, are nigh,
Nor trees with tempest rock'd, nor human cry:
But safe repose, without an air of breath,
Dwells here, and a dumb quiet next to death
   An arm of Lethe, with a gentle flow,
Arising upwards from the rock below,
The palace moats, and o'er the pebbles creeps,
And with soft murmurs calls the coming sleeps;
Around its entry nodding poppies grow,
And all cool simples that sweet rest bestow;
Night from the plants their sleepy virtue drains,
And passing, sheds it on the silent plains:
No door there was the unguarded house to keep,
On creaking hinges turn'd to break his sleep.
   But in the gloomy court was rais'd a bed,
Stuff'd with black plumes, and on an ebon sted:
Black was the covering too, where lay the god,
And slept supine, his limbs display'd abroad.
About his head fantastic visions fly,
Which various images of things supply,
And mock their forms; the leaves on trees not more,
Nor bearded ears in fields, nor sands upon the shore."

               Ovid (Dryden's tr.).

All around the bed and over it hovered throngs of exquisite spirits, the Dreams, who stooped to whisper their pleasant messages in his ear; while in the distant corners of the apartment lurked the hideous Nightmares. The Dreams were often despatched to earth under Mercury's charge, to visit mortals.

Two gates led out of the valley of sleep,—one of ivory, and the other of horn. The Dreams which passed through the glittering gates of ivory were delusive, while those which passed through the homely gate of horn were destined to come true in the course of time.

   " Of dreams, O stranger, some are meaningless
     And idle, and can never be fulfilled.
   Two portals are there for their shadowy shapes,

Of ivory one, and one of horn. The dreams
That come through the carved ivory deceive
With promises that never are made good;
But those which pass the doors of polished horn,
And are beheld of men, are ever true."

Homer (Bryant's tr.).

Dreams were also frequently sent through the gates
of horn to prepare mortals for misfortunes, as in the
case of Halcyone.

Ceyx and Halcyone

Ceyx, King of Thessaly, was once forced to part from
his beloved wife, Halcyone, to travel off to Delphi to
consult the oracle.   With many tears this loving couple
parted, and Halcyone watched the lessening sail until
it had quite vanished from sight; then she returned to
her palace to pray for her husband's safe return.   But,
alas ! the gods had decreed they should never meet
again on earth; and, even while Halcyone prayed, a
tempest arose which wrecked Ceyx's vessel, and caused
him and all his crew to perish in the seething waves.

Day after day the queen hastened down to the sea-
shore, followed by her attendants, to watch for the returning sails of her husband's vessel ; and night after
night she lay on her couch, anxiously expecting the
morrow, which she ever fancied would prove auspicious.
The gods, seeing her anxiety, and wishing to prepare
her to receive the news of his death, and especially to
view with some composure his corpse, which they had
decided should be washed ashore, sent a Dream to
visit her.

After assuming the face and form of Ceyx, the Dream
glided away through the gate of horn, hastened to
Halcyone's bedside, and whispered that her husband
was dead, and that his body was even now being cast

up on the smooth, sandy beach by the salt sea waves. With a wild cry of terror and grief, Halcyone awoke, and hastened to the sea-shore to convince herself that the dream had been false; but she had no sooner reached the beach, than the waves washed her husband's corpse to her feet.

To endure life without him seemed too great a task for poor Halcyone, who immediately cast herself into the sea, to perish beside him. Touched by grief so real and intense, the gods changed both bodies into birds, since known as Halcyon birds, and decreed they should ever live on the waters. These birds were said to build their nests and hatch their young on the heaving billows, and to utter shrill cries of warning to the seamen whenever a storm threatened, bidding them prepare for the blast, and hasten to shelter in port, if they would not encounter the mournful fate of poor Ceyx.

Mors, god of death, occupied one of the corners of Somnus' cave. He was a hideous, cadaverous-looking deity, clad in a winding-sheet, and held an hour-glass and a scythe in his hand. His hollow eyes were fixed upon the sands of time; and when they had run out, he knew some life was about to end, and sallied forth, scythe in hand, to mow down his prey with relentless joy.

Needless to say, this cruel deity was viewed by the ancients with fear and dislike, and no homage was offered him.

These two divinities were, however, but of slight importance in the general scheme of ancient mythology, in which Proserpina was generally regarded as the emblem of death, and they were therefore little more than local divinities. The Lacedæmonians paid the most heed to them, and invariably placed their statues side by side.

CEYX AND HALCYONE

As for Morpheus, the son as well as the prime minister of Somnus, he was also called the god of sleep, and mortals were wont to intercede for his good offices. He is generally represented as a sleeping child of great corpulence, and with wings. Morpheus held a vase in one hand, and poppies in the other, which he gently shook to induce a state of drowsiness,—according to him, the acme of bliss.

CHAPTER XVIII : ÆOLUS

The Home of Æolus

NOT very far away from the quiet realm of Somnus and Mors, but on the surface of the earth, were the Æolian Islands, now known as the Lipari Islands, where Æolus, god of the storm and winds, governed a very unruly and turbulent population.

He is said to have received his royal dignity from the fair hands of Juno, and he was therefore specially eager to obey all her behests. He is commonly reputed to have married Aurora, or Eos, who gave him six sons : *i.e.*, Boreas, the north wind ; Corus, the north-west wind ; Aquilo, the west wind ; Notus, the south-west wind ; Eurus, the east wind ; and lastly, Zephyrus, the gentle and lovable south wind, whose mission it was to announce to mortals the return of ever-welcome spring.

Æolus' five elder sons were of a noisy, roving, mis-chievous, turbulent disposition, and peace and quiet were utterly impossible to them. To prevent their causing serious disasters, he therefore ruled them with a very strict hand, kept them closely confined in a great cave, and let them loose only one at a time, to stretch their limbs and take a little exercise.

> " Æolus in a cavern vast
> With bolt and barrier fetters fast
> Rebellious storm and howling blast.
> They with the rock's reverberant roar
> Chafe blustering round their prison door :
> He, throned on high, the sceptre sways,
> Controls their moods, their wrath allays."
> *Virgil (Conington's tr.).*

Although very unruly indeed, the winds always

" Tempestuous Corus rears his dreadful head "

Hercules and·the Hydra

obeyed their father's voice, and at his command, however reluctant, returned to their gloomy prison, where they expended their impotent rage in trying to shake its strong walls.

According to his own mood, or in conformity with the gods' request, Æolus either sent the gentler winds to play among the flowers, or, recalling them, let the fiercest of all his children free, with orders to pile up the waves mountain-high, lash them to foam, tear the sails of all the vessels at sea, break their masts, uproot the trees, tear the roofs off the houses,—in short, to do all the harm they possibly could.

> " Now rising all at once, and unconfin'd,
> From every quarter roars the rushing wind:
> First, from the wide Atlantic Ocean's bed,
> Tempestuous Corus rears his dreadful head,
> Th' obedient deep his potent breath controls,
> And, mountain-high, the foamy flood he rolls;
> Him the North-east encountering fierce, defied,
> And back rebuffeted the yielding tide.
> The curling surges loud conflicting meet,
> Dash their proud heads, and bellow as they beat;
> While piercing Boreas, from the Scythian strand,
> Ploughs up the waves and scoops the lowest sand.
> Nor Eurus then, I ween, was left to dwell,
> Nor showery Notus in th' Æolian cell,
> But each from every side, his power to boast,
> Ranged his proud forces to defend the coast."
>
> *Lucan.*

Æolus, king of the winds, shared with Dædalus the honour of inventing the sails which propel the ships so swiftly over the tide. It was he, too, who, according to Homer, bound all his children but one in a leather bag, which he gave to Ulysses when the latter visited Æolia. Thanks to this gift, Ulysses reached the shores of Ithaca, and would have landed in safety, had not his men, in view of port, untied the sack to

185

investigate its contents, and thus set free the angry winds, who stirred up the most frightful tempest in mythic annals.

The ancients, and especially the Athenians, paid particular attention to the winds, to whom they dedicated a temple, which still remains, and is generally known as the Tower of the Winds, or the Temple of Æolus. This temple is hexagonal, and on each side a flying figure of one of the winds is represented.

Eurus, the east wind, was generally depicted "as a young man flying with great impetuosity, and often appearing in a playful and wanton humour." Notus, or Auster, the south-west wind, "appeared generally as an old man, with grey hair, a gloomy countenance, a head covered with clouds, a sable vesture, and dusky wings," for he was considered the dispenser of rain and of all sudden and heavy showers. Zephyrus, mild and gentle, had a lapful of flowers, and, according to the Athenian belief, was wedded to Flora, with whom he was perfectly happy, and visited every land in turn. Corus, the north-west wind, drove clouds of snow before him ; while Aquilo, dreadful in appearance, caused cold shivers to run down one's back at his mere sight. Boreas, rough and shivering too, was the father of rain, snow, hail, and tempests, and was therefore generally represented as veiled in impenetrable clouds. His favourite place of abode was in the Hyperborean Mountains, from whence he sallied forth on wild raids. During one of these excursions he carried off Orithyia, who always fled at his approach. But all her fleetness could not save her : she was overtaken, and borne away to the inaccessible regions of snow and ice, where he detained her, and made her his wife. She became the mother of Zetes and Calais,—who took part in the Argonautic expedition, and drove

186

away the Harpies,—and of two daughters, Cleopatra and Chione.

On another occasion, Boreas, having changed him self into a horse and united himself to the mares of Dardanus, King of Troy, became the father of twelve steeds so swift that none could overtake them.

CHAPTER XIX : HERCULES

Hercules and the Serpents

> " Unto this thy son it shall be given,
> With his broad heart to win his way to heaven;
> Twelve labours shall he work ; and all accurst
> And brutal things o'erthrow, brute men the worst;
> And in Trachinia shall the funeral pyre
> Purge his mortalities away with fire ;
> And he shall mount amid the stars, and be
> Acknowledg'd kin to those who envied thee,
> And sent these den-born shapes to crush his destiny."
>
> *Theocritus (Hunt's tr.).*

THE ancients were not content to worship the gods only, but also offered up sacrifices to a few mortals, who, by their heroic deeds and virtuous lives, had won both admiration and respect. Foremost among these heroes—generally designated by the title of demi-gods—is Hercules (Heracles, Alcides), son of Jupiter and Alcmene, a mortal princess.

As soon as the tidings of Hercules' birth reached Olympus, Juno began to plot how to destroy her rival's child. Two colossal serpents with poisonous fangs were therefore despatched by her orders to attack the babe in its cradle. The monsters crept along noiselessly, entered the palace unseen, twined themselves around the cradle, and were about to crush the child to death in their folds, when, to the utter astonishment of the helpless attendants, little Hercules caught them fast by the neck in each tiny hand and strangled them, thus giving the first proof of the marvellous strength which was to make him famous.

> " First two dread Snakes at Juno's vengeful nod
> Climb'd round the cradle of the sleeping God ;
> Waked by the shrilling hiss, and rustling sound,
> And shrieks of fair attendants trembling round,

HERCULES' CHOICE

Their gasping throats with clenching hands he holds:
And Death untwists their convoluted folds."

Darwin.

When Juno perceived how easily Hercules had escaped from the danger which threatened him, she deemed it useless to make another attempt to take his life, but decided to vex his proud spirit by inflicting many petty annoyances, and to prevent his enjoying any lasting peace or happiness.

To achieve this purpose, she first extorted from Jupiter a decree that condemned Hercules to serve his cousin Eurystheus—a mean and cowardly prince who ruled over the kingdom of Argos—for a certain number of years.

Hercules' education was carefully attended to by Chiron, a learned Centaur, who taught him how to use all the different weapons, and trained him in all kinds of athletic sports. The years passed by happily and swiftly, until the time came when Hercules' education was completed, and the whole world lay before him, full of pleasant possibilities, and rich with many attractions.

Hercules' Choice

The youthful hero, dismissed by his instructor, now set out to seek his fortunes. He had not gone very far, however, before he met two beautiful women, who immediately entered into conversation with him, and drew from him a confession that he was in search of adventures. The women, Arete (Virtue) and Kakia (Vice), each offered to be his guide, but bade him choose which he preferred to follow.

Kakia, to induce him to follow her guidance, promised riches, ease, consideration, and love ; while Arete, a modest maiden, warned him that in her wake he would be obliged to wage incessant war against evil, to endure

189

hardships without number, and spend his days in toil and poverty.

Silently Hercules pondered for a while over these two so dissimilar offers, and then, mindful of his tutor's oft-repeated instructions, rose from his seat by the wayside, and, turning to Arete, declared himself ready to obey any command she might choose to give him.

> "Young Hercules with firm disdain
> Braved the soft smiles of Pleasure's harlot train;
> To valiant toils his forceful limbs assign'd,
> And gave to Virtue all his mighty mind."
>
> *Darwin.*

Courageously he then trod along the rough and thorny path she pointed out, and patiently performed the various tasks she assigned him, delivering the oppressed, defending the weak, and redressing all wrongs.

In reward for these good actions he received the hand of Megara, daughter of Creon, King of Thebes, in marriage, and by her had three children, whom he tenderly loved. But Juno was not at all satisfied to see him leading such a peaceful and prosperous life, and to interrupt its even course drove the hero mad.

Hercules' Madness

In a fit of delirium he threw his offspring into the fire, and, we are told, slew his dearly beloved wife. Then only he recovered his senses, and suffered agonies of sorrow and remorse for the terrible crimes he had unwittingly committed. In his grief he withdrew to the mountain solitudes, where he would probably have lingered all the remainder of his life, had not Mercury brought to him the decision of the gods that he was to serve Eurystheus, King of Argos, for a twelvemonth.

The messenger god then offered to lead him to his appointed taskmaster. But when Hercules learned he

THE HYDRA OF LERNA

was doomed to be a slave, he fell into such a passion that he nearly lost his reason again ; and instead of killing noxious beasts, and winning the people's blessings by his deeds of kindness, he wandered about stupidly and aimlessly, until he finally perceived how vain was his attempt to struggle against fate, and, urged by his chosen adviser, Arete, voluntarily offered his services to Eurystheus, who informed him that he must accomplish twelve great labours ere he could again be free.

The Nemean Lion

Eager to begin the appointed tasks, Hercules set out first to find and destroy a monstrous lion, whose den was in the Nemean Forest. Far and wide, throughout the whole neighbourhood, this monster committed his depredations, carrying off cattle and sheep, men, women, and children, to devour at his ease. All warned Hercules of the danger and difficulty of the undertaking, described the failure of countless previous attempts to slay the monster, and prophesied that he would never return alive. The hero would not be dissuaded, but entered the forest, tracked the lion to his den, grasped him by the throat, and strangled him as he had strangled the snakes in his infancy. He then skinned the monster, whose shaggy pelt became his favourite covering.

> " So from Nemea's den Alcides strode,
> The lion's yellow spoil around his shoulders flow'd."
> *Flaccus (Elton's tr.).*

The Hydra of Lerna

On his return to Argos to report the successful termination of his first task, Hercules was told to repair to the marshes of Lerna, where lurked a seven-headed serpent, the Hydra, and put an end to its career of rapacity, for this snake devoured man and beast Armed

191

with a great sword, Hercules succeeded in cutting off one of the seven heads; but he had no sooner done so, than, to his dismay, he saw seven other heads suddenly spring from the bleeding stump. To prevent a repetition of this unpleasant miracle, Hercules bade his friend Iolaus, who had accompanied him thither to view his prowess, take a lighted brand and sear the wounds as soon as inflicted. Thanks to this wise plan, the monster was finally slain, although a friendly crab sent by Juno to defend Hydra continually pinched Hercules' feet. The hero, angry at this intervention, crushed the crab, which, however, received its reward, for the Queen of Heaven placed it in the sky as the constellation of Cancer (the Crab). The country was thus freed from its long state of thraldom; but, before leaving the scene of his second labour, Hercules dipped his arrows in the Hydra's venomous blood, knowing well that any wound they might inflict, however slight, would be sure to prove fatal.

The Stag of Cerynea

The third task appointed by Eurystheus was the capture of the golden-horned, brazen-footed stag of Cerynea, whose fleetness was such that he seemed scarcely to touch the ground. Hercules was obliged to pursue this animal for many a weary mile before he could overtake him; and he only managed the capture by driving him into a deep snowdrift, in a distant northern land, from which he extricated him, and carried him home in triumph.

The Erymanthian Boar

The same success crowned his fourth labour, the capture of the wild boar of Erymanthus in Arcadia. Attacked by the Centaurs during the performance of

192

this labour, Hercules turned his deadly arrows upon them, and accidentally wounded his beloved tutor Chiron, who was coming to settle the dispute. Vainly the hero applied every healing herb. The wound was mortal, and Chiron died ; but in reward for his good offices the gods transferred him to the sky, where he is known as the constellation Sagittarius.

The Augean Stables

Hercules was next sent to Augeas, King of Elis, who had immense droves of cattle. The stables usually occupied by these animals were in an incredibly filthy state, as they had not been cleaned for years ; and now Hercules was given the task to remove the accumulated filth, and make a complete purification of the building.

Close by these stables rushed a torrent, or rather a river, the Alpheus. Hercules, with one glance, saw the use he could make of this rushing stream, which he dammed and turned aside from its course, so that the waters passed directly through the stables, carrying away all impurities, and finally washing them perfectly clean.

> " Nothing else
> Could clean the Augean stables."
> *Wordsworth.*

When Hercules saw that the work of purification was thoroughly accomplished, he guided the stream back to its original bed, and returned home to announce that the fifth labour was accomplished. The fabulous filth of the Augean stables, and the radical methods employed for their cleansing, have given rise to proverbial expressions still in current use.

The Cretan Bull

Hercules next journeyed off to Crete to accomplish his sixth task, the capture of a mad bull given by

Neptune to Minos, king of the island. The god had sent the animal with directions that he should be offered up in sacrifice; but Minos, charmed with his unusual size and beauty, resolved to keep him, and substituted a bull from his own herds for the religious ceremony.

Angry at seeing his express command so wantonly disobeyed, Neptune maddened the bull, which rushed wildly all over the island, causing great damage. This animal Hercules, with his usual strength and skill, caught and bound fast, thus finishing the sixth task.

The Steeds of Diomedes

He then hastened on to Thrace, where Diomedes, the king, kept some fine coursers, which were fed on human flesh. In order to obtain a sufficient supply of fresh meat for his horses, Diomedes had decreed that all strangers who ventured into his kingdom should be seized, and, when sufficiently fat, executed, and served up in his horses' mangers. To punish Diomedes for this long-continued barbarity, Hercules threw him to his own horses, which were then led off to Eurystheus, as a token that the seventh labour was completed.

Hippolyte's Girdle

Now, at the court of Eurystheus was his beautiful daughter, Admete, a vain princess, who delighted in dress and jewels, and who was never happier than when she obtained some new ornament or article of apparel. One day Admete heard a traveller describe a girdle worn by Hippolyte, queen of the Amazons, and was immediately seized by the desire to possess the ornament.

She imparted this wish to Eurystheus, who, delighted to gratify her as long as he could do so without taking any personal risk or trouble, sent Hercules in quest of the coveted jewel. The journey to the land of the

194

THE STYMPHALIAN BIRDS

Amazons—a fierce, warlike nation of women—was long and dangerous ; but Hercules travelled on undaunted, nor paused, except when his services were needed in furthering some good work for mortals, until he reached their land, presented himself before their queen, and boldly explained the cause of his presence. Hippolyte listened to his explanation and request with queenly condescension, promised to consider the matter, and meanwhile bade him feast and rest in her palace.

Hercules would have succeeded in this undertaking without any trouble, had not Juno suddenly remembered his existence, and resolved to continue her never entirely forgotten persecutions In the guise of an Amazon, she mingled among the women, and artfully spread the report that Hercules had really come to kidnap their queen, and that the pretended quest of the girdle was a mere excuse, and only intended to distract their attention from his real purpose. The Amazons yielded implicit belief to these rumours, flew to arms, and surrounded their queen.

> " The Amazons array their ranks,
> In painted arms of radiant sheen
> Around Hippolyte the queen."
>
> *Virgil (Conington's tr.).*

The assembled force then attacked Hercules, who met their onslaught single-handed, defeated them, and finally bore away the prize he had risked so much to obtain. It was on his homeward journey from this expedition that he saved Hesione, Laomedon's daughter, from the jaws of the sea monster who was about to devour her, as he had devoured many a fair Trojan maid before.

The Stymphalian Birds

Eurystheus, well pleased with the manner in which Hercules had accomplished eight out of the twelve tasks, bade him now go forth and slay the dangerous, brazen-clawed birds which hovered over the stagnant waters of Lake Stymphalus. The poisoned arrows now served him in good stead, and enabled him to put a speedy end to the whole flock.

> " His arrows slew
> The monsters hov'ring fell Stymphalus round."
>
> *Catullus,*

The Cattle of Geryones

Hercules was next told to capture the divine cattle of Geryones, a giant of Erythea. On his way home with this marvellous herd, Hercules paused on Mount Aventine, where, during the night, the loathsome giant Cacus stole some of his cows. To punish him for this theft Hercules forced his way into his cave, attacked him, and, after a memorable encounter, slew him. The animals were soon after delivered into the hands of Eurystheus, who then sent Hercules in search of the Golden Apples of the Hesperides, daughters of Hesperus, god of the West, and also known as the Evening Star.

> " O Hesperus ! thou bringest all things home;
> All that the garish day hath scattered wide;
> The sheep, the goat, back to the welcome fold;
> Thou bring'st the child, too, to his mother's side."
>
> *Sappho (W. H. Appleton's tr.).*

The Hesperian Apples

This commission sadly perplexed Hercules, for he did not know in what portion of the world he would find these apples, which had been given to Juno as a wedding present, and which she had entrusted to the care of the Hesperides. After numerous journeys and many inquiries, Hercules discovered that these maidens had carried these apples off to Africa, hung them on a tree in their garden, and placed the dragon Ladon at its foot to guard their treasures night and day. Unfortu-

nately, no one could tell Hercules in what part of Africa
the garden of the Hesperides might be situated: so he
set out at a venture, determined to travel about until
he gained some information. On his way he met with
many adventures, and saw many strange sights. For
instance, he first met the nymphs of the Eridanus River,
and, questioning them about the golden apples, was told
to consult old Nereus, god of the sea, who would probably be able to give him some information on the subject.

Hercules, having surprised this aged divinity while
asleep on the sea-shore, held him fast, in spite of the
multitudinous transformations he underwent in the
vain hope of frightening his would-be interlocutor
away. In answer to Hercules' question, he finally very
reluctantly bade him seek Prometheus, who alone would
be able to direct him aright.

In obedience to this advice, Hercules went to the
Caucasian Mountains, where, on the brink of a mighty
precipice, he found Prometheus, still bound with
adamantine chains, and still a prey to the ravenous
vulture. To spring up the mountain-side, kill the
cruel bird, snap the adamantine chains, and set free
the benefactor of all mankind, was the work of but a
few minutes for such a hero as Hercules ; and, in gratitude for the deliverance he had so long sought in vain,
Prometheus directed Hercules to his brother Atlas,
telling him he would be sure to know where the apples
could be found.

Hercules wended his way to Africa, where Atlas
dwelt, and on his way passed through the land of a
diminutive race of men, called Pygmies, who were so
small that they lived in constant dread of their neighbours, so much larger and stronger than they, and of
the cranes, which passed over their country in great
flocks, and sometimes alighted to devour their harvests.

To guard against these constant inroads, the Pygmies finally accepted the services of Antæus, a giant son of Gæa, who generously offered to defend them against all their enemies. When these little people, therefore, saw Hercules' mighty form looming up in the dim distance, they called aloud for fear, and bade Antæus go forth and kill the new invader, who, they wrongly fancied, had evil designs against them.

Proud of his strength, Antæus went to meet Hercules, and defied him. A fierce struggle was the immediate result of this challenge, and, as the combatants were of equal size and strength, the victory seemed very uncertain. At last Hercules felt his great strength begin to fail, and noticed that every time his adversary touched the ground he seemed to renew his vigour. He therefore resolved to try and win by strategy, and, watching his opportunity, seized Antæus round the waist, raised him from the ground, and held him aloft in his powerful embrace.

The giant struggled with all his might to get free ; but Hercules held him fast, and felt him grow weaker and weaker, now that he was no longer sustained by his mother Earth, from whom he derived all his strength, until at last his struggles ceased, and he hung limp and lifeless in Hercules' crushing embrace.

"Lifts proud Antæus from his mother-plains,
    And with strong grasp the struggling giant strains;
    Back falls his fainting head and clammy hair,
    Writhe his weak limbs, and flits his life in air."

Darwin.

Now that the gigantic defender of the Pygmies no longer blocked his way, Hercules travelled onward in search of Atlas, whom he finally found supporting the heavens on his broad shoulders. Atlas listened attentively to all Hercules had to say, declared he knew where

Atlas

Hercules' Struggle with Death

the apples could be found, and promised to get them if the hero would only relieve him of his burden for a little while. Glad to accomplish his purpose so easily, Hercules allowed the burden of the heavens to be transferred to his shoulders, and Atlas hastened off to fulfil his part of the agreement.

From afar the giant saw the golden fruit glittering in the sunshine. Stealthily he drew near, entered the gardens, slew the dragon in his sleep, plucked the apples, and returned unmolested to the place where he had left Hercules. But his steps became slower and slower; and as he neared the hero, he could not help thinking with horror of the burden he must so soon resume, and bear for centuries, perhaps, without relief.

This thought oppressed him. Freedom was so sweet that he resolved to keep it, and, coolly stepping up to Hercules, announced that he would carry the golden apples to Eurystheus, and leave him to support the heavens in his stead. Feigning a satisfaction which he was very far from feeling, Hercules acquiesced, but detained Atlas for a moment, asking him to hold the heavens until he could place a cushion on his shoulders. Good-natured, as giants proverbially are, Atlas threw the apples on the grass beside him, and assumed the incumbent weight; but Hercules, instead of preparing to resume it, picked up the apples, leaving Atlas alone, in the same plight as he had found him, there to remain until some more compassionate hero should come and set him free.

> "There Atlas, son of great Iapetus,
>   With head inclined and ever-during arms,
>   Sustains the spacious heavens."
>
> *Hesiod.*

It was during the course of one of his mighty labours that Hercules, with one wrench of his powerful arm, tore a cleft in the mountains, and allowed the waters of the Sea to flow into Oceanus; and ever since, the rocks on either side of the Strait of Gibraltar have borne the name of Hercules' Pillars.

The twelfth and last task appointed by Eurystheus was the most difficult of all to perform. Hercules was commanded to descend into Hades and bring up the dog Cerberus, securely bound.

> "But for the last, to Pluto's drear abode
> Through the dark jaws of Tænarus he went,
> To drag the triple-headed dog to light."
>
> *Euripides (Potter's tr.).*

This command, like all the others, was speedily obeyed; but Eurystheus was so terrified at the aspect of the triple-headed dog, from the foam of whose dripping jaws the nightshade sprang, that he took refuge in a huge jar, and refused to come out until Hercules had carried the monster back to his cave.

The twelve appointed labours were finished; the time of bondage was ended; and Hercules, a free man, could wander at his own sweet will, and enjoy the happiness of freedom. A roaming existence had, from force of habit, become a necessity: so the hero first journeyed to Olympia, where he instituted games to be celebrated every fifth year in honour of Jupiter, his father. Thence he wandered from place to place, doing good, and came to the house of Admetus, where he was surprised to find all the court in mourning.

His sympathetic inquiries soon brought forth a full account of Alcestis' sacrifice of her own life to ensure the immortality of her husband. The hero's heart was touched by the king's loneliness; and he again braved the terrors of Hades, and brought Alcestis back from the grave, and restored her to her husband's arms.

HERCULES AND DEIANEIRA

Hercules took a prominent part in many heroic enterprises. Among others, he joined in the Argonautic expedition, in the battle between the Centaurs and Lapithæ, in the war of the gods and giants, and in the first siege of Troy, which proved successful

Hercules and Omphale

But the hero, although so lately escaped from servitude, was soon obliged to return into bondage; for in a fit of anger he slew a man, and was condemned by the assembled gods to serve Omphale, Queen of Lydia, for a certain period of time.

No great deeds were now required of Hercules, whose strength was derided by his new mistress, and who, governing him easily by his admiration for her, made him submit to occupations unworthy of a man, and, while he was busy spinning, decked herself in his lion's skin, and brandished his renowned club.

> "His lion spoils the laughing Fair demands,
> And gives the distaff to his awkward hands."
> *Darwin.*

However unworthy these effeminate tasks may seem for such a hero, they proved very agreeable indeed to Hercules, who, having fallen in love with his new mistress, seemed to wish nothing better than to remain her slave for ever, and end his days in idleness and pleasure. Great labours were awaiting his mighty arm, however; and the gods, at the appointed time, freed him from his bondage to the Lydian queen, and bade him go forth and do all the good in his power.

Hercules and Deianeira

In the course of his wanderings, Hercules next met Deianeira, daughter of Œneus, and, having fallen in love with her, expressed a desire to marry her. But unfortunately another suitor, the river god Achelous, had already won the father's consent.

> Achelous came,
> The river god, to ask a father's voice,
> And snatched me to his arms."
>
> *Sophocles (Francklin's tr.).*

So sure was this suitor of his attractions, that he did not even deem it necessary to secure the maiden's good graces , and when Hercules made known his love, she immediately promised to marry him if he would only free her from the lover her father would fain force upon her. Delighted to be able to win his bride and punish his rival at the same time, Hercules challenged Achelous ; and now began a wrestling match, the fame of which has come down to us through all the intervening centuries.

Achelous was an opponent worthy of Hercules, and, besides, took advantage of his power to change his form at will, further to perplex and harass the sturdy hero. At last he assumed the shape of a bull, and with lowered horns rushed toward Hercules, intending to toss him aside. The hero, skilfully avoiding his first onset, seized him by one of his great thick-set horns, and held it so firmly that all the bull's efforts to free himself from his powerful grasp were vain, until the horn broke.

The Goddess of Plenty, the Attican Fortuna, a witness of this strange combat, appropriated the broken horn, stuffed her treasures in its hollow, and was so well pleased with the effect, that she decreed it should henceforth be one of her attributes. The fight, only temporarily suspended, was now resumed with re-

THE STORY OF NESSUS

doubled ardour, for each of the lovers was intent upon winning the hand of the fair Deianeira.

> " Warm, and more warm the conflict grows:
> Dire was the noise of rattling bows,
> Of front to front opposed, and hand to hand:
> Deep was the animated strife
> For love, for conquest, and for life."
>
> Sophocles (*Francklin's tr.*).

The victory, though long uncertain, finally rested with Hercules, who triumphantly departed with his hard-won bride, for his destiny would not permit him to tarry long in any place. Instead of wandering alone now, with none to cheer or sympathise, Hercules had Deianeira ever at his side; and after many days they came to the river Evenus, whose usually shallow and peaceful waters were swollen and turbid, for violent rain-storms had recently swept over that portion of the country.

The Story of Nessus

Hercules paused for a moment to contemplate the stream, and glanced about for some safe mode to transport Deianeira across. While he was thus considering, a Centaur by the name of Nessus came to his assistance, and proposed to carry the fair young bride to the other shore in complete safety, if she would but consent to mount upon his broad back.

> " The hoary centaur, who was wont for hire
> To bear the traveller o'er the rapid flood
> Of deep Evenus: not with oars or sail
> He stemm'd the torrent, but with nervous arm
> Opposed and pass'd it: me, when first a bride
> I left my father's hospitable roof
> With my Alcides, in his arms he bore
> Athwart the current."
>
> Sophocles (*Francklin's tr.*).

Hercules, only too glad to avail himself of the Centaur's kind offer of assistance, quickly helped Deianeira to mount, saw them descend into the water, and prepared to follow, holding his bow and arrows aloft in one hand, and breasting the waves with the other.

Now, the Centaur Nessus did not often have the good fortune to carry such a pretty passenger as Deianeira over the river, and as he swam he made up his mind to gallop off with her as soon as he reached the opposite shore. All his strength and energy, therefore, were called into requisition · and when he reached the shore, instead of pausing to allow his fair burden to dismount, he set off as fast as he could run.

A loud shriek from Deianeira attracted Hercules' attention, and a second later one of his poisoned arrows had brought the would-be ravisher to the ground, pierced through the heart. With dying accents the Centaur Nessus professed repentance, and bade Deianeira take his robe,—but slightly stained with the blood which gushed from the wound inflicted by the poisoned arrow,—and keep it carefully, for it had magic power; and if she ever found her husband's love waning, he assured her that, could she but induce him to put it on, all his early affection would revive, as pure and fervent as during their courtship.

> "'Take
> This white robe. It is costly. See, my blood
> Has stained it but a little. I did wrong .
> I know it, and repent me. If there come
> A time when he grows cold—for all the race
> Of heroes wander, nor can any love
> Fix theirs for long—take it and wrap him in it,
> And he shall love again.'"
>
> *Lewis Morris.*

Deianeira gratefully accepted the proffered gift, and promised to treasure it up carefully, although she

sincerely hoped she would never be called upon to
make use of it. Years passed by. Hercules often left
Deianeira to deliver the oppressed and relieve the
suffering, for people came from great distances to ask
for his aid ; and although his absences were sometimes
prolonged, he always returned to her side, as loving as
ever, and she had no cause for complaint. Finally duty
took him back to the court of Eurytus, where he beheld
Iole, whom he had seen and loved in the beginning of
his career, but whom he had been obliged to leave to
fulfil his arduous tasks. She was still young and
charming, and his first glance into her sweet face
rekindled all his former passion. Day after day he
lingered by her side, forgetful of duty, Deianeira, and
all but his first dream of love and happiness. When
absent, Deianeira was wont to hear rumours of his
heroic achievements ; but on this occasion the only
report which reached her ear was that he had returned
to his allegiance to his first love, and this roused her
jealousy, so long dormant.

Finally she heard that Hercules was wending his way
homeward again, and her heart bounded with joy, but
only to sink more heavily when told that he was accompanied by Iole and a numerous train. Then she remembered the long-forgotten gift of the Centaur. With
trembling hands she sought the glittering robe, gave it
to a messenger, and bade him hasten to meet Hercules,
and prevail upon him to wear it for his triumphant
return. The messenger, Lichas, hastened to do her
bidding, and Deianeira waited with fast-beating heart
for the success of her venture.

> "I only wish the charm may be of power
> To win Alcides from this virgin's love,
> And bring him back to Deianeira's arms."
> *Sophocles (Francklin's tr.).*

Lichas acquitted himself faithfully of his errand ; and Hercules, viewing the costly garment, and anxious to appear to his best advantage before the bright eyes of Iole, immediately donned the richly embroidered robe.

He had no sooner put it on, than the Centaur's poisoned blood began its deadly work. First he experienced a burning, stinging sensation, which ran like fire through every vein. Vainly he tried to tear off the fatal garment. It clung to his limbs, and the poison ate its way into his flesh, until the pain was greater than he could bear.

In his rage at the trick which had been played upon him, he seized Lichas—the unfortunate bearer of the poisoned robe—by the foot, and flung him from the heights of Mount Œta down into the sea, where he perished.

> "And Lichas from the top of Œta threw
> Into th' Euboic Sea."

Milton.

The Death of Hercules

Then, resolved to end these unendurable torments by a death worthy of his whole life, Hercules called his servants, and bade them build his funeral pyre on the mountain peak; but they, in tears, refused to obey, for they could not bear the thought of parting with their beloved master. Commands and entreaties alike failed to move them : so Hercules climbed up the mountain side alone, tore up the huge oaks by their roots, flung them one upon the other until he had raised a mighty pile, upon which he stretched his colossal, pain-racked limbs, and bade his friend Philoctetes set fire to the stupendous mass.

At first Philoctetes also refused to do his bidding ; but, bribed by the promise of the world-renowned poisoned arrows, he finally consented to do as Hercules wished, and the red flames rose higher and higher, the wood crackled and burned, and the hero was soon enveloped in sheets of flames, which purged him from all mortality.

Then Jupiter came down from his glorious abode, caught the noble soul in his mighty arms, and bore it off to Olympus, there to dwell in happiness for ever with Hebe, the fair goddess of youth, whose hand was given him in marriage.

> " Till the god, the earthly part forsaken,
>   From the man in flames asunder taken,
>   Drank the heavenly ethers' purer breath.
> Joyous in the new, unwonted lightness,
>   Earth's dark, heavy burden lost in death.
> High Olympus gives harmonious greeting
>   To the hall where reigns his sire adored ;
> Youth's bright goddess, with a blush at meeting,
>   Gives the nectar to her lord."
>
> *Schiller* (*S. G. B.'s tr.*)

Hercules, the special divinity of athletic sports and of strength, was principally worshipped by young men. He is generally represented in art as a tall, powerfully built man, with a small, bearded head, a lion's skin carelessly thrown over his shoulder, and leaning upon a massive club.

> "Great Alcides, stooping with his toil,
>   Rests on his club.'
>
> *Pope.*

It is said that some of the games celebrated at Olympia were held in his honour, although originally instituted by him in honour of Jupiter, his father. The Nemean Games, celebrated in the forest of Nemea, the scene of his first great labour, were the principal games held in Greece in commemoration of his noble deeds and early death.

CHAPTER XX : PERSEUS

Acrisius and Danae

THE life of Acrisius, King of Argos, had been a burden to him ever since the unfortunate day when an oracle had predicted that he would be killed by his grandson. Until then the king had been very fond of his only child, Danae, and until then, too, had thought with pride of the time when he would bestow her hand in marriage upon the noblest of all who came to woo.

Now his plans were all changed, and his only wish was to keep her unmated,—a somewhat difficult task, for the maiden was very fair, and Acrisius knew that the wily God of Love would endeavour to find some way to outwit him and bring his plans to naught. After much thought, Acrisius decided to lock Danae up in a brazen tower, around which he stationed guards to prevent any one from even approaching the captive princess.

But, although safely concealed from the eyes of men, Danae was plainly seen by the everlasting gods ; and Jupiter, looking down from Olympus, beheld her in all her loveliness and in all her loneliness. She was seated on top of her brazen tower, her eyes wistfully turned toward the city, where girls of her age enjoyed freedom, and were allowed to marry when they pleased.

The Shower of Gold

Jupiter, pitying her isolation and admiring her beauty, resolved to go down and converse with her for a little while. To avoid being seen, he changed himself into a golden shower, and gently dropped down on the turret beside her, where his presence and spirited conversation soon won the maiden's heart.

208

Danaë and the Tower of Brass

Perseus and the Hesperides

DANAE AND HER BABE

"Danae, in a brazen tower
Where no love was, loved a shower."
Shelley.

This first successful visit was frequently repeated, and Danae no longer felt lonely and deserted, for Jupiter spent most of his time with her, pursuing his courtship most diligently, and finally winning her to a secret marriage, to which no one offered the slightest objection, as no one suspected his visits, which he continued quite unmolested.

But one morning the guards rushed in terror to Acrisius' palace to announce that Danae, his daughter, had given birth to a son, who, on account of his beauty, was called Perseus. The king no sooner learned this astonishing news, than he flew into a great rage, vowed that mother and child should perish, and despatched the guards to fetch the unfortunate victims.

Danae and her Babe

Acrisius, however, was not cruel enough to stain his own hands with his child's blood, or to witness her execution : so he ordered that she should be placed in an empty cask with her helpless infant, and exposed to the fury of the waves. These orders were speedily executed ; and Danae's heart sank with terror when she felt the cask buffeted about by the great waves far out of sight of land, and out of all reach of help. Clasping her babe close to her bosom, she fervently prayed the gods to watch over them both, and bring them in safety to some hospitable shore.

"When round the well-fram'd ark the blowing blast
Roar'd, and the heaving whirlpools of the deep
With rough'ning surge seem'd threatening to o'erturn
The wide-tost vessel, not with tearless cheeks
The mother round her infant gently twined

THE CLASSICAL MYTHS

> Her tender arm, and cried, 'Ah me! my child!
> What sufferings I endure! thou sleep'st the while,
> Inhaling in thy milky-breathing breast
> The balm of slumber.' "
>
> *Simonides (Elton's tr.).*

Her piteous prayer was evidently heard, for, after much tossing, the cask was finally washed ashore on the Island of Seriphus, where Polydectes, the king, kindly received mother and child. Here Perseus, the golden-haired, grew to manhood, and here made his first appearance in games and combats.

In the meanwhile Polydectes had fallen in love with Danae, and expressed his desire to marry her; but Danae did not return his affection, and would not consent. Angry at her persistent refusal of his proposals, Polydectes wished to compel her to obey, and thereby incurred the wrath of young Perseus, who loudly declared that none should dare force his mother as long as he were there to defend her. This boast did not at all allay the monarch's wrath; and, hoping to get rid of the young boaster, he bade him go forth and slay Medusa, if he wished to convince people that his bravery was real.

The Gorgons

This Medusa was one of the three Gorgons. Her sisters, Euryale and Stheno, although immortal, had never had any claims to beauty; but Medusa, when only a girl, had been considered very handsome indeed. Her home, in a land where the sun never shone, was very distasteful to her, so she entreated Minerva to let her go and visit the beautiful sunny south.

But when Minerva refused to grant her wish, she reviled the goddess, and declared that nothing but a conviction that mortals would no longer consider her

210

beautiful if they but once beheld Medusa, could have prompted this denial. This presumptuous remark so incensed Minerva, that, to punish her for her vanity, she changed her beautiful curling locks into hissing, writhing serpents, and decreed that one glance into her still beautiful face would suffice to change the beholder into stone.

> "Fatal Beauty! thou didst seem
> The phantom of some fearful dream.
> Extremes of horror and of love
> Alternate o'er our senses move,
> As, rapt and spellbound, we survey
> The horrid coils which round thee play,
> And mark thy wild, enduring smile,
> Lit by no mortal fire the while,
> Formed to attract all eyes to thee,
> And yet their withering blight to be;
> Thy power mysterious to congeal
> And from life's blood its warmth to steal,
> To petrify the mortal clay
> In its first gleam of wild dismay,
> Is a dread gift to one like thee,
> Cursed with a hateful destiny."
>
> *Mrs. St. John.*

The gods, who had carefully watched over Perseus through his childhood and youth, now decided to lend him their aid, so that he might successfully accomplish the great task of slaying Medusa. Pluto lent him a magic helmet, which made the wearer invisible at will; Mercury attached his own winged sandals to the youth's heels, to endow him with great rapidity of flight; while Minerva armed him with her own mirrorlike shield, the dreadful Ægis.

> "Minerva thus to Perseus lent her shield;
> Secure of conquest, sent him to the field:
> The hero acted what the queen ordain'd,
> So was his fame complete."
>
> *Prior.*

Another account relates that Perseus received the sandals and helmet, together with a magic pouch in which to carry the head of Medusa, from the Hesperides.

Thus equipped, Perseus flew northward until he came to the land of perpetual darkness, the home of the Grææ, three horrible sisters, who possessed but one eye and one tooth, which they handed about and used in turn, and who were the only living beings cognisant of the place where Medusa dwelt.

Invisible by virtue of his magic helmet, Perseus drew near the cave without fear of detection, and intercepted the eye while on its way from one sister to another. As soon as it was safe in his possession, he spoke to them, promising to restore it if they would only give him accurate directions for finding Medusa. The sisters, eager to recover the treasured eye, immediately gave the desired information ; and Perseus, having honourably fulfilled his share of the contract, departed in search of Medusa.

Perseus at last perceived the Gorgons' home in the dim distance ; and, as he was fully aware of Medusa's petrifying proclivities, he advanced very cautiously, holding his shield before him at such an angle that all surrounding objects were clearly reflected on its smooth, mirrorlike surface.

He thus discovered Medusa asleep, raised his sword, and, without looking at anything but her mirrored form, severed her head from her body, seized it in one hand, and, holding it persistently behind his back, flew away in great haste, lest the two remaining Gorgons should fall upon him and attempt to avenge their sister's death.

Perseus then swiftly winged his way over land and sea, carefully holding his ghastly trophy behind him ; and as he flew, Medusa's blood trickled down on the hot African sand, where it gave birth to a race of

Perseus and the Graeæ

Perseus and Andromeda

poisonous reptiles destined to infest the region in future ages, and cause the death of many an adventurous explorer. The drops which fell into the sea were utilised by Neptune, who created from them the famous winged steed called Pegasus.

> " And the life drops from thy head
> On Libyan sands, by Perseus shed,
> Sprang a scourging race from thee—
> Fell types of artful mystery."
>
> *Mrs. St. John.*

Perseus and Atlas

The return journey was long and wearisome, and on his way the hero had many adventures. Once, when flying high above a mountainous country, he caught a glimpse of Atlas, his pale face turned up to the heavens, whose weight he had patiently borne for many a long year,—a burden which seemed all the more grievous after the short taste of freedom he had enjoyed while Hercules stood in his place,—

> " Supporting on his shoulders the vast pillar
> Of Heaven and Earth, a weight of cumbrous grasp."
>
> *Æschylus (Potter's tr.).*

When Atlas saw Perseus flying toward him, hope revived, for he remembered that fate had decreed that it was this hero who was to slay the Gorgon ; and he thought that, if he could but once gaze upon her stony face, he would be free from pain and weariness for ever. As soon as the hero was within hearing, Atlas therefore addressed him as follows :

" ' Hasten now, Perseus, and let me look upon the Gorgon's face, for the agony of my labour is well-nigh greater than I can bear.' So Perseus hearkened unto the word of Atlas, and he unveiled before him the dead face of Medusa. Eagerly he gazed for a moment on

213

THE CLASSICAL MYTHS

the changeless countenance, as though beneath the blackness of great horror he yet saw the wreck of her ancient beauty and pitied her for her hopeless woe. But in an instant the straining eyes were stiff and cold; and it seemed to Perseus, as he rose again into the pale yellow air, that the grey hairs which streamed from the giant's head were like the snow which rests upon the peak of a great mountain, and that in place of the trembling limbs he saw only the rents and clefts on a rough hillside."

Thus the mere sight of Medusa changed Atlas into the rugged mountains which have since borne his name; and, as their summits are lost in the clouds, the ancients supposed they sustained the full weight of the heavenly vault.

The Story of Andromeda

Thence Perseus flew on until he reached the sea-shore, where a strange sight greeted him. Away down on the "rock-bound coast," so near the foaming billows that their spray continually dashed over her fair limbs, a lovely maiden was chained fast to an overhanging rock. This maiden was the princess Andromeda. To atone for the vanity of her mother, Cassiopeia, who claimed she was fairer than any of the sea nymphs, she had been exposed there as prey for a terrible sea monster sent to devastate the homes along the coast.

An oracle, when consulted, declared that the monster would not depart until Andromeda was sacrificed to his fury; and Perseus could even now perceive the receding procession which had solemnly accompanied her to the appointed place of sacrifice, and chained her fast.

At the same time, too, he saw the waters below the maiden lashed to foam by the monster's tail, and the scales of his hideous body slowly rising out of the

214

water. Fascinated by this horrible sight, the maiden's eyes were fixed on the monster. She did not see the rapid approach of her deliverer, who, dauntless, drew his sword from its scabbard, and, swooping down, attacked the monster, cheered by the shouts of the people, who had seen him, and now rushed back to witness the slaying of their foe.

> " On the hills a shout
> Of joy, and on the rocks the ring of mail;
> And while the hungry serpent's gloating eyes
> Were fixed on me, a knight in casque of gold
> And blazing shield, who with his flashing blade
> Fell on the monster. Long the conflict raged,
> Till all the rocks were red with blood and slime,
> And yet my champion from those horrible jaws
> And dreadful coils was scathless."
>
> *Lewis Morris.*

Of course, this fierce struggle could have but one conclusion; and when Perseus had slain the monster, freed Andromeda from her chains, and restored her to the arms of her overjoyed parents, they immediately offered any reward he might be pleased to claim. When he, therefore, expressed a desire to marry the maiden he had so bravely rescued, they gladly gave him her hand, although in early youth the princess had been promised to her uncle Phineus.

Preparations for the marriage were immediately begun; and the former suitor, who had been too cowardly to venture a single blow to deliver her from the monster, prepared, nevertheless, to fight the rival who was about to carry off his promised bride. Unbidden he came to the marriage feast with a number of armed followers, and was about to carry off Andromeda, when Perseus, bidding his adherents stand behind him, suddenly unveiled the Medusa head, and, turning its baleful face toward Phineus and his followers, changed them all into stone.

> "'Mid the fabled Libyan bridal stood
> Perseus in stern tranquillity of wrath,
> Half stood, half floated on his ankle plumes
> Out-swelling, while the bright face on his shield
> Looked into stone the raging fray."
>
> *Milman.*

The interrupted marriage feast was now resumed; and when it was over, Perseus took his bride to Seriphus. There, hearing that Polydectes had dared to ill-treat his mother because she still refused to accede to his wishes and become his wife, he changed the importunate king into a rock by showing him his Medusa trophy, gave the kingdom to the king's brother, and, accompanied by wife and mother, returned to his native land. The borrowed helmet, sandals, and shield were all duly restored to their respective owners, and the Medusa head was given to Minerva in token of gratitude for her help. Greatly pleased with this gift, the goddess set it in the centre of her terrible Ægis, where it retained all its petrifying power, and served her in many a fight.

Arrived at Argos, Perseus discovered that a usurper had claimed his grandfather's throne. To hurl the unlawful claimant from his exalted seat, and compel him to make full restitution and atonement, was but a trifle for the hero who had conquered Medusa; and Acrisius, now old and weak, was taken from the prison where he languished, and restored to his wonted honours, by the very youth he had been taught to fear.

But the gods' decree was always sure to be fulfilled sooner or later; and one day, when Perseus was playing quoits, he accidentally killed his grandfather. To

Perseus

The Minotaur

remain at Argos, haunted by the memory of this involuntary crime, was too painful for him : so he
exchanged his kingdom for another, that of Mycenæ,
which he ruled wisely and well. When Perseus died,
after a long and glorious reign, the gods, who had
always loved him, placed him among the stars, where
he can still be seen, with his wife Andromeda, and
mother-in-law Cassiopeia.

CHAPTER XXI : THESEUS

The Childhood of Theseus

WHEN yet but a very young man, Ægeus, King of Athens, journeyed off to Trœzene, where he fell in love with and married a beautiful young princess by the name of Æthra. For some reason, which mythologists do not make known, the king was forced to return alone to Athens; but ere he departed he concealed his sword and sandals beneath a stone, bidding his wife remember, that, as soon as the strength of their son Theseus permitted, he must raise the rock, take the sword and sandals, and come and join him in Athens, where he should be introduced to the people as his son and heir. These instructions given, Ægeus bade a fond farewell to his wife and infant son, and returned home.

As the years passed by, they brought strength, beauty, and wisdom to Theseus, whose fame began to be published abroad. At last Æthra deemed him strong enough to raise the rock beneath which his father's trusty weapon lay; and, conducting him to the spot where it was, she told him the whole story, and bade him try his strength.

Theseus immediately obeyed. With a mighty effort he raised the rock, and, to his great satisfaction, found the sword and sandals in a perfect state of preservation. Sword in hand, he then set out for Athens,—a long and dangerous journey. He proceeded slowly and cautiously, for he knew that many dangers lurked along his pathway, and that ere he reached his father's city he would have to encounter both giants and monsters, who would strive to bar his way.

He was not at all mistaken in his previsions; for Trœzene was scarcely lost to sight ere he came across the giant Periphetes, son of Vulcan, who stood in the road and attacked with a huge club, whose blows were generally fatal, all who strove to pass. Adroitly evading the giant's first onslaught, Theseus plunged his sword deep into his huge side ere he could renew the attack, and brought him lifeless to the ground.

Theseus then disarmed his fallen foe, and, retaining the club for future use, continued his journey in peace, until he came to the Isthmus of Corinth, where two adventures awaited him. The first was with a cruel giant named Sinis, nicknamed The Pine-bender, whose usual practice was to bend some huge pine until its top touched the ground, and call to any unsuspecting passer-by to seize it and lend him a helping hand for a moment. Then, as soon as the innocent stranger had complied with his request, he would suddenly let go the pine, which, freed from his gigantic grasp, sprang back to its upright position, and hurled the unfortunate traveller away up into the air, to be dashed to pieces against the rocky mountain-side.

Theseus, who had already heard of the giant's stratagem, skilfully eluded the danger, and finally caused Sinis to perish by the same cruel death which he had dealt out to so many others.

In one place the Isthmus of Corinth was exceedingly narrow, and the only practicable pathway led along a rocky ledge, guarded by a robber named Sciron, who forced all who tried to pass him to wash his feet. While the traveller was thus engaged, and knelt in the narrow pathway to do his bidding, he would suddenly raise his foot, kick him over the side, and hurl him down into the sea below, where a huge tortoise was ever waiting with gaping jaws to devour the victims.

Instead of yielding to Sciron's exactions, Theseus drew his sword, and by his determined bearing so terrified the robber, that he offered him a free passage. This offer, however, did not satisfy Theseus, who said he would sheathe his sword only on condition that Sciron performed for him the menial office he had imposed upon so many others. Sciron dared not refuse, and obeyed in fear and trembling ; but he was doomed never to molest any one again, for Theseus kicked him over the precipice, into the breakers, where the tortoise feasted upon his remains with as keen a relish as upon former victims.

After disposing of another world-renowned robber, Cercyon (The Wrestler), Theseus encountered Procrustes (The Stretcher), a cruel giant, who, under pretext of entertainment, deluded travellers into entering his home, where he had two beds of very different dimensions,—one unusually short, the other unusually long. If the unfortunate traveller were a short man, ne was put to bed in the long bedstead, and his limbs were pulled out of joint to make him fit it ; but if, on the contrary, he were tall, he was assigned the short bed, and the superfluous length of limb were lopped off under the self-same pretext. Taking Procrustes quite unawares, Theseus gave him a faint idea of the sufferings he had inflicted upon others by making him try each bed in turn, and then, to avoid his continuing these evil practices, put an end to his wretched existence.

Theseus successfully accomplished a few more exploits of a similar character, and finally reached Athens, where he found that his fame had preceded him.

The first thing that he heard upon his arrival was that Ægeus had just married Medea, the enchantress ; but, although the news was very unwelcome, he hastened to his father's court, to make himself known, and receive the welcome promised so many years before. Medea, seated by Ægeus' side, no sooner saw the young stranger draw near, then she knew him, and foresaw that he had come to demand his rights. To prevent his making known claims which might interfere with the prospects of her future offspring, she hastily mixed a deadly poison in a cup, which she filled with fragrant wine, and bade Ægeus offer it to the stranger.

The monarch was about to execute her apparently hospitable purpose, when his eye suddenly rested upon the sword at Theseus' side, which he immediately recognised. One swift glance into the youth's open face convinced him that Æthra's son stood before him, and he eagerly stretched out his arms to clasp him to his heart. This sudden movement upset the goblet, and the poisonous contents, falling upon a dog lying at the king's feet, caused his almost instantaneous death. Seeing her crime discovered and Theseus recognised, Medea quickly mounted her magic dragon car, and fled to Media, whence she never returned.

One day, some time after his arrival at Athens, Theseus heard a sound of weeping and great lamentation throughout all the city, and in reply to his wondering inquiries was told, that ever since an unfortunate war between the Cretans and Athenians, the latter, who had been vanquished, were obliged to pay a yearly tribute of seven youths, and as many maidens, destined to serve as food for the Minotaur. Further questions elicited the fact that the Minotaur was a hideous monster, kept by Minos, King of Crete, in an intricate labyrinth, constructed for that express purpose by Dædalus, the far-famed architect.

"There lived and flourished long ago, in famous Athens town,
One Dædalus, a carpenter of genius and renown;
('Twas he who with an augur taught mechanics how to bore,—
An art which the philosophers monopolised before.)"

Saxe.

Dædalus and Icarus

This labyrinth was so very intricate, that those who
entered could not find their way out ; and even
Dædalus and his son Icarus, after many days' attempt,
found they could not leave it. Rather than remain
imprisoned for ever, Dædalus then manufactured wings
for himself and for his son, and determined to make
use of them to effect his escape.

> " Now Dædalus, the carpenter, had made a pair of wings,
> Contrived of wood and feathers and a cunning set of springs,
> By means of which the wearer could ascend to any height,
> And sail about among the clouds as easy as a kite."
>
> *Saxe.*

After repeated cautions to his son not to venture too
high, lest the sun's heat should melt the wax which fixed
the feathers to the frame, Dædalus bade Icarus don his
plumage and fly to a country where they would be free,
promising to follow him thither very shortly.

> " ' My Icarus ! ' he says; ' I warn thee fly
> Along the middle track: nor low, nor high ;
> If low, thy plumes may flag with ocean's spray ;
> If high, the sun may dart his fiery ray.' "
>
> *Ovid (Elton's tr.).*

Delighted with this new mode of travel, Icarus flew
swiftly along. Little by little he forgot the danger and
his father's caution, and rose up higher and higher,
until he could bask in the direct rays of the ardent
sun. The heat, which seemed so grateful after his chilly
flight, soon softened and melted the wax on his wings ;
and Icarus, no longer supported by the light feathers,
sank down faster and faster, until he fell into the sea,
where he was drowned, and which, in memory of him,
bears the name of Icarian to this day.

> " His scattered plumage danced upon the wave,
> And sorrowing Nereids decked his watery grave'.

The Lament for Icarus

Ariadne in Naxos

O'er his pale corse their pearly sea-flowers shed,
And strewed with crimson moss his marble bed;
Struck in their coral towers the passing bell,
And wide in ocean tolled his echoing knell."

Darwin.

The Minotaur

This terrible story kindled Theseus' love of adventure, and still further strengthened him in his sudden resolve to join the mournful convoy, try his strength against the awful Minotaur, and, if possible, save his country from further similar exactions.

"While Attica thus groan'd, with ills opprest;
His country's wrongs inflam'd brave Theseus' breast;
Instant his gen'rous soul resolv'd to save
Cecrops' great offspring from a timeless grave."

Catullus.

Even his father's tears and entreaties were powerless to move him from his purpose, and, the hour having come, he embarked upon the black-sailed vessel which was to bear the yearly tribute to Crete, promising to change the black sails for snowy white ones if he were fortunate enough to return victorious.

Favourable winds soon wafted the galley to distant Crete, and as they sailed along the coast, searching for the harbour, they were challenged by the brazen giant Talus, who walked daily thrice around the whole island, killing, by contact with his red-hot body, all who had no business to land on that coast. Knowing, however, that the black-sailed galley brought a fresh supply of youths and maidens for the terrible Minotaur, Talus let it pass unharmed; and the victims were brought into the presence of Minos, who personally inspected each new freight-load, to make sure he was not being cheated by the Athenians.

At the monarch's side stood his fair daughter Ariadne,

whose tender heart was filled with compassion when she beheld the frail maidens and gallant youths about to perish by such a loathsome death. Theseus, by right of his birth, claimed the precedence, and proffered a request to be the first victim—a request which the king granted with a sardonic smile, ere he returned unmoved to his interrupted feast.

Unnoticed by all, Ariadne slipped out of the palace, and, under cover of the darkness, entered the prison where Theseus was confined. There she tremblingly offered him a ball of twine and a sharp sword, bidding him tie one end of the twine to the entrance of the labyrinth, and keep the other in his hand as a clue to find the way out again should the sword enable him to kill the dreaded Minotaur. In token of gratitude for this timely assistance, Theseus solemnly promised Ariadne to take her with him to Athens as his bride, were he only successful in his undertaking.

At dawn the next day Theseus was conducted to the entrance of the labyrinth, and there left to await the tender mercies of the Minotaur. Like all heroes, he preferred to meet any danger rather than remain inactive : so, mindful of Ariadne's instructions, he fastened his twine to the entrance, and then boldly penetrated into the intricate ways of the labyrinth, where many whitening bones plainly revealed the fate of all who had preceded him.

He had not gone very far before he encountered the Minotaur,—a creature more hideous than fancy can paint,—and he was obliged to use all his skill and ingenuity to avoid falling a prey to the monster's appetite, and all his strength to lay him low at last.

THE ESCAPE FROM CRETE

The Escape from Crete

The Minotaur slain, Theseus hastily retraced his footsteps.

> " And the slender clue,
> Prepar'd in secret by th' enamour'd maid,
> Thro' the curv'd labyrinth his steps convey'd."
>
> *Catullus.*

Arrived at the place where his ship rode at anchor, he found his companions and Ariadne awaiting him, and, springing on board, bade the sailors weigh anchor as quickly as possible. They were almost out of reach of the Cretan shores, when Talus came into view, and, perceiving that his master's prisoners were about to escape, leaned forward to catch the vessel by its rigging. Theseus, seeing this, sprang forward and dealt the giant such a blow, that he lost his balance and fell into the deep sea, where he was drowned, and where thermal springs still bear witness to the heat of his brazen body.

The returning vessel, favoured by wind and tide, made but one port, Naxos ; and here youths and maidens landed to view the beautiful island. Ariadne strayed apart, and threw herself down upon the ground to rest, where, before she was aware of it, sleep overtook her. Now, although very brave, Theseus was not very constant. He had already grown weary of Ariadne's love ; and, when he saw her thus asleep, he basely summoned his companions, embarked with them and set sail, leaving her alone upon the island, where Bacchus soon came to console her for the loss of her faithless lover.

Theseus, having committed a deed heinous in the eyes of gods and men, was doomed to suffer just punishment. In his preoccupation he entirely forgot his promise to change the black sails for white ; and

225

Ægeus, from Attica's rocky shore, seeing the sable sails when the vessel was yet far from land, immediately concluded that his son was dead, and in his grief cast himself into the sea, since known as the Ægean, where he perished.

> " As from a mountain's snowy top are driv'n
> The rolling clouds, by the rude blasts of heav'n
> So from the mem'ry of lost Theseus fled
> Those dictates, which before his reason sway'd:
> But now his father from the ramparts' height,
> All bath'd in tears, directs his eager sight;
> O'er the wide sea, distended by the gale,
> He spies, with dread amaze, the lurid sail."
>
> *Catullus.*

Theseus, on entering the city, heard of his father's death; and when he realised that it had been caused by his carelessness, he was overwhelmed with grief and remorse. All the cares of royalty and the wise measures he introduced for the happiness of his people could not divert his mind from this terrible catastrophe: so he finally resolved to resign his authority and set out again in search of adventures, which might help him forget his woes. He therefore made an excursion into the land of the Amazons, where Hercules had preceded him, and whence he brought back Hippolyte, whom he married. Theseus was now very happy indeed, and soon all his hopes were crowned by the birth of a son, whom he called Hippolytus. Shortly after this joyful event, the Amazons invaded his country under pretext of rescuing their kidnapped queen, and in the battle which ensued Hippolyte was accidentally wounded by an arrow, and breathed her last in Theseus' arms.

Theseus next set out with an Athenian army to fight Pirithous, king of the Lapithæ, who had dared to declare war; but when the armies were face to face, the two chiefs, seized with a sudden liking for each other, simultaneously cast down their weapons, and, falling on each other's necks, embraced, and swore an eternal friendship.

The Centaurs and the Lapithæ

To show his devotion to this newly won friend, Theseus consented to accompany him to the court of Adrastus, King of Argos, and witness his marriage to Hippodamia, daughter of the king. Many guests were, of course, present to witness the marriage ceremony, among others Hercules and a number of the Centaurs. The latter, struck with admiration for the bride's unusual beauty, made an attempt to kidnap her, which was frustrated by the Lapithæ, seconded by Theseus and Hercules. The terrible struggle which ensued between the conflicting parties has ever been a favourite subject in art, and is popularly known as the "Battle between the Centaurs and Lapithæ."

The hotly contested bride did not, however, enjoy a very long life, and Pirithous soon found himself, like Theseus, a disconsolate widower. To avoid similar bereavement in future, they both resolved to secure goddesses, who, being immortal, would share their thrones for ever. Aided by Pirithous, Theseus carried off Helen, the daughter of Jupiter, and, as she was still but a child, entrusted her to the care of his mother, Æthra, until she attained a suitable age for matrimony. Then, in return for Pirithous' kind offices, he accompanied him to Hades, where they intended to carry off Proserpina.

While they were thus engaged, Helen's twin brothers, Castor and Pollux, came to Athens, delivered her from captivity, and carried her home in triumph. As for Theseus and Pirithous, their treacherous inten-

tion was soon discovered by Pluto, who set the first on
an enchanted rock, from which he could not descend
unassisted, and bound the second to the constantly
revolving wheel of his father, Ixion.

When Hercules was in Hades in search of Cerberus
he delivered Theseus from his unpleasant position,
and thus enabled him to return to his own home,
where he now expected to spend the remainder of his
life in peace.

Although somewhat aged by this time, Theseus was
still anxious to marry, and looked about him for a wife
to cheer his loneliness. Suddenly he remembered that
Ariadne's younger sister, Phædra, must be a charming
young princess, and sent an embassy to obtain her hand
in marriage. The embassy proved successful, and
Phædra came to Athens; but, young and extremely
beautiful, she was not at all delighted with her aged husband, and, instead of falling in love with him, bestowed
all her affections upon his son, Hippolytus, a virtuous
youth, who utterly refused to listen to her proposals to
elope. In her anger at finding her advances scorned,
Phædra went to Theseus and accused Hippolytus of
attempting to kidnap her. Theseus, greatly incensed at
what he deemed his son's dishonourable behaviour, implored Neptune to punish the youth, who was even then
riding in his chariot close by the shore. In answer to
this prayer, a great wave suddenly arose, dashed over
the chariot, and drowned the young charioteer, whose
lifeless corpse was finally flung ashore at Phædra's feet.
When the unfortunate queen saw the result of her false
accusations, she confessed her crime, and, in her remorse
and despair, hung herself.

As for Theseus, soured by these repeated misfortunes, he grew so stern and tyrannical, that he gradually
alienated his people's affections, until at last they hated

228

him, and banished him to the Island of Scyros, where, in obedience to a secret order, Lycomedes, the king, treacherously slew him by hurling him from the top of a steep cliff into the sea. As usual, when too late, the Athenians repented of their ingratitude, and in a fit of tardy remorse deified this hero, and built a magnificent temple on the Acropolis in his honour. This building, now used as a museum, contains many relics of Greek art. Theseus' bones were piously brought back, and interred in Athens, where he was long worshipped as a demi-god.

CHAPTER XXII : JASON

The Education of Jason

AT Iolcus, in Thessaly, there once reigned a virtuous king, Æson, with his good wife, Alcimede. Their happiness, however, was soon disturbed by Pelias, the king's brother, who, aided by an armed host, took forcible possession of the throne. Æson and Alcimede, in fear of their lives, were forced to resort to a hasty and secret flight, taking with them their only son, Jason.

The king and queen soon found a place of refuge, but, afraid lest their hiding-place should be discovered and they should all be slain by the cruel Pelias, they entrusted their son to the Centaur Chiron, revealing to him alone the secret of the child's birth, and bidding him train him up to avenge their wrongs.

Chiron discharged his duties most faithfully, trained the young prince with great care, and soon made him the wisest and most skilful of his pupils. The years spent by Jason in the diligent acquisition of knowledge, strength, and skill passed very quickly; and at last the time came when Chiron made known to him the secret of his birth, and the story of the wrongs inflicted by Pelias, the usurper, upon his unfortunate parents.

This tale aroused the young prince's anger, and made him solemnly vow to punish his uncle, or perish in the attempt. Chiron encouraged him to start, and in parting bade him remember that Pelias alone had injured him, but that all the rest of the human race were entitled to any aid he could bestow. Jason listened respectfully to his tutor's last instructions; then, girding on his sword and putting on his sandals, he set out on his journey to Iolcus.

JASON AND JUNO

Jason and the Goddess Juno

It was early in the spring, and the young man had not gone very far before he came to a stream, which, owing to the unusual freshets of the season, was almost impassable. Jason, however, quite undaunted by the rushing, foaming waters, was about to attempt the crossing, when he saw an aged woman not far from him, gazing in helpless despair at the waters she could not cross.

Naturally kind-hearted and helpful, and, moreover, mindful of Chiron's last recommendation, Jason offered the old woman his assistance, proposing to carry her across on his back if she would but lend him her staff to lean upon. The old woman gladly accepted this offer; and a few moments later, Jason, bending beneath his strange load, was battling with the rapid current.

After many an effort, breathless and almost exhausted, Jason reached the opposite bank, and, after depositing his burden there, scrambled up beside her, casting a rueful glance at the torrent, which had wrenched off one of his golden sandals. He was about to part from the old dame with a kindly farewell, when she was suddenly transformed into a tall, handsome, imperious-looking woman, whom, owing to the peacock by her side, he immediately recognised as Juno, queen of heaven. He bent low before her, and claimed her aid and protection, which she graciously promised ere she vanished from his sight.

With eager steps Jason now pressed onward, nor paused until he came in view of his native city. As he drew near, he noticed an unusual concourse of people, and upon inquiry discovered that Pelias was celebrating a festival in honour of the immortal gods. Up the steep ascent leading to the temple Jason hastened, and pressed on to the innermost circle of spectators, until

231

he stood in full view of his enemy Pelias, who, unconscious of coming evil, continued offering the sacrifice.

At last the ceremony was completed, and the king cast an arrogant glance over the assembled people. His eyes suddenly fell upon Jason's naked foot, and he grew pale with horror as there flashed into his memory the recollection of an ancient oracle, warning him to beware of the man who appeared before him wearing but one sandal. Pelias tremblingly bade the guards bring forth the uninvited stranger. His orders were obeyed; and Jason, confronting his uncle boldly, summoned him to make a full restitution of the power he had so unjustly seized.

Phryxus and Helle

To surrender power and wealth, and return to obscurity was not to be thought of; but Pelias artfully concealed his displeasure, and told his nephew that they would discuss the matter and come to an amicable understanding after the banquet, which was already spread and awaiting their presence. During the festive meal, bards sang of all the heroic deeds accomplished by great men; and Pelias, by judicious flattery, stimulated Jason to attempt similar feats. At last the musicians recited the story of Phryxus and Helle, the son and daughter of Athamas and Nephele, who, to escape the cruel treatment of their stepmother, Ino, mounted a winged, golden-fleeced ram sent by Neptune to transport them to Colchis.

The ram flew over land and sea; but Helle, frightened at the sight of the waves tossing far beneath her, suddenly lost her hold on the golden fleece, and tumbled off the ram's back into a portion of the sea since known as the Hellespont,

> " Where beauteous Helle found a watery grave."
>
> *Meleager.*

THE QUEST OF THE GOLDEN FLEECE

Phryxus, more fortunate than his sister, reached Colchis in safety, and in gratitude to the gods sacrificed the ram they had sent to deliver him, and hung its golden fleece on a tree, near which he stationed a dragon to guard it night and day. The bards then went on to relate that the glittering trophy still hung there, awaiting a hand bold enough to slay the dragon and bear it off.

This tale and his liberal potations greatly excited the youth Jason; and Pelias, perceiving it, hypocritically regretted his inability to win the golden fleece, and softly insinuated that young men of the present generation were not brave enough to risk their lives in such a glorious cause. The usurper's crafty remarks had the desired effect; for Jason suddenly sprang from his seat, and vowed he would go in quest of the golden fleece. Pelias, quite certain that the rash youth would lose his life in the attempt, and thus cause no more trouble, with much difficulty restrained all expressions of joy, and dared him to make the attempt.

> " With terror struck, lest by young Jason's hand
> His crown should be rent from him, Pelias sought
> By machinations dark to slay his foe.
> From Colchis' realm to bring the golden fleece
> He charged the youth."
>
> *Orphic Argonautics.*

The Quest of the Golden Fleece

When Jason, sobered and refreshed by a long night's rest, perceived how foolish had been his vow, he would fain have recalled it; but, mindful of Chiron's teachings ever to be true to his word, he resolved to depart for Colchis. To secure Juno's assistance, he began by visiting her shrine at Dodona, where the oracle, a Speaking Oak, assured him of the goddess's goodwill and efficacious protection. Next the Speaking Oak bade

233

him cut off one of its own mighty limbs, and carve from it a figure-head for the swift-sailing vessel which Minerva, at Juno's request, would build for his use from pine-trees grown on Mount Pelion.

Jason, having finished his figure-head, found that it too had the gift of speech, and that it would occasion-ally vouchsafe sage counsel in the direction of his affairs. When quite completed, Jason called his vessel the *Argo* (swift-sailing), and speedily collected a crew of heroes as brave as himself, among whom were Hercules, Castor, Pollux, Peleus, Admetus, Theseus, and Orpheus, who were all glad to undertake the perilous journey to lands unknown. To speed them on their way, Juno then bargained with Æolus for favourable winds, and forbade any tempest which might work them harm.

> "Then with a whistling breeze did Juno fill the sail,
> And *Argo*, self-impell'd, shot swift before the gale."
>
> *Onomacritus (Elton's tr.).*

The Story of Hylas

On several occasions the heroes landed, either to renew their stock of provisions or to recruit their strength, but in general every delay brought them some misfortune. Once Hercules, having landed with a youth named Hylas to cut wood for new oars, bade the youth go to a neighbouring spring and draw a pitcher of water to quench the thirst produced by his exertions. The youth promptly departed ; but as he bent over the fountain, the nymphs, enamoured of his beauty, drew him down into their moist abode to keep them company. Hercules, after vainly waiting for Hylas' return, went in search of him, but, finding no trace of his young friend, in his grief and disappointment he refused to continue the expedition, and, deserting the Argonauts, made his way home alone and on foot.

THE STORY OF HYLAS

On another occasion, when Jason visited Phineus, the blind king of Thrace, he heard that this monarch's life was embittered by the Harpies, vile monsters, part woman, part bird, who ate or befouled all the food placed before him, and never let him eat a mouthful in peace. Having repeated this tale to his companions, the two sons of Boreas, who were also in the *Argo*, begged permission to drive them away. Jason could not refuse their request; and the two youths, with drawn swords, pursued the Harpies to the Strophades Islands, where the birds promised to remain.

Jason, sailing on in the meantime, was attacked by a flock of brazen-feathered birds, which rained their sharp plumage down upon the Argonauts, wounding many of them sorely. The captain of the expedition, seeing weapons were of no avail against these foes, consulted the figure-head, and, in obedience to its directions, clashed his arms against his shield, until, terrified by the din, the brazen-feathered birds flew rapidly away, uttering discordant cries of terror.

Some time during the course of their journey the Argonauts came to the Symplegades—floating rocks which continually crashed together, and ground to powder all objects caught between them. Jason knew he was obliged to pass between these rocks or give up the expedition : so, calculating that the speed of his vessel was equal to that of a dove on the wing, he sent one out before him. The dove flew safely between the rocks, losing only one of its tail-feathers as they again clashed together. Watching his opportunity, therefore, Jason bade his men row swiftly. The *Argo* darted through the opening, and, when the rocks again came into contact, they merely grazed the rudder. Thus, as a vessel had passed between them unharmed, their power for evil left them, and they were chained fast to the bottom of the sea, near the mouth of the Bosphorus, where they remained immovable like any other rocks.

The Argonauts, after other adventures far too numerous to recount in detail, reached the Colchian shores, and presented themselves before Æetes, the king, to whom they made known their errand. Loath to part with his golden treasure, Æetes declared that, before Jason could obtain the fleece, he must catch and harness two wild, fire-breathing bulls dedicated to Vulcan, and make use of them to plough a stony piece of ground sacred to Mars. This done, he must sow the field with some dragon's teeth, as Cadmus had done, conquer the giants which would spring up, and, last of all, slay the guardian dragon, or the fleece would never be his.

The Princess Medea

One of these tasks would have sufficed to dismay most youths, however brave, but Jason was of hero mould, and merely hastened down to his vessel to ask the figure-head how he had better proceed. On his way to the sea-shore he met the king's daughter, Medea, a beautiful young sorceress, who had been charmed by his modest but firm bearing, and who was quite ready to bring her magic to his aid if he would but promise to marry her. Jason, susceptible to her attractions, and free from any conflicting ties, readily agreed to her proposal, and, carrying out her directions, caught and harnessed the fiery bulls, ploughed the field, and sowed it with the dragon's teeth.

> "And how he yoked the bulls, whose breathings fiery glow'd,
> And with the dragons' teeth the furrow'd acres sow'd."
>
> *Onomacritus (Elton's tr.).*

But when he saw glittering spears and helmets grow out of the ground, and beheld the close ranks of giants

in full armour, he was filled with dismay, and would
have fled had it been possible. However, aware that
such a performance would ensure his ruin, he stood his
ground, and, when the phalanx was quite near him,
threw a handful of dust full in the giants' faces.
Blinded with the sand, the giants attacked one another,
and in a short time were exterminated.

> " They, like swift dogs,
> Ranging in fierceness, on each other turn'd
> Tumultuous battle. On their mother earth
> By their own spears they sank ; like pines, or oaks,
> Strew'd by a whirlwind in the mountain dale."
>
> *Apollonius Rhodius* (*Elton's tr.*).

Accompanied by Medea, Jason next hastened to the
tree where the dragon kept guard over his treasure.
An opiate prepared by Medea's magic skill soon made
the dragon forget his charge in a profound sleep, and
enabled Jason to draw near enough to sever his frightful head from his hideous trunk. Jason then tore the
coveted fleece from the branch where it had hung for
many a year, and bore it in triumph to the *Argo*.

> " Exulting Jason grasped the shining hide,
> His last of labours, and his envied pride.
> Slow from the groaning branch the fleece was rent."
>
> *Flaccus* (*Elton's tr.*).

His companions, who had made ready for a hasty
departure, were already seated at their oars ; and as soon
as he had embarked with Medea and her attendants,
the *Argo* shot out of the Colchian harbour.

> " How softly stole from home the luckless-wedded maid,
> Through darkness of the night, in linen robe array'd ;
> By Fate to *Argo* led, and urged by soft desire,
> Nor yet regarding aught her father's furious ire."
>
> *Onomacritus* (*Elton's tr.*).

When morning dawned and Æetes awoke, he heard

that the dragon was slain, the fleece stolen, his daughter gone, and the Grecian ship far out of sight. No time was lost in useless wailing, but a vessel was hurriedly launched and manned, and the king in person set out in pursuit of the fugitives, who had, moreover, taken his most precious treasure, his only son and heir, Absyrtus. Although the Colchian men were good sailors and skilful rowers, they did not catch sight of the *Argo* until they came near the mouth of the Danube, and Æetes wildly called to his daughter to return to her home and to her father.

> " ' Stay thy rash flight ! and, from the distant main,—
> For oh ! thou canst, my daughter,—turn again.
> Whither depart ? the vessel backward steer ;
> Thy friends, thy still fond father, wait thee here.' "
>
> *Flaccus (Elton's tr.).*

The Death of Absyrtus

But Medea had no wish to be torn away from Jason's arms, and, instead of listening to her father's entreaties, urged the Argonauts to redoubled efforts. Little by little the distance between the two vessels grew less ; the Colchian rowers were gaining upon the Greek ; and Medea saw that, unless she found means to delay her father, he would overtake her and compel her to return. With her own hands she therefore slew her little brother, Absyrtus, and cut his body into pieces, which she dropped over the side of the vessel one by one. Æetes, a helpless witness of this cruel, awful deed, piously collected his son's remains, and, in pausing to do so, lost sight of the *Argo*, and all hope of recovering his unnatural daughter : so he returned sadly to Colchis, where he buried his son's remains with due solemnity.

Meanwhile, Pelias had reigned contentedly over Thessaly, confident that Jason would never return. Imagine his dismay, therefore, when he heard that the

Medea and Absyrtus

Atalanta's Race

Argo had arrived, bearing Jason, now the proud possessor of the renowned golden fleece. Ere he could take measures to maintain his usurped authority, Jason appeared, and compelled him to resign the throne in favour of the rightful king, Æson.

Unfortunately, Æson was now so old and decrepit, that power had no charms for him : so Jason begged Medea to use her magic in his behalf, and restore him to the vigour and beauty of his early manhood. To gratify Jason, Medea called all her magic into play, and by some mysterious process restored Æson to all his former youth, strength, activity, and grace.

> " Medea's spells dispersed the weight of years,
> And Æson stood a youth 'mid youthful peers."
> *Wordsworth.*

As soon as Pelias daughters heard of this miraculous transformation, they hastened to Medea and implored her to give them the recipe, that they might rejuvenate their father also. The sorceress maliciously bade them cut their father's body into small pieces, and boil them in a cauldron with certain herbs, declaring that, if the directions were carefully carried out, the result would be satisfactory ; but, when the too credulous maidens carried out these instructions, they only slew the father whom they had so dearly loved.

Days and years now passed happily and uneventfully for Jason and Medea ; but at last their affection for each other cooled, and Jason fell in love with Glauce, or Creusa. Frantic with jealousy, Medea prepared and sent the maiden a magic robe, which she no sooner donned than she was seized with terrible convulsions, in which she died. Medea, still full of resentment against Jason, then slew her own children, and, mounting her dragon car, departed, leaving a message for

Jason, in which she warned him that the *Argo* would yet cause his death.

Jason, a victim of remorse and despair, now led a weary and sorrowful life, and every day he wandered down to the shore, where he sat under the shade of the *Argo's* hulk, which was slowly rotting away. One day, while he was sitting there musing over his youthful adventures and Medea's strange prophecy, a sudden gale detached a beam, which, falling on his head, fractured his skull and caused instantaneous death.

The Argonautic expedition is emblematic of the first long maritime voyage undertaken by the Greeks for commercial purposes ; while the golden fleece which Jason brought back from Colchis is but a symbol of the untold riches they found in the East, and carried to their native land.

CHAPTER XXIII : THE CALYDONIAN HUNT

The Birth of Meleager

OENEUS and Althæa, King and Queen of Calydon, in Ætolia, were very happy in the possession of a little son, Meleager, only a few days old, until they heard that the Fates had decreed the child should live only as long as the brand then smoking and crackling on the hearth. The parents were motionless with grief, until Althæa, with true mother's wit, snatched the brand from the fire, plunged it into an earthen jar filled with water, quenched the flames which were consuming it, and, carefully laying it aside, announced her intention to keep it for ever.

Meleager, thus saved from an untimely death by his mother's presence of mind, grew up a brave and handsome youth, and joined the Argonautic expedition. While he was absent, his father omitted the yearly sacrifice to Diana, who, enraged at his neglect, sent a monstrous boar to devour his subjects and devastate his realm. Meleager, on his return, gathered together all the brave men of the country, and instituted a great hunt, whose main object was the capture or death of the obnoxious boar.

Jason, Nestor, Peleus, Admetus, Theseus, Pirithous, and many other great heroes, came at his call; but the attention of all the spectators was specially attracted by Castor and Pollux, and by the fair Atalanta, daughter of Iasius, King of Arcadia. This princess had led a very adventurous life, for when but a babe, her father, disappointed to see a daughter instead of the longed-for son, had exposed her on Mount Parthenium to the fury of wild beasts. Some hunters, passing there shortly after this, found a she-bear suckling the babe, who evinced no sign of fear, and in compassion they carried her home, where they trained her to love the chase.

The grand Calydonian Hunt was headed by Meleager and Atalanta, who were very fond of each other, and who boldly led the rest in pursuit of the boar. From one end of the Calydonian forest to the other the boar fled, closely pursued by the hunt, and was at last brought to bay by Atalanta, who succeeded in dealing him a mortal wound. But even in his dying struggles the boar would have killed her, had not Meleager come to her rescue and given him his death-blow.

All the hunt now gathered round the boar's corpse, and watched Meleager take its spoil, which he gallantly bestowed upon Atalanta. Althæa's two brothers were present at the hunt, and, as they wished to possess the skin, they bitterly reproved their nephew on their way home for giving it to a stranger. They added taunts to this reproof, which so angered Meleager that, in a sudden fit of passion, he slew them both. When Althæa saw her brothers' corpses, and heard that they had been slain by her son, she vowed to avenge their death, drew the carefully cherished brand from its hiding-place, and threw it upon the fire burning brightly on her hearth. When the last bit of the precious wood crumbled away into ashes, Meleager died. All Althæa's affection for her son returned when his lifeless corpse was brought to her, and in her despair she committed suicide.

Atalanta's Race

Meanwhile, Atalanta, proud of her skill and of her spoil, had returned to her father's court, where no other heir having appeared, she was joyfully received, and entreated to marry. Many suitors came to woo the fair princess, but most of them refrained from pressing their suit when they heard what conditions were imposed upon all who would obtain her hand; for Atalanta, disapproving of marriage, and anxious to keep her freedom, had decreed that she should marry only the suitor who could beat her in a foot-race. It was decreed, moreover, that every unsuccessful suitor should pay for his defeat by forfeiting his life.

In spite of these barbarous terms, a few youths had tried to outrun her; but they failed, and their lifeless heads were exposed on the racing ground to deter all other suitors. Undaunted by these ghastly trophies, Hippomenes, or Milanion, came one day to Atalanta and expressed a desire to race with her. This youth had previously obtained Venus' protection, and had received from her the gift of three golden apples. Atalanta, as usual, passed her rival easily; but as she did so he cast one of the golden apples at her feet. For a moment she paused, then stopped and picked it up ere she resumed the race. The delay, short as it was, had given her adversary an advantage; but she soon overtook him, whereupon a second golden apple cast in the same way caused a second delay. Notwithstanding this, the maiden would have reached the goal first, as usual, had not a third golden treasure tempted her to pause, and enabled Hippomenes to win the race.

> " Hippomenes turns her astray
> By the golden illusions he flings on her way."
> *Moore.*

Atalanta could now no longer refuse to marry, and her nuptials were soon celebrated. In his happiness at having won such a peerless bride, Hippomenes forgot to pay the promised thanks to Venus, for which offence he and his wife were severely punished by being transformed into a pair of lions, and doomed to drag Cybele's car.

Castor and Pollux

The twin brothers Castor and Pollux, the Dioscuri,
or Gemini, who had greatly distinguished themselves by
their daring in the Calydonian Hunt, were made the
deities of boxing, wrestling, and all equestrian exercises.

> " Leda's sons I'll sound,
> Illustrious twins, that are
> For wrestling, this and for the race renown'd."
>
> *Horace.*

One of these twins, Castor, was a mortal, and in a
combat with the sons of Aphareus was slain. Pollux,
who was immortal, then implored Jupiter to allow him
to die also, that he might not be parted from his
brothers—a proof of brotherly affection which so
touched the father of the gods, that he permitted Castor
to return to life on condition that Pollux would spend
half his time in Hades.

Later on, satisfied that even this sacrifice was none
too great for their fraternal love, he translated them
both to the skies, where they form a bright constellation,
one of the signs of the zodiac. Castor and Pollux are
generally represented as handsome youths, mounted on
snowy chargers.

> " So like they were, no mortal
> Might one from other know:
> White as snow their armour was:
> Their steeds were white as snow."
>
> *Macaulay.*

Their appearance under certain circumstances foretold
success in war, and the Romans believed that they
fought at the head of their legions at the celebrated
battle of Lake Regillus. Their name was also given to
meteors, sometimes seen at sea, which attach themselves

like balls of fire to the masts of ships,—a sure sign, according to the sailors, of fine weather and an auspicious journey.

"Safe comes the ship to haven,
    Through billows and through gales,
If once the Great Twin Brethren
    Sit shining on the sails."

Macaulay.

Festivals celebrated in honour of these twin brethren, and called the Dioscuria, were held in many places, but specially in Sparta, their birthplace, where they had world renowned wrestling matches.

CHAPTER XXIV : ŒDIPUS

The Destiny of Œdipus

LAIUS and Jocasta, King and Queen of Thebes, in Bœotia, were greatly delighted at the birth of a little son. In their joy they sent for the priests of Apollo, and bade them foretell the glorious deeds their heir would perform ; but all their joy was turned to grief when told that the child was destined to kill his father, marry his mother, and bring great misfortunes upon his native city.

> " Laius once,
> Not from Apollo, but his priests, receiv'd
> An oracle, which said, it was decreed
> He should be slain by his own son."
>
> *Sophocles (Francklin's tr.).*

To prevent the fulfilment of this dreadful prophecy, Laius bade a servant carry the new-born child out of the city, and end its feeble little life. The king's mandate was obeyed only in part ; for the servant, instead of killing the child, hung it up by its ankles to a tree in a remote place, and left it there to perish from hunger and exposure if it were spared by the wild beasts.

When he returned, none questioned how he had performed the appointed task, but all sighed with relief to think that the prophecy could never be accomplished. The child, however, was not dead, as all supposed. A shepherd in quest of a stray lamb had heard his cries, delivered him from his painful position, and carried him to Polybus, King of Corinth, who, lacking an heir of his own, gladly adopted the little stranger. The Queen of Corinth and her hand-maidens hastened with tender concern to bathe the swollen ankles, and called the babe Œdipus (swollen-footed).

THE DESTINY OF ŒDIPUS

Years passed by. The young prince grew up in total ignorance of the unfortunate circumstances under which he had made his first appearance at court, until one day at a banquet one of his companions, heated by drink, began to quarrel with him, and taunted him with his origin, declaring that those whom he had been accustomed to call parents were in no way related to him.

> " A drunken rev'ller at a feast proclaim'd
>   That I was only the supposèd son
>   Of Corinth's king."
>
> *Sophocles (Francklin's tr.).*

These words, coupled with a few meaning glances hastily exchanged by the guests, excited Œdipus' suspicions, and made him question the queen, who, afraid lest he might do himself an injury in the first moment of his despair if the truth were revealed to him, had recourse to prevarication, and quieted him by the assurance that he was her beloved son.

Something in her manner, however, left a lingering doubt in Œdipus' mind, and made him resolve to consult the oracle of Delphi, whose words he knew would reveal the exact truth. He therefore went to this shrine; but, as usual, the oracle answered somewhat ambiguously, and merely warned him that fate had decreed he should kill his father, marry his mother, and cause great woes to his native city.

> " I felt
> A secret anguish, and unknown to them
> Sought out the Pythian oracle; in vain;
> Touching my parents, nothing could I learn;
> But dreadful were the mis'ries it denounc'd
> Against me; 'twas my fate, Apollo said,
> To wed my mother, to produce a race
> Accursed and abhorr'd; and last, to slay
> My father."
>
> *Sophocles (Francklin's tr.).*

What! kill Polybus, who had ever been such an indulgent father, and marry the queen, whom he revered as his mother! Never! Rather than perpetrate these awful crimes, and bring destruction upon the people of Corinth, whom he loved, he would wander away over the face of the earth, and never see city or parents again.

> " Lest I should e'er fulfil the dire prediction,
> Instant I fled from Corinth, by the stars
> Guiding my hapless journey."
>
> *Sophocles (Francklin's tr.).*

But his heart was filled with intense bitterness, and as he journeyed he did not cease to curse the fate which drove him away from home. After some time, he came to three cross-roads; and while he stood there, deliberating which direction to take, a chariot, wherein an aged man was seated, came rapidly toward him. The herald who preceded it haughtily called to the youth to stand aside and make way for his master; but Œdipus, who, as Polybus' heir, was accustomed to be treated with deference, resented the commanding tone, and refused to obey. Incensed at what seemed unparalleled impudence, the herald struck the youth, who, retaliating, stretched his assailant lifeless at his feet.

Œdipus slays his Father

This affray attracted the attention of the master and other servants. They immediately attacked the murderer, who slew them all, thus unconsciously accomplishing the first part of the prophecy; for the aged man was Laius, his father, journeying in disguise from Thebes to Delphi, where he wished to consult the oracle.

Œdipus then leisurely pursued his way until he came to the gates of Thebes, where he found the whole city

in an uproar, " because the king had been found lifeless
by the roadside, with all his atttendants slain beside
him, presumably the work of a band of highway robbers
or assassins."

> " He fell
> By strangers murdered, for so fame reports,
> By robbers in the place where three ways meet."
>
> *Sophocles (Francklin's tr.)*

Of course, Œdipus did not connect the murder of
such a great personage as the King of Thebes by an
unknown band of robbers with the death he had dealt
to an arrogant old man, and he therefore composedly
inquired what other calamity had befallen them.

The Sphinx

With lowered voices, as if afraid of being overheard,
the Thebans described the woman's head, bird's wings
and claws, and lion's body, which were the outward
presentment of a terrible monster called the Sphinx,
which had taken up its station without the city gates
beside the highway, and would allow none to pass in or
out without propounding a difficult riddle. Then, if
any hesitated to give the required answer, or failed to
give it correctly, they were mercilessly devoured by
the terrible Sphinx, which no one dared attack or could
drive away.

While listening to these tidings, Œdipus saw a
herald pass along the street, proclaiming that the
throne and the queen's hand would be the reward of
any man who dared encounter the Sphinx and was
fortunate enough to free the country of its terrible
presence.

As Œdipus attached no special value to the life
made desolate by the oracle's predictions, he resolved
to slay the dreaded monster, and, with that purpose in

249

view, advanced slowly, sword in hand, along the road where lurked the Sphinx. He soon found the monster, which from afar propounded the following enigma, warning him, at the same time, that he forfeited his life if he failed to give the right answer.

> " Tell me, what animal is that
> Which has four feet at morning bright,
> Has two at noon, and three at night ? "
>
> *Prior.*

Œdipus was not devoid of intelligence, by any manner of means, and soon concluded that the animal could only be man, who in infancy, when too weak to stand, creeps along on hands and knees, in manhood walks erect, and in old age supports his tottering steps with a staff.

This reply, evidently as correct as unexpected, was received by the Sphinx with a hoarse cry of disappointment and rage as it turned to fly ; but ere it could effect its purpose, it was stayed by Œdipus, who drove it at his sword's point over the edge of a neighbouring precipice, where it was killed.

Œdipus marries his Mother

On his return to the city, Œdipus was received with cries of joy, placed on a chariot, crowned King of Thebes, and married to his own mother, Jocasta, unwittingly fulfilling the second fearful clause of the prophecy.

A number of happy and moderately uneventful years now passed by, and Œdipus became the father of two manly sons, Eteocles and Polynices, and two beautiful daughters, Ismene and Antigone ; but prosperity was not doomed to favour him long.

Just when he fancied himself most happy, and looked

forward to a peaceful old age, a terrible scourge visited
Thebes, causing the death of many faithful subjects,
and filling the hearts of all with great terror. The
people now turned to him, beseeching him to aid them,
as he had done once before when threatened by the
Sphinx ; and Œdipus sent messengers to consult the
Delphic oracle, who declared the plague would cease
only when the former king's murderers had been found
and punished.

> "The plague, he said, should cease,
> When those who murder'd Laius were discover'd,
> And paid the forfeit of their crime by death,
> Or banishment."
>
> *Sophocles (Francklin's tr.).*

Messengers were sent in every direction to collect
all possible information about the murder committed so
long ago, and after a short time they brought unmis-
takable proofs which convicted Œdipus of the crime.
At the same time the guilty servant confessed that he
had not killed the child, but had exposed it on a mountain, whence it was carried to Corinth's king.

The chain of evidence was complete, and now
Œdipus discovered that he had involuntarily been
guilty of the three crimes to avoid which he had fled
from Corinth. The rumour of these dreadful dis-
coveries soon reached Jocasta, who, in despair at finding
herself an accomplice, committed suicide.

Œdipus, apprised of her intention, rushed into her
apartment too late to prevent its being carried out, and
found her lifeless. This sight was more than the poor
monarch could bear, and in his despair he blinded himself with one of her ornaments.

> " He pluck'd from off the robe she wore
> A golden buckle that adorn'd her side,
> And buried in his eyes the sharpen'd point,
> Crying, he ne'er again would look on her,

Never would see his crimes or mis'ries more,
Or those whom guiltless he could ne'er behold,
Or those to whom he now must sue for aid."

Sophocles (Francklin's tr.).

Penniless, blind, and on foot, he then left the scene of his awful crimes, accompanied by his daughter Antigone, the only one who loved him still, and who was ready to guide his uncertain footsteps wherever he wished to go. After many days of weary wandering, father and daughter reached Colonus, where grew a mighty forest sacred to the avenging deities, the Furies, or Eumenides.

Here Œdipus expressed his desire to remain, and, after bidding his faithful daughter an affectionate farewell, he groped his way into the dark forest alone. The wind rose, the lightning flashed, the thunder pealed; but although, as soon as the storm was over, a search was made for Œdipus, no trace of him was ever found, and the ancients fancied that the Furies had dragged him down to Hades to receive the punishment of his unwitting crimes.

Eteocles and Polynices

Antigone, no longer needed by her unhappy father, slowly wended her way back to Thebes, where she found that the plague had ceased, but that her brothers had quarrelled about the succession to the throne. A compromise was finally decided upon, whereby it was decreed that Eteocles, the elder son, should reign one year, and at the end of that period resign the throne to Polynices for an equal space of time, each brother thus exercising the royal authority in turn. This arrangement seemed satisfactory to Eteocles; but when, at the end of the first year, Polynices returned from his travels in foreign lands to claim the sceptre, Eteocles refused to relinquish it, and, making use of his power, drove the claimant away.

> " Thou seest me banish'd from my native land,
>   Unjustly banish'd, for no other crime
>   But that I strove to keep the throne of Thebes,
>   By birthright mine, from him who drove me thence,
>   The young Eteocles : not his the claim
>   By justice, nor to me his fame in arms
>   Superior ; but, by soft, persuasive arts
>   He won the rebel city to his love."
>
> *Sophocles (Francklin's tr.).*

The Seven Chiefs

Polynices' nature was not one to endure such a slight patiently ; and he hastened off to Argos, where he persuaded Adrastus, the king, to give him his daughter in marriage, and aid him to recover his inheritance. True to his promise, Adrastus soon equipped a large army, which was led by seven determined and renowned chiefs, ready to risk all in the attempt, and either win or perish.

> " Seven valiant leaders march
> To Thebes, resolved to conquer or to die."
>
> *Sophocles (Francklin's tr.).*

Their bravery was of no avail, however, for Thebes was well fortified and defended ; and after a seven-years' siege they found themselves no nearer their goal than at the beginning of the war. Weary of the monotony of this quarrel, the conflicting armies finally decreed that the difference should be settled by a duel between the inimical brothers, who no sooner found themselves face to face, than they rushed upon each other with such animosity that both fell.

By order of Jocasta's father, Creon, the corpse of Eteocles received all the honours of a Greek burial, while that of Polynices was left on the plain, a prey to the birds and wild beasts.

> "Polynices' wretched carcass lies
> Unburied, unlamented, left expos'd
> A feast for hungry vultures on the plain."
>
> *Sophocles (Francklin's tr.).*

Antigone's Devotion

Then a proclamation was issued, that, if any dared bury the body of the fallen prince, he would incur the penalty of being buried alive. Heedless of this injunction and of Ismene's prayers to refrain from endangering her own life, Antigone dug a grave for her brother's remains, and, unaided, fulfilled the various customary funeral rites. Her task was almost completed, when the guards discovered her, and dragged her into the presence of Creon, who, although she was a relative and the promised wife of his son Hæmon, condemned her to death.

> "Let her be carried instant to the cave,
> And leave her there alone, to live, or die;
> Her blood rests not on us : but she no longer
> Shall breathe on earth."
>
> *Sophocles (Francklin's tr.).*

Hæmon pleaded passionately for her life; but, when he saw his prayers were vain, he ran to the place where Antigone was confined, sprang into her narrow cell, wound his arms closely around her, and refused to leave her. There they were walled in: Antigone's sufferings were cut mercifully short by asphyxiation; and, when Hæmon saw she was no more, he, in utter despair, thrust his dagger into his side, and perished too.

> "On himself bent all his wrath,
> Full in his side the weapon fix'd, but still,
> Whilst life remain'd, on the soft bosom hung

ANTIGONE'S DEVOTION

Of the dear maid, and his last spirit breath'd
O'er her pale cheek, discolour'd with his blood.
Thus lay the wretched pair in death united,
And celebrate their nuptials in the tomb."

Sophocles (Francklin's tr.).

Ismene, the last of Œdipus' unfortunate race, died of grief, and thus the prophecy was fully accomplished. The Theban war was not, however, entirely ended, for, when both brothers fell, the two armies flew to attack each other; and such was their courage that many fell, and only one of the seven chiefs returned to Argos. There he patiently waited until the children of these brave captains were old enough to bear arms, and then proposed to them to attack Thebes and avenge their fathers' death.

The Epigoni (or those who come after), as these youths are collectively designated, received this proposal with rapture; and Thebes, again besieged, fell into their hands, and was duly sacked, burned, and destroyed, as the Delphic oracle had foretold so many years before.

CHAPTER XXV : BELLEROPHON

The Flight of Bellerophon

BELLEROPHON, a brave young prince, the grandson of Sisyphus, King of Corinth, had the great misfortune to kill his own brother while hunting in the forest. His grief was, of course, intense; and the horror he felt for the place where the catastrophe had occurred, added to his fear lest he should incur judicial punishment for his involuntary crime, made him flee to the court of Argos, where he took refuge with Prœtus, the king, who was also his kinsman

Anteia's Treachery

He had not sojourned there very long before Anteia, the queen, fell in love with him; and although her husband, Prœtus, treated her with the utmost kindness, she made up her mind to desert him, and tried to induce Bellerophon to elope with her. Too honest to betray a man who had treated him as a friend, the young prince refused to listen to the queen's proposals. His refusal was to cost him dear, however, for, when Anteia saw that the youth would never yield to her wishes, she became very angry indeed, sought her husband, and accused the young stranger of crimes he had never even dreamed of committing.

Prœtus, indignant at what he deemed deep treachery on the part of an honoured guest, yet reluctant to punish him with his own hand as he deserved, sent Bellerophon to Iobates, King of Lycia, with a sealed message bidding him put the bearer to death.

Quite unconscious of the purport of this letter, Bellerophon presented himself before Iobates, who received him very hospitably, and, without inquiring his

Bellerophon and Anteia

Homer

name or errand, entertained him royally for many days. After some time, Bellerophon suddenly remembered the sealed message entrusted to his care, and hastened to deliver it to Iobates, with many apologies for his forgetfulness.

With blanched cheeks and every outward sign of horror, the king read the missive, and then fell into a deep reverie. He did not like to take a stranger's life, and still could not refuse to comply with Prœtus' urgent request; so, after much thought, he decided to send Bellerophon to attack the Chimæra, a terrible monster with a lion's head, a goat's body, and a dragon's tail.

> " Dire Chimæra's conquest was enjoin'd ;
> A mingled monster, of no mortal kind ;
> Behind, a dragon's fiery tail was spread ;
> A goat's rough body bore a lion's head ;
> Her pitchy nostrils flaky flames expire ;
> Her gaping throat emits infernal fire."
>
> *Homer (Pope's tr.)*.

His principal motive in choosing this difficult task was, that, although many brave men had set forth to slay the monster, none had ever returned, for one and all had perished in the attempt.

The Chimæra

Although very courageous, Bellerophon's heart beat fast with fear when told what great deed he must accomplish ; and he left Iobates' palace very sorrowfully, for he had fallen deeply in love with the king's fair daughter, Philonoe, and was afraid he would never see her again.

While thus inwardly bewailing the ill-luck which had persistently dogged his footsteps, Bellerophon suddenly saw Minerva appear before him in all her splendour, and heard her inquire in gentle tones the cause of his too evident dejection. He had no sooner apprised her of the difficult task appointed him, than she promised him her aid, and before she vanished gave him a beautiful golden bridle, which she bade him use to control Pegasus.

Bridle in hand, Bellerophon stood pondering her words, until he remembered that Pegasus was a wonderful winged steed, born from the blood which fell into the foam of the sea from Medusa's severed head. This horse, as white as snow, and gifted with immortal life as well as incredible speed, was the favourite mount of Apollo and the Muses, who delighted in taking aërial flights on his broad back ; and Bellerophon knew that from time to time he came down to earth to drink of the cool waters of the Hippocrene (a fountain which had bubbled forth where his hoofs first touched the earth), or to visit the equally limpid spring of Pirene, near Corinth.

Bellerophon proceeded, therefore, to the latter fountain, where, after lingering many days in the vain hope of catching even a glimpse of the winged steed, he finally beheld him sailing downward in wide curves, like a bird of prey. From his place of concealment in a neighbouring thicket, Bellerophon watched for an opportunity which came at last, and, while the winged steed was grazing, he vaulted boldly upon his back.

Pegasus had never before been ridden by a mortal, and he reared and pranced, and flew up to dizzy heights ; but all his efforts failed to unseat the brave rider, who, biding his time, finally thrust Minerva's golden bit between his teeth, whereupon the steed immediately became gentle and tractable. Thus mounted, Bellerophon now went in search of the Chimæra, who had given birth to the Nemean lion and to the riddle-loving Sphinx, and from an unclouded sky he swooped suddenly and unexpectedly down upon the winged monster, whose fiery breath and great strength were of no avail; for after a protracted struggle Bellerophon and Pegasus were victorious, and the monster lay lifeless upon the blood-soaked ground.

This mighty deed of valour accomplished, Bellerophon returned to Iobates, to report the success of his undertaking; and, although the king was heartily glad to know the Chimæra was no more, he was very sorry to see Bellerophon safe and sound, and tried to devise some other plan to get rid of him.

He therefore sent him to fight the Amazons; but the hero, aided by the gods, defeated these warlike women also, and returned to Lycia, where, after escaping from an ambush posted by the king for his destruction, he again appeared victorious at court.

These repeated and narrow escapes from certain death convinced Iobates that the youth was under the special protection of the gods; and this induced the king not only to forego further attempts to slay him, but also to bestow upon the young hero his daughter's hand in marriage.

Bellerophon's Fall

Bellerophon, having now attained his dearest wishes, might have settled down in peace; but his head had been utterly turned by the many lofty flights he had taken upon Pegasus' back, and, encouraged by the fulsome flattery of his courtiers, he finally fancied himself the equal of the immortal gods, and wished to join them in their celestial abode.

Summoning his faithful Pegasus once more, he rose higher and higher, and would probably have reached Olympus' heights, had not Jupiter sent a gadfly, which stung poor Pegasus so cruelly, that he shied viciously, and flung his too confident rider far down to the earth below.

> " Bold Bellerophon (so Jove decreed
> In wrath) fell headlong from the fields of air."
>
> *Wordsworth.*

This fall, which would doubtless have killed any one but a mythological hero, merely deprived Bellerophon of his eyesight; and ever after he groped his way disconsolately, thinking of the happy days when he rode along the paths of air and gazed upon the beautiful earth at his feet.

Bellerophon, mounted upon Pegasus, winging his flight through the air or fighting the Chimæra, is a favourite subject in sculpture and painting, which has frequently been treated by ancient artists, a few of whose most noted works are still extant in various museums.

This story, like many others, is merely a sun myth, in which Bellerophon, the orb of day, rides across the sky on Pegasus, the fleecy white clouds, and slays Chimæra, the dread monster of darkness, which he alone can overcome. Driven from home early in life, Bellerophon wanders throughout the world like his brilliant prototype, and like it, ends his career in total darkness.

CHAPTER XXVI : MINOR DIVINITIES

Their Provinces and Duties

ACCORDING to the ancients' belief, every mountain, valley, plain, lake, river, grove, and sea was provided with some lesser deity, whose special duty was assigned by the powerful gods of Olympus. There were, for instance, the Naiades, beautiful water nymphs, who dwelt in the limpid depths of the fountains, and were considered local patrons of poetry and song.

The Oreades, or mountain nymphs, were supposed to linger in the mountain solitudes and guide weary travellers safely through their rocky mazes.

> "Mark how the climbing Oreads
> Beckon thee to their Arcades!"
> *Emerson.*

As for the Napææ, they preferred to linger in the valleys, which were kept green and fruitful by their watchful care, in which task they were ably seconded by the Dryades, the nymphs of vegetation.

The very trees in the forest and along the roadside were supposed to be each under the protection of a special divinity called Hamadryad, said to live and die with the tree entrusted to her care.

> "When the Fate of Death is drawing near,
> First wither on the earth the beauteous trees,
> The bark around them wastes, the branches fall,
> And the nymph's soul, at the same moment, leaves
> The sun's fair light."
> *Homer.*

The Story of Dryope

A sweet and touching story was told by the ancients of a mortal who was changed into a Hamadryad. This young girl, whose name was Dryope, was a beautiful young princess, the daughter of Baucis, so bright and clever that all who knew her loved her dearly. Of course, as soon as she was old enough to think of marriage, a host of suitors asked her hand, each eager to win for his bride one so beautiful and gifted.

> " No nymph of all Œchalia could compare,
> For beauteous form, with Dryope the fair."
>
> *Ovid (Pope's tr.).*

Fully aware of the importance of making a wise choice, Dryope took her time, and finally decided to marry Andræmon, a worthy young prince, who possessed every charm calculated to win a fair girl's heart. The young people were duly married, and daily rejoiced in their happiness, which seemed almost too great for earth when they became the parents of a charming little son.

Every day Dryope carried the child along the banks of a little lake close by the palace, where bloomed a profusion of gay-coloured flowers.

> " A lake there was, with shelving banks around,
> Whose verdant summit fragrant myrtles crown'd.
> Those shades, unknowing of the Fates, she sought,
> And to the Naiads flowery garlands brought ;
> Her smiling babe (a pleasing charge) she press'd
> Between her arms."
>
> *Ovid (Pope's tr.).*

One day, while wandering there as usual, accompanied by her sister, she saw a lotus blossom, and pointed it out to her little son. He no sooner saw the brilliant flower, than he stretched out his little hands. To please him, the fond mother plucked it and gave it to him.

She had scarcely done so, when she noticed drops of blood trickling from the broken stem ; and while she stood there, speechless with wonder, a voice was heard accus-

ing her of having slain Lotis, a nymph, who, to escape
the pursuit of Priapus, god of the shade, had assumed
the guise of a flower.

> " Lotis the nymph (if rural tales be true),
>   As from Priapus' lawless love she flew,
>   Forsook her form ; and fixing here became
>   A flowery plant, which still preserves her name."
>
> *Ovid (Pope's tr.).*

Recovering from her first speechless terror, Dryope
turned to flee, with a pitiful cry of compassion on her
pale lips, but, to her astonishment, she could not leave
the spot : her feet seemed rooted to the ground.   She
cast a rapid glance downward to ascertain what could so
impede her progress, and noticed the rough bark of a
tree growing with fearful rapidity all around her.

Higher and higher it rose, from her knees to her
waist, and still it crept upward, in spite of her frantic
attempts to tear it away from her shapely limbs.   In
despair she raised her trembling hands and arms to
heaven to implore aid ; but, ere the words were spoken,
her arms were transformed into twisted branches, and
her hands were filled with leaves.

Nothing human now remained of poor Dryope
except her sweet, tear-stained face ; but this too would
soon vanish under the all-involving bark. She therefore
took hasty leave of her father, sister, husband, and son,
who, attracted by her first cry, had rushed to give her
all the assistance in their power.   The last words were
quickly spoken, but none too soon, for the bark closed
over the soft lips and hid the lovely features from view.

> " She ceased at once to speak, and ceased to be,
>   And all the nymph was lost within the tree :
>   Yet latent life through her new branches reign'd,
>   And long the plant a human heat retain'd."
>
> *Ovid (Pope's tr.).*

One of Dryope's last requests had been that her child might often play beneath her shady branches; and when the passing winds rustled through her leaves, the ancients said it was "Dryope's lone lulling of her child."

The Story of Rhœcus

Another exquisite story is told of Rhœcus, who saved an oak from falling, and thus preserved the life of the Hamadryad within the tree. Filled with gratitude, the nymph bade Rhœcus name his reward, whereupon he asked for her love, which she consented to bestow, provided he would remain constant and undivided in his affection. She bade him come to her an hour before sunset, but promised to send her messenger, the bee, to him before that time.

Filled with pleasure at the thought of his love, Rhœcus returned to the city with a light heart, and as the hours dragged, he sought some companions, whom he joined in a game of dice. Becoming absorbed in the varying fortunes of the game, he hardly noticed the bee which was incessantly buzzing about his ears, until, becoming suddenly aware of its attentions, he brushed it impatiently aside with his hand.

Out through the open window sped the little creature, and as Rhœcus looked after it to mark its flight, his eyes fell upon the distant line of hills against which the sun was just setting, and the sudden recollection of the events of the morning drove the blood from his heart. Without a word to his fellows, he rushed off to find his love, and

> "Quite spent and out of breath he reached the tree,
> And, listening fearfully, he heard once more
> The low voice murmur, 'Rhœcus!' close at hand:
> Whereat he looked around him, but could see
> Naught but the deepening glooms beneath the oak.
> Then sighed the voice, 'O Rhœcus! nevermore

PAN

Shalt thou behold me or by day or night,
Me, who would fain have blessed thee with a love
More ripe and bounteous than ever yet
Filled up with nectar any mortal heart ;
But thou didst scorn my humble messenger
And sent'st him back to me with bruisèd wings.'

Then Rhœcus beat his breast, and groaned aloud
And cried, ' Be pitiful ! forgive me yet
This once, and I shall never need it more !'
' Alas !' the voice returned, ' 'tis thou art blind,
Not I unmerciful ; I can forgive,
But have no skill to heal thy spirit's eyes.'

                    Above, the sky,
With all its bright sublimity of stars,
Deepened, and on his forehead smote the breeze :
Beauty was all around him and delight,
But from that eve he was alone on earth."

Lowell.

This modern rendering of the story is more spiritual than the ancient versions, in which Rhœcus was deprived of physical sight.

Pan

The male divinities of the woods, which were also very numerous, were mostly Satyrs,—curious beings with a man's body and a goat's legs, hair, and horns. They were all passionately fond of music and revelry, and were wont to indulge in dancing at all times and in all places. The most famous among all the Satyrs was Silenus, Bacchus' tutor ; and Pan, or Consentes, god of the shepherds, and the personification of nature. The latter was the reputed son of Mercury and a charming young nymph named Penelope ; and we are told that, when his mother first beheld him, she was aghast, for he was the most homely as well as the most extraordinary little creature she had ever seen. His body was all

265

covered with goat's hair, and his feet and ears were also those of a goat.

Amused at the sight of this grotesque little divinity, Mercury carried him off to Olympus, where all the gods turned him into ridicule. Pan was widely worshipped in olden times, however; and the ancients not only decked his altars with flowers, but sang his praises, and celebrated festivals in his honour.

> " He is great and he is just,
> He is ever good, and must
> Thus be honoured.   Daffodillies,
> Roses, pinks, and lovèd lilies,
> Let us fling,
> Whilst we sing,
> Ever holy,
> Ever holy,
> Ever honoured ! ever young,
> The great Pan is ever sung ! "
>
> *Beaumont and Fletcher.*

The Story of Syrinx

Pan was equally devoted to music, the dance, and pretty nymphs.   He saw one of the nymphs, Syrinx whom he immediately loved ; but unfortunately for him she, frightened at his appearance, fled.   Exasperated by her persistent avoidance of him, Pan once pursued and was about to overtake her, when she paused, and implored Gæa to protect her.   The prayer was scarcely ended, when she found herself changed into a clump of reeds, which the panting lover embraced, thinking he had caught the maiden, who had stood in that very spot a few moments before.

His deception and disappointment were so severe that they wrung from him a prolonged sigh, which, passing through the rustling reeds, produced plaintive tones.   Pan, seeing Syrinx had gone for ever, took seven pieces of the reed, of unequal lengths, bound

THE STORY OF SYRINX

them together, and fashioned from them a musical instrument, which was called by the name of the fair nymph.

> "Fair, trembling Syrinx fled
> Arcadian Pan, with such a fearful dread.
> Poor nymph !—poor Pan !—how he did weep to find
> Naught but a lovely sighing of the wind
> Along the reedy stream ; a half-heard strain
> Full of sweet desolation—balmy pain."
>
> *Keats.*

Pan was supposed to delight in slyly overtaking belated travellers and inspiring them with sudden and unfounded fears,—from him called "panic." He is generally represented with a syrinx and shepherd's crook, and a pine garland around his misshapen head.

> "He tore out a reed, the great god Pan,
>   From the deep cool bed of the river.
> The limpid water turbidly ran,
> And the broken lilies a dying lay,
> And the dragon-fly had fled away,
>   Ere he brought it out of the river.
>
> This is the way, laughed the great god Pan
>   (Laughed while he sate by the river !),
> ' The only way since gods began
> To make sweet music they could succeed.'
> Then, dropping his mouth to a hole in the reed
>   He blew in power by the river.
>
> Sweet, sweet, sweet, O Pan,
>   Piercing sweet by the river !
> Blinding sweet, O great god Pan !
> The sun on the hill forgot to die,
> And the lilies revived, and the dragon-fly
>   Came back to dream on the river.
>
> Yet half a beast is the great god Pan
>   To laugh, as he sits by the river,
> Making a poet out of a man.
> The true gods sigh for the cost and pain,—
> For the reed that grows nevermore again
>   As a reed with the reeds in the river."
>
> *E. B. Browning.*

The Romans also worshipped three other divinities of nature entirely unknown to the Greeks, *i.e.*, Silvanus, Faunus, and Fauna, the latter's wife, who had charge over the woods and plants. Priapus, god of the shade, was also a rural deity, but his worship was only known along the shores of the Hellespont.

The fairest among all the lesser gods was doubtless Flora, goddess of flowers, who married Zephyrus, the gentle god of the south wind, and wandered happily with him from place to place, scattering her favours with lavish generosity. She was principally worshipped by young girls, and the only offerings ever seen on her altars were fruits and garlands of beautiful flowers. Her festivals, generally celebrated in the month of May, were called the Floralia.

> " Crowds of nymphs,
> Soft voiced, and young, and gay,
> In woven baskets bringing ears of corn,
> Roses and pinks and violets to adorn
> The shrine of Flora in her early May."
>
> *Keats.*

Vertumnus and Pomona

Vertumnus and Pomona were the special divinities of the garden and orchard. They are represented with pruning-knives and shears, gardening implements, and fruits and flowers. Pomona was very coy indeed, and had no desire to marry. Vertumnus, enamoured of her charms, did his best to make her change her mind, but she would not even listen to his pleadings.

At last the lover had recourse to stratagem, disguised himself as an aged crone, entered Pomona's garden, and inquired how it happened that such a very charming young woman should remain so long unmarried. Then, having received a mocking answer, he began to argue with her, and finally extracted an avowal that, among

268

all the suitors, one alone was worthy of her love, Vertumnus. Vertumnus seized the favourable opportunity, revealed himself, and clasped her to his breast. Pomona, perceiving that she had hopelessly betrayed herself, no longer refused to wed, but allowed him to share her labours, and help her turn the luscious fruit to ripen in the autumn sunshine.

The lesser divinities of the sea were almost as numerous as those of the land, and included the lovely Oceanides and Nereides, together with their male companions the Tritons, who generally formed Neptune's regal train.

The Story of Glaucus

One of the lesser sea gods, Glaucus, was once a poor fisherman, who earned his daily bread by selling the fish he caught in his nets. On one occasion he made a very fine haul, and threw his net full of fish down upon a certain kind of grass, which the flapping fish immediately nibbled, and, as if endowed with extraordinary powers, bounded back into the waves and swam away.

Greatly surprised at this occurrence, Glaucus began chewing a few blades of this peculiar grass, and immediately felt an insane desire to plunge into the sea,—a desire which soon became so intense that he could no longer resist it, but dived down into the water. The mere contact with the salt waves sufficed to change his nature; and swimming about comfortably in the element, where he now found himself perfectly at home, he began to explore the depths of the sea.

> " ' I plung'd for life or death. To interknit
>   One's senses with so dense a breathing stuff
>   Might seem a work of pain ; so not enough
>   Can I admire how crystal-smooth it felt,
>   And buoyant round my limbs. At first I dwelt

THE CLASSICAL MYTHS

Whole days and days in sheer astonishment ;
Forgetful utterly of self-intent ;
Moving but with the mighty ebb and flow,
Then, like a new fledg'd bird that first doth show
His spreaded feathers to the morrow chill,
I try'd in fear the pinions of my will.
'Twas freedom ! and at once I visited
The ceaseless wonders of this ocean-bed.' "

Keats.

Glaucus was worshipped most particularly by the
fishermen and boatmen, whose vessels he was supposed
to guard from evil, and whose nets were often filled to
overflowing through his intervention.

CHAPTER XXVII; THE TROJAN WAR

Jupiter and Thetis

JUPITER, father of the gods, once fell deeply in love with a beautiful sea nymph named Thetis, the daughter of Nereus and Doris,—

> "Thetis of the silver feet, and child
> Of the gray Ancient of the Deep."
> *Homer (Bryant's tr.).*

He was very anxious indeed to marry her, but, before taking such an important step, deemed it prudent to consult the Fates, who alone could inform him whether this union would be for his happiness or not. It was very fortunate for him that he did so, for the three sisters told him that Thetis was destined to be the mother of a son who would far outshine his father.

Jupiter carefully pondered this reply, and concluded to renounce the marriage rather than run any risk of being forced to surrender his power to one greater than he. Thetis' hand he then decreed should be given in marriage to Peleus, King of Phthia, who had loved her faithfully, and had long sued in vain.

Thetis, however, was not at all anxious to accept the hand of a mere mortal after having enjoyed the attention of the gods (for Neptune also had wooed her), and demurred, until Jupiter promised his own and the gods' attendance at the marriage feast. The prospect of this signal honour reconciled the maiden, and the wedding preparations were made in the coral caves of her father, Nereus, beneath the foam-crested waves.

Thither, mindful of his promise, came Jupiter, with all the gods of Olympus.

> "Then, with his Queen, the Father of the gods
> Came down from high Olympus' bright abodes;
> Came down, with all th' attending deities."
> *Catullus.*

The guests took their seats, and pledged the bride and groom in brimming cups of wine,—Bacchus' wedding gift to Thetis. All was joy and merriment, when an uninvited guest suddenly appeared in the banquet-hall. All present immediately recognised Eris (Discordia, Ate), goddess of discord, whose snaky locks, sour looks, and violent temper had caused her to be omitted from the wedding list,—

> "The Abominable, that uninvited came
> Into the fair Peleian banquet-hall."
>
> *Tennyson.*

The Apple of Discord

This omission angered her, and made her determine to have her revenge by troubling the harmony which evidently reigned among all the guests. For a moment she stood beside the bountiful board, then threw upon it a golden apple, and, exhaling over the assembly her poisoned breath, she vanished. The general attention was, of course, turned upon the golden fruit, whereon the inscription " To the fairest " was clearly traced.

All the ladies were at first inclined to contend for the prize; but one by one each claimant withdrew except Juno, Minerva, and Venus, who hotly disputed for its possession. Juno declared that the queen of the gods, in her majesty and power, surely had the best right; Minerva, that the beauty of wisdom and know-ledge far surpassed external charms; and Venus smiled, and archly requested to be informed who might assert greater claims than the goddess of beauty.

The dispute grew more and more bitter, and the irate goddesses called upon the guests to award the prize to the most deserving; but the guests, one and all, refused to act as umpires, for the apple could be given to but one, and the two others would be sure to vent their anger and disappointment upon the judge who passed over their charms in favour of a third. The final decision was therefore referred to Paris, who, although performing the lowly duties of a shepherd, was the son of Priam and Hecuba, King and Queen of Troy.

When but a babe, Paris had been exposed on a mountain to perish, because an oracle had predicted that he would cause the death of his family and the downfall of his native city. Although thus cruelly treated, he had not perished, having been found and adopted by a shepherd, who made him follow his own calling.

When Paris reached manhood, he was a very handsome and attractive young man, and he won the love of Œnone, a beautiful nymph, to whom he was secretly united. Their happiness, however, was but fleeting, for the Fates had decreed that Paris' love for the fair Œnone would soon die.

> " The Fate,
> That rules the will of Jove, had spun the days
> Of Paris and Œnone."
>
> *Quintus Smyrnæus (Elton's tr.)*

The Judgment of Paris

Instead of lingering by the fair nymph's side, Paris wandered off to a lonely mountain top, where the three goddesses besought him to judge their quarrel. Minerva, in glittering armour, first appeared before his dazzled eyes, and proffered the bribe of supreme wisdom if he would but give her the preference.

Juno, queen of heaven, next appeared in royal robes and insignia, and whispered that he should have great wealth and unlimited power were he to award the prize to her.

> " She to Paris made
> Proffer of royal power, ample rule
> Unquestion'd, overflowing revenue
> Wherewith to embellish state, ' from many a vale

And river-sunder'd champaign clothed with corn,
Or labour'd mine undrainable of ore.
Honour,' she said, 'and homage, tax and toll,
From many an inland town and haven large,
Mast-throng'd beneath her shadowing citadel
In glassy bays among her tallest towers.'"

Tennyson.

But all Minerva's and Juno's charms and bribes were forgotten when Venus, in her magic cestus, appeared before the judge. This artful simplicity was the result of much thought, for we are told that

"Venus oft with anxious care
Adjusted twice a single hair."

Cowper.

Then, trembling lest her efforts should prove vain, she gently drew near the youth, and softly promised him a bride as fair as herself in return for the coveted golden apple.

Won either by her superior attractions or by her alluring bribe, Paris no longer hesitated, but placed the prize in her extended palm.

"Ere yet her speech was finished, he consign'd
To her soft hand the fruit of burnished rind ;
And foam-born Venus grasp'd the graceful meed,
Of war, of evil war, the quickening seed."

Coluthus (Elton's tr.).

This act of partiality, of course, called down upon him the wrath and hatred of Juno and Minerva, who, biding their time, watched for a suitable opportunity to avenge themselves ; while Venus, triumphant, and anxious to redeem her promise, directed Paris to return to Troy, make himself known to his parents,—who, the goddess promised, would welcome him warmly,— and obtain from them a fleet in which he might sail to Greece.

THE JUDGMENT OF PARIS

In obedience to these instructions, Paris ruthlessly abandoned the fair and faithful Œnone, and, joining a band of youthful shepherds, went to Troy, under pretext of witnessing a solemn festival. There he took part in the athletic games, distinguished himself, and attracted the attention of his sister Cassandra. This princess was noted for her beauty, and it is said had even been wooed by Apollo, who, hoping to win her favour, bestowed upon her the gift of prophecy. For some reason the god's suit had not prospered ; and, as he could not take back the power conferred, he annulled it by making her hearers refuse to credit her words.

Cassandra immediately called her parents' attention to the extraordinary likeness Paris bore to her other brothers ; and then, breaking out into a prophetic strain, she foretold that he would bring destruction upon his native city. Priam and Hecuba, scorning her prophecy, joyfully received their long-lost son, lovingly compelled him to take up his abode in their palace, and promised to atone for their past neglect by granting his every wish.

Still advised by Venus, Paris soon expressed a desire to sail for Greece, under the pretext of rescuing Hesione, his father's sister, whom Hercules had carried off, after besieging Troy. He was promptly provided with several well-manned galleys, and soon after appeared at the court of Menelaus, King of Sparta, whose young wife, Helen, was the most beautiful woman of her time, if we are to believe the testimony of her contemporaries,

> " Full threescore girls, in sportive flight we stray'd,
> Like youths anointing, where along the glade
> The baths of cool Eurotas limpid play'd.
> But none, of all, with Helen might compare,
> Nor one seem'd faultless of the fairest fair.
> As morn, with vermeil visage, looks from high,
> When solemn night has vanished suddenly;

When winter melts, and frees the frozen hours,
And spring's green bough is gemm'd with silvery flowers:
So bloom'd the virgin Helen in our eyes,
With full voluptuous limbs, and towering size :
In shape, in height, in stately presence fair,
Straight as a furrow gliding from the share ;
A cypress of the gardens, spiring high,
A courser in the cars of Thessaly.
So rose-complexion'd Helen charm'd the sight;
Our Sparta's grace, our glory, and delight."

Theocritus (Elton's tr.).

Helen's Suitors

A daughter of Jupiter and Leda (whom Jove had courted in the guise of a snow-white swan), Helen had many suitors who ardently strove to win her favour. The noblest, bravest, and best came to woo and hoped to win; but all were left in suspense, as the maiden did not show any preference, and refused to make known her choice.

Tyndareus, Helen's stepfather, thinking the rejected suitors might attempt to steal her away from any husband she selected, proposed that all the candidates for her hand should take a solemn oath, binding themselves to respect the marital rights of the favoured suitor, and help him regain possession of his wife should any one venture to kidnap her.

" This was cause
To Tyndarus her father of much doubt,
To give, or not to give her, and how best
To make good fortune his : at length this thought
Occurr'd, that each to each the wooers give
Their oath, and plight their hands, and on the flame
Pour the libations, and with solemn vows
Bind their firm faith that him, who should obtain
The virgin for his bride, they all would aid ;
If any dar'd to seize and bear her off,
And drive by force her husband from her bed,
All would unite in arms, and lay his town,
Greek or Barbaric, level with the ground."

Euripides (Potter's tr.).

The Rape of Helen

Iphigenia

THE ABDUCTION OF HELEN

All agreed to this proposal, the oath was taken, and Helen, whose deliberations had come to an end, bestowed her hand upon Menelaus, King of Sparta.

The Abduction of Helen

On his arrival at Sparta, in Lacedæmonia, Paris was received with graceful hospitality by Menelaus and Helen. He had not sojourned there many days, however, before the king was called away from home, and departed, confiding to his wife the care of entertaining his princely guest. During his absence, Paris, urged by Venus, courted Helen so successfully that she finally consented to elope with him, and allowed herself to be borne away in triumph to Troy.

> " Then from her husband's stranger-sheltering home
> He tempted Helen o'er the ocean foam."
> *Coluthus* (*Elton's tr.*).

Menelaus, on his return from Crete, discovered his guest's treachery, and swore never to rest satisfied until he had recovered his truant wife and punished her seducer. Messengers were sent in haste in every direction, to summon Helen's former suitors to keep their oath, and join Menelaus at Aulis with men and weapons. All came promptly at his call except Ulysses, King of Ithaca, who, to console himself for Helen's refusal of his suit, had married her cousin, Penelope, and had now no dearer wish than to linger by her side and admire his infant son, Telemachus.

In the presence of the messenger Palamedes, Ulysses feigned insanity, hoping thereby to elude the tedious journey to Troy; but the messenger was not so easily duped, and cleverly determined to ascertain the truth by stratagem. One day, therefore, when the king was ploughing the sea-shore with an ox and horse harnessed together, and sowing this strange field with salt, Palamedes placed the babe Telemachus in the furrow, directly in front of the plough, and marked how skilfully Ulysses turned his ill-assorted team aside to avoid harming his heir. This action sufficed to prove to Palamedes that the king had not lost all control of his senses, and enabled him to force Ulysses to obey Menelaus' summons.

At Aulis the assembled army with unanimous consent elected Agamemnon, Menelaus' brother, chief of the expedition, which numbered, among many others, Nestor, noted for his wise counsel; Ajax, gigantic in strength and courage; and Diomedes, the renowned warrior.

The troops were assembled, the vessels freighted; but before they departed, the chiefs considered it expedient to consult an oracle, to ascertain whether their expedition was destined to succeed. In a somewhat veiled and ambiguous manner, they received answer that Troy could never be taken without the aid of the son of Peleus and Thetis, Achilles, of whom the Fates had predicted he would surpass his father in greatness.

The Hero Achilles

Thetis loved this only child so dearly, that when he was but a babe, she had carried him to the banks of the Styx, whose waters had the magic power of rendering all the parts they touched invulnerable. Premising that her son would be a great warrior, and thus exposed to great danger, she plunged him wholly into the tide with the exception of one heel, by which she held him, and then returned home.

Some time after an oracle foretold that Achilles would die beneath the walls of Troy from a wound in his heel, the only vulnerable part of his body. With many tears

278

THE HERO ACHILLES

Thetis vowed that her son should never leave her to encounter such a fate, and entrusted the care of his education to the Centaur Chiron, who had taught all the greatest heroes in turn.

From this instructor Achilles learned the arts of war, wrestling, poetry, music and song—all, in short, that an accomplished Greek warrior was expected to know —and, when his studies were finished, returned to his father's court to gladden his fond mother's heart by his presence.

Thetis' joy was all turned to grief, however, when rumours of the war imminent between Greece and Troy came to her ears. She knew her son would soon be summoned, and to prevent his going, sent him off to the court of Lycomedes, where, under some pretext, he was prevailed upon to assume a disguise and mingle with the king's daughters and their handmaidens.

One messenger after another was despatched to summon Achilles to join the fleet at Aulis, but one after another returned without having seen him or being able to ascertain where he was hiding. The Greeks, however anxious to depart, dared not sail without him. They were in despair, until Ulysses, the wily, proposed a plan, and offered to carry it our.

> " Ulysses, man of many arts,
>   Son of Laertes, reared in Ithaca,
>   That rugged isle, and skilled in every form
>   Of shrewd device and action wisely planned."
>   *Homer (Bryant's tr.).*

Arrayed in pedlar's garb, with a pack upon his shoulders, Ulysses entered Lycomedes' palace, where he shrewdly suspected Achilles was concealed, and offered his wares for sale. The maidens selected trinkets ; but one of them, closely veiled, seized a weapon concealed among the ornaments, and brandished

279

it with such skill that Ulysses saw through the assumed disguise, explained his presence and purpose, and by his eloquence persuaded the young Achilles to accompany him to Aulis.

The Greeks were now ready to embark ; but no favourable wind came to swell the sails, which day after day hung limp and motionless against the tall masts of their vessels.

> " The troops
> Collected and embodied, here we sit
> Inactive, and from Aulis wish to sail
> In vain."

Euripides (Potter's tr.).

The Sacrifice of Iphigenia

Calchas, the soothsayer of the expedition, was again consulted, to discover how they might best win the favour of the gods ; and the purport of the reply given was that no favourable wind would blow until Iphigenia, daughter of Agamemnon, were offered up in sacrifice to appease the everlasting gods.

Many other propitiatory methods were tried ; but as they all proved ineffective, Agamemnon, urged by his companions, sent for his daughter, feigning that he wished to celebrate her nuptials with Achilles before his departure.

> " I wrote, I seal'd
> A letter to my wife, that she should send
> Her daughter, to Achilles as a bride
> Affianc'd."

Euripides (Potter's tr.).

Iphigenia came to her father secretly delighted at being the chosen bride of such a hero ; but, instead of being led to the hymeneal altar, she was dragged to the place of sacrifice, where the priest, with uplifted knife, was about to end her sufferings, when Diana suddenly appeared, snatched her up in a cloud, and

left in her stead a deer, which was duly sacrificed, while
Iphigenia was borne in safety to Taurus, where she
became a priestess in one of the goddess's temples.

The gods were now propitious, and the wind slowly
rose, filled the sails of the waiting vessels, and wafted
them swiftly and steadily over the sea to the Trojan
shores, where an army stood ready to prevent the
Greek troops from disembarking. The invaders were
eager to land to measure their strength against the
Trojans ; yet all hesitated to leave the ships, for an
oracle had foretold that the first warrior who attempted
to land would meet with instant death.

> " ' The Delphic oracle foretold
> That the first Greek who touched the Trojan strand
> Should die.' "
>
> *Wordsworth.*

Protesilaus and Laodamia

Protesilaus, a brave chief, seeing his comrades'
irresolution, and animated by a spirit of self-sacrifice,
sprang boldly ashore, and perished, slain by the enemy,
as soon as his foot had touched the foreign soil.
When the tidings of his death reached his beloved wife,
Laodamia, whom he had left in Thessaly, her heart
was well-nigh broken ; and in her despair she entreated
the gods to let her die, or allow her to see her lord once
more, were it but for a moment. Her appeal was so
touching, that the gods could not refuse to hear it, and
bade Mercury conduct her husband's shade back to earth,
to tarry with her for three hours' time.

> " ' Such grace hath crowned thy prayer,
> Laodamia ! that at Jove's command
> Thy husband walks the paths of upper air :
> He comes to tarry with thee three hours' space ;
> Accept the gift, behold him face to face ! ' "
>
> *Wordsworth.*

THE CLASSICAL MYTHS

With an inarticulate cry of joy, Laodamia beheld the beloved countenance of Protesilaus once more, and from his own lips heard the detailed account of his early death. The three hours passed all too quickly in delicious intercourse; and when Mercury reappeared to lead him back to Hades, the loving wife, unable to endure a second parting, died of grief.

The same grave, it is said, was the resting-place of this united pair, and kind-hearted nymphs planted elm trees over their remains. These trees grew "until they were high enough to command a view of Troy, and then withered away, while fresh branches sprang from the roots."

> "Upon the side
> Of Hellespont (such faith was entertained)
> A knot of spiry trees for ages grew
> From out the tomb of him for whom she died;
> And ever, when such stature they had gained
> That Ilium's walls were subject to their view,
> The trees' tall summits withered at the sight;
> A constant interchange of growth and blight!"
>
> *Wordsworth.*

Hostilities had now begun, and the war between the conflicting hosts was waged with equal courage and skill. During nine long years of uninterrupted strife, the Greeks' effort to enter Troy, or Ilium, as it was also called, were vain, as were also the Trojans' attempts to force the foe to leave their shores. This memorable struggle is the theme of many poems. The oldest and most renowned of all, the Iliad, begins with the story of the tenth and last year's events.

Chryseis and Briseis

Among a number of captives taken in a skirmish by the Hellenic troops were two beautiful maidens, Chryseis, daughter of Chryses, priest of Apollo, and Briseis. The prisoners were, as usual, allotted to various chiefs, and Agamemnon received the priest's daughter as reward for his bravery, while Achilles triumphantly led to his tent the equally fair Briseis.

When Chryses heard that his child had fallen into the hands of the enemy, he hastened to Agamemnon's tent to offer a rich ransom for her recovery; but the aged father's entreaties were all unheeded, and he was dismissed with many heartless taunts. Exasperated by this cruel treatment, he raised his hands to heaven, and implored Apollo to avenge the insults he had received by sending down upon the Greeks all manner of evil. This prayer was no sooner heard than answered, by the sun god's sending a terrible plague to decimate the enemy's troops.

> " The aged man indignantly withdrew ;
> And Phœbus—for the priest was dear to him—
> Granted his prayer, and sent among the Greeks
> A deadly shaft. The people of the camp
> Were perishing in heaps."
>
> *Homer (Bryant's tr.).*

The Greeks, in terror, now consulted an oracle to know why this calamity had come upon them, and how they might check the progress of the deadly disease which was so rapidly reducing their forces. They were told that the plague would never cease until Agamemnon surrendered his captive, and thus disarmed Apollo's wrath, which had been kindled by his rude refusal to comply with the aged priest's request.

All the Greek chiefs, assembled in council, decided to send Achilles to Agamemnon to apprise him of their wish that he should set Chryseis free,—a wish which he immediately consented to grant, if Briseis were given him in exchange.

The plague was raging throughout the camp; the cries of the sufferers rent the air; many had already succumbed to the scourge, and all were threatened with an inglorious death. Achilles, mindful of all this, and anxious to save his beloved companions, consented to comply with this unreasonable request; but at the same time he swore that, if Agamemnon really took his captive away, he would not strike another blow.

Chryseis was immediately consigned to the care of a herald, who led her back to her aged father's arms. Ready to forgive all, now that his child was restored to him, Chryses implored Apollo to stay his hand, and the plague instantly ceased.

As for Agamemnon, he sent his slaves to Achilles' tent to lead away Briseis; and the hero, true to his promise, laid aside his armour, determined to fight no more.

> " The great Achilles, swift of foot, remained
> Within his ships, indignant for the sake
> Of the fair-haired Briseis."
>
> *Homer (Bryant's tr.).*

Thetis, hearing of the wanton insult offered her son, left her coral caves, ascended to Olympus, cast herself at Jupiter's feet, and with many tears tremulously prayed he would avenge Achilles and make the Greeks fail in all their attempts as long as her son's wrath remained unappeased.

Jupiter, touched by her beauty and distress, frowned until the very firmament shook, and swore to make the Greeks rue the day they left their native shores,

> " To give Achilles honour and to cause
> Myriads of Greeks to perish by their fleet."
>
> *Homer (Bryant's tr.).*

In consequence of a treacherous dream purposely sent by Jupiter to delude him, Agamemnon again assembled his troops, and proposed a new onslaught upon the Trojan forces. But when the army was drawn up in

Helen on the Walls of Troy

Laocoön

battle array, Hector, the eldest son of Priam, and therefore leader of his army, stepping forward, proposed that the prolonged quarrel should be definitely settled by a single combat between Paris and Menelaus.

> "Hector then stood forth and said :
> ' Hearken, ye Trojans and ye nobly-armed
> Achaians, to what Paris says by me.
> He bids the Trojans and the Greeks lay down
> Their shining arms upon the teeming earth,
> And he and Menelaus, loved of Mars,
> Will strive in single combat, on the ground
> Between the hosts, for Helen and her wealth ;
> And he who shall o'ercome, and prove himself
> The better warrior, to his home shall bear
> The treasure and the woman, while the rest
> Shall frame a solemn covenant of peace.' "
>
> *Homer (Bryant's tr.).*

This proposal having been received favourably, Menelaus and Paris soon engaged in a duel, which was witnessed by both armies, by Helen and Priam from the Trojan walls, and by the everlasting gods from the wooded heights of Mount Ida ; but in the very midst of the fight, Venus, seeing her favourite about to succumb, suddenly snatched him away from the battlefield, and bore him unseen to his chamber, where he was joined by Helen, who bitterly reproached him for his cowardly flight.

Indignant at this interference on Venus' part, the gods decreed that the war should be renewed; and Minerva, assuming the form of a Trojan warrior, aimed an arrow at Menelaus, who was vainly seeking his vanished opponent. This act of treachery was the signal for a general call to arms and a renewal of hostilities. Countless deeds of valour were now performed by the heroes on both sides, and also by the gods, who mingled in the ranks and even fought against each

285

other, until recalled by Jupiter, and forbidden to fight any more.

For a little while fortune seemed to favour the Greeks; and Hector, hastening back to Troy, bade his mother go to the temple with all her women, and endeavour by her prayers and gifts to propitiate Minerva and obtain her aid. Then he hastened off in search of his wife Andromache and little son Astyanax, whom he wished to embrace once more before rushing out to battle and possible death.

Hector and Andromache

He found his palace deserted, and, upon questioning the women, heard that his wife had gone to the Scæan Gate, where he now drove as fast as his noble steeds could draw him. There, at the gate, took place the parting scene, which has deservedly been called the most pathetic in all the Iliad, in which Andromache vainly tried to detain her husband within the walls, while Hector gently reproved her, and demonstrated that his duty called him out upon the field of battle, where he must hold his own if he would not see the city taken, the Trojans slain, and the women, including his mother and beloved Andromache, borne away into bitter captivity.

> " Andromache
> Pressed to his side meanwhile, and, all in tears,
> Clung to his hand, and, thus beginning, said :—
> ' Too brave ! thy valour yet will cause thy death.
> Thou hast no pity on thy tender child,
> Nor me, unhappy one, who soon must be
> Thy widow. All the Greeks will rush on thee
> To take thy life. A happier lot were mine,
> If I must lose thee, to go down to earth,
> For I shall have no hope when thou art gone,—
> Nothing but sorrow. Father have I none,
> And no dear mother.

HECTOR AND ANDROMACHE

" Hector, thou
Art father and dear mother now to me,
And brother and my youthful spouse besides.
In pity keep within the fortress here,
Nor make thy child an orphan nor thy wife
A widow.'
     Then answered Hector, great in war : ' All this
I bear in mind, dear wife ; but I should stand
Ashamed before the men and long-robed dames
Of Troy, were I to keep aloof and shun
The conflict, coward-like.' "

Homer (Bryant's tr.).

Then he stretched out his arms for his infant son,
who, however, shrank back affrighted at the sight of
his brilliant helmet and nodding plumes, and would not
go to him until he had set the gleaming headdress aside.
After a passionate prayer for his little heir's future
welfare, Hector gave the child back to Andromache,
and, with a farewell embrace, sprang into his chariot
and drove away.

" ' Sorrow not thus, beloved one, for me.
No living man can send me to the shades
Before my time ; no man of woman born,
Coward or brave, can shun his destiny.
But go thou home, and tend thy labours there,
The web, the distaff,—and command thy maids
To speed the work. The cares of war pertain
To all men born in Troy, and most to me.' "

Homer (Bryant's tr.).

Paris, ashamed now of his former flight, soon joined
his brother upon the battlefield, and together they performed many deeds of valour. The time had now
come when Jupiter was about to redeem the promise
given to Thetis, for little by little the Greeks were
forced to yield before the might of the Trojans, who,
stimulated by their partial success, and fired by Hector's
example, performed miracles of valour, and finally drove
their assailants into their entrenchments.

287

Death and defeat now dogged the very footsteps of the Greek forces, who were driven, inch by inch, away from the walls, ever nearer the place where their vessels rode at anchor. They now ardently longed for the assistance of Achilles, whose mere presence, in days gone by, had filled the Trojan hearts with terror; but the hero, although Briseis had been returned unmolested, paid no heed to their entreaties for aid, and remained a sullen and indifferent spectator of their flight, while the Trojans began to set fire to some of the vessels of their fleet.

> "The goddess-born Achilles, swift of foot,
> Beside his ships still brooded o'er his wrath,
> Nor came to counsel with the illustrious chiefs,
> Nor to the war, but suffered idleness
> To eat his heart away ; for well he loved
> Clamour and combat."
>
> *Homer (Bryant's tr.).*

Discouraged by all these reverses, in spite of their brave resistance, the Greeks, in despair, concluded that the gods had entirely forsaken them, and beat a hasty and ignominious retreat to the shore, closely followed by the enemy, who uttered loud cries of triumph.

Patroclus, Achilles' intimate friend, then hastened to the hero's side to inform him of his comrades' flight, and implore him once more to rescue them from inevitable death. But Achilles, summoning all his pride to his assistance, did not waver in his resolve. Suddenly Patroclus remembered that the mere sight of Achilles' armour might suffice to arrest the enemy's advance and produce a diversion in favour of the Greeks ; so he asked permission to wear it and lead the Myrmidons, Achilles' trusty followers, into the fray.

> "Send me at least into the war,
> And let me lead thy Myrmidons, that thus

HECTOR AND ANDROMACHE

The Greeks may have some gleam of hope.   And give
The armour from thy shoulders.   I will wear
Thy mail, and then the Trojans, at the sight,
May think I am Achilles, and may pause
From fighting, and the warlike sons of Greece,
Tired as they are, may breathe once more, and gain
A respite from the conflict."

Homer (Bryant's tr.)

Achilles had sworn, it is true, not to return to the
scene of strife, but was quite willing to lend men and
arms, if they might be of any use, and immediately
placed them at his friend's disposal.   Hastily Patroclus
donned the glittering armour, called aloud to the
Myrmidons to follow his lead, and rushed forth to
encounter the enemy.

The Trojans paused in dismay, thinking Achilles had
come, and were about to take flight, when all at once
they discovered the fraud.   With renewed courage
they opposed the Greek onslaught.   Many heroes bit
the dust in this encounter, among others Sarpedon, the
son of Jupiter and Europa—whose remains were borne
away from the battlefield by the twin divinities Sleep
and Death—ere Hector, son of Priam, and chief among
the Trojan warriors, challenged Patroclus to single
combat.   Needless to say, the two closed in deadly
battle, and fought with equal valour, until Patroclus,
already exhausted by his previous efforts, and betrayed
by the gods, finally succumbed.

" The hero fell
With clashing mail, and all the Greeks beheld
His fall with grief."

Homer (Bryant's tr.).

With a loud cry of victory, Hector wrenched the
armour off the mangled corpse, and quickly withdrew
to array himself in the brilliant spoils.   The tidings of
Patroclus' fall spread rapidly through all the Grecian

camp, and reached Achilles, who wept aloud when he heard that his beloved friend, who had left him but a short time before full of life and energy, was now no more. So loudly did the hero mourn his loss, that Thetis, in the quiet ocean depths, heard his groans, and rushed to his side to ascertain the cause.

Into his mother's sympathetic ear Achilles poured the whole story of his grief and loss, while she gently strove to turn his thoughts aside from the sad event, and arouse an interest for some pursuit less dangerous than war. All her efforts were vain, however; for Achilles' soul thirsted for revenge, and he repeatedly swore he would go forth and slay his friend's murderer.

> "No wish
> Have I to live, or to concern myself
> In men's affairs, save this: that Hector first,
> Pierced by my spear, shall yield his life, and pay
> The debt of vengeance for Patroclus slain."
>
> *Homer (Bryant's tr.).*

The Armour of Achilles

Then, in sudden dread lest Hector should fall by another's hand, or withdraw from the battlefield and thus escape his vengeance, Achilles would have rushed from his tent unarmed; but his mother prevailed upon him to wait until the morrow, when she promised to bring him a full suit of armour from Vulcan's own hand. Rapidly Thetis then traversed the wide space which separates the coast of Asia Minor from Mount Ætna, where Vulcan laboured at his forge.

> "She found him there
> Sweating and toiling, and with busy hand
> Plying the bellows."
>
> *Homer (Bryant's tr.).*

Arrived before him, she breathlessly made known her errand, and the god promised that the arms should be ready within the given time, and immediately set to work to fashion them. By his skilful hands the marvellous weapons were forged ; and when the first streak of light appeared above the horizon, he consigned them to Thetis, who hastened back to her son's tent, where she found him still bewailing the loss of Patroclus.

During Thetis' absence, messengers had come to Achilles' tent to warn him that Patroclus' body was still in the enemy's hands, and to implore him to come and rescue the precious corpse. Mindful of his promise to his mother, Achilles still refused to fight, but, springing upon the rampart, uttered his mighty war-cry, the sound of which filled the enemy's hearts with terror, and made them yield to the well-directed onslaught of Ajax and Diomedes, who finally succeeded in recovering the body, which they then reverently bore to Achilles' tent.

To console Achilles for his friend's death, Thetis exhibited the glorious armour she had just obtained, helped him to put it on, and then bade him go forth and conquer.

> " ' Leave we the dead, my son, since it hath pleased
> The gods that he should fall ; and now receive
> This sumptuous armour, forged by Vulcan's hand,
> Beautiful, such as no man ever wore.' "
>
> Homer (*Bryant's tr.*).

The Death of Hector

Thus armed, mounted in his chariot drawn by his favourite steeds, and driven by his favourite charioteer Automedon, Achilles went forth to battle, and at last seeing Hector, whom alone he wished to meet, he rushed upon him with a hoarse cry of rage. The Trojan hero, at the mere sight of the deadly hatred which shone in Achilles' eyes, turned to flee. Achilles pursued him, and taunted him with his cowardice, until Hector turned and fought with all the courage and recklessness of despair.

Their blows fell like hail, a cloud of dust enveloped their struggling forms, and the anxious witnesses only heard the dull thud of the blows and the metallic clash of the weapons. Suddenly there came a loud cry, then all was still ; and when the dust-cloud had blown away, the Trojans from the ramparts, where they had waited in agony for the issue of the fight, beheld Achilles tear the armour from their champion's body, bind the corpse to his chariot, and drive nine times round the city walls, Hector's princely head dragging in the dust. Priam, Hecuba, and Andromache, Hector's wife, were agonised spectators of this ignominious treatment, and finally they saw Achilles drive off to the spot where Patroclus' funeral pile was laid, and there abandon the corpse.

Achilles then returned to his tent, where for a long time he continued to mourn his friend's untimely end, refusing to be comforted.

The gods, from their celestial abode, had also witnessed this heartrending scene, and now Jupiter sent Iris to Thetis, and bade her hasten down to Achilles and command him to restore Hector's body to his mourning family. He also directed Mercury to lead Priam, unseen, into Achilles' tent, to claim and bear away his son's desecrated corpse. Thetis, seeking Achilles in his tent, announced the will of Jove :

> " I am come
> A messenger from Jove, who bids me say
> The immortals are offended, and himself
> The most, that thou shouldst in thy spite detain
> The corse of Hector at the beaked ships,
> Refusing its release. Comply thou, then,
> And take the ransom and restore the dead."
>
> Homer (*Bryan tr.*).

THE DEATH OF ACHILLES

Mercury acquitted himself with his usual despatch and soon guided Priam in safety through the Grecian camp to Achilles' tent, where the aged king fell at the hero's feet, humbly pleading for his son's body, and proffering a princely ransom in exchange.

Achilles, no longer able to refuse this entreaty, and touched by a father's tears, consigned Hector's corpse to the old man's care, and promised an armistice of fourteen days, that the funeral rites in both camps might be celebrated with all due pomp and solemnity; and with the burial of Hector the Iliad comes to a close.

At the end of the truce the hostilities were renewed, and the Trojans were reinforced by the arrival of Penthesilea, queen of the Amazons, who, with a chosen troop of warrior maidens, came to offer her aid. The brave queen afforded them, however, only temporary relief, as she was slain by Achilles in their very first encounter.

He, too, however, was doomed to die "in the flower of his youth and beauty," and the Fates had almost finished spinning his thread of life. In an early skirmish, while in close pursuit of the Trojans, Thetis' son had once caught sight of Polyxena, daughter of Priam, and had been deeply smitten by her girlish charms. He now vainly tried to make peace between the conflicting nations, hoping that, were the war but ended, he might obtain her hand in marriage.

The Death of Achilles

His efforts to make peace failed; but at last he prevailed upon Priam to celebrate his betrothal with Polyxena, with the stipulation that the marriage would take place as soon as the war was over. The betrothal ceremony was held without the city gates;

and Achilles was just about to part from his blushing betrothed, when Paris, ever treacherous, stole behind him and shot a poisoned arrow into his vulnerable heel, thus slaying the hero who had caused so many brave warriors to bite the dust.

> "Thus great Achilles, who had shown his zeal
> In healing wounds, died of a wounded heel."
> *O. W. Holmes.*

His armour—the glorious armour forged by Vulcan—was hotly contested for by Ulysses and Ajax. The former finally obtained the coveted weapons; and Ajax' grief at their loss was so intense, that he became insane, and killed himself in a fit of frenzy, while Polyxena, inconsolable at her betrothed's death, committed suicide on the magnificent tomb erected over his remains on the Trojan plain. Another version has it that Polyxena was torn from the arms of Hecuba and offered up as a sacrifice upon the tomb of Achilles by his son Pyrrhus.

Philoctetes

The oracles, silent so long, now announced that Troy could never be taken without the poisoned arrows of Hercules, then in the keeping of Philoctetes. This hero had started with the expedition, but had been put ashore on the Island of Lemnos on account of a wound in his foot, which had become so offensive that none of the ship's company could endure his presence on board.

Ten long years had already elapsed since then, and although a party of Greeks immediately set out in search of him, they had but little hope of finding him alive. They nevertheless wended their way to the cave where they had deposited him, where, to their

294

THE DEATH OF PARIS

unbounded surprise, they still found him. The wound had not healed, but he had managed to exist by killing such game as came within reach of his hand.

> " Exposed to the inclement skies,
> Deserted and forlorn he lies ;
> No friend or fellow-mourner there,
> To soothe his sorrows, and divide his care ;
> Or seek the healing plant, of power to 'suage
> His aching wound, and mitigate its rage."
> *Sophocles* (*Francklin's tr.*).

Incensed by the Greeks' former cruel desertion, no entreaty could now induce Philoctetes to accompany the messengers to Troy, until Hercules appeared to him in a dream, and bade him go without delay, for there he would find Machaon, Æsculapius' son, who was to heal his wound.

The Death of Paris

The dream was realised. Philoctetes, whole once more, joined the Greek host, and caused great dismay in the enemy's ranks with his poisoned arrows. One of his deadly missiles even struck Paris, and, as the poison entered his veins, it caused him grievous suffering. Paris then remembered that his first love Œnone, who knew all remedies and the best modes of applying them, had once told him to send for her should he ever be wounded. He therefore sent for Œnone ; but she, justly offended by the base desertion and long neglect of her lover, refused her aid, and let him die in torture. When he was dead, Œnone repented this decision ; and when the flames of his funeral pyre rose around him, she rushed into their midst, and was burned to death on his corpse.

> " But when she gain'd the broader vale and saw
> The ring of faces redden'd by the flames

295

Infolding that dark body which had lain
Of old in her embrace, paused—and then ask'd
Falteringly, ' Who lies on yonder pyre ? '
But every man was mute for reverence.
Then moving quickly forward till the heat
Smote on her brow, she lifted up a voice
Of shrill command, ' Who burns upon the pyre ? '
Whereon their oldest and their boldest said,
' He whom thou would'st not heal ! ' and all at once
The morning light of happy marriage broke,
Thro' all the clouded years of widowhood,
And muffling up her comely head, and crying
' Husband ! ' she leapt upon the funeral pile,
And mixt herself with *him* and past in fire."

Tennyson.

Two of Priam's sons had already expired, and yet
Troy had not fallen into the hands of the Greeks, who
now heard another prophecy, to the effect that Troy
could never be taken as long as the Palladium—a sacred
statue of Minerva, said to have fallen from heaven—
remained within its walls.   So Ulysses and Diomedes in
disguise effected an entrance into the city one night, and
after many difficulties succeeded in escaping with the
precious image.

The Wooden Horse

Men and chiefs, impatient of further delay, now joyfully hailed Ulysses' proposal to take the city by stratagem.   They therefore secretly built a colossal wooden
horse, within whose hollow sides a number of brave
warriors might lie concealed.   The main army feigned
weariness of the endless enterprise, and embarked,
leaving the horse as a pretended offering to Neptune ;
while Sinon, a shrewd slave, remained to persuade the
Trojans to drag the horse within their gates and keep
him there, a lasting monument of their hard-won
triumph.

296

THE STORY OF LAOCOON

To the unbounded joy of the long-besieged Trojans, the Greek fleet then sailed away, until the Island of Tenedos hid the ships from view. All the inhabitants of Troy poured out of the city to view the wooden horse and question Sinon, who pretended to have great cause of complaint against the Greeks, and strongly advised them to secure their last offering to Neptune.

The Story of Laocoon

The Trojans hailed this idea with rapture; but Laocoon, Neptune's priest, implored them to leave the horse alone, lest they should bring untold evil upon their heads.

> " 'Wretched countrymen,' he cries,
> ' What monstrous madness blinds your eyes?
>
> .   .   .   .
>
> Perchance—who knows?—these planks of deal
> A Grecian ambuscade conceal,
> Or 'tis a pile to o'erlook the town,
> And pour from high invaders down;
> Or fraud lurks somewhere to destroy:
> Mistrust, mistrust it, men of Troy!' "
>
> *Virgil (Conington's tr.).*

Deaf to all warnings and entreaties, they dragged the colossal image into the very heart of their city, tearing down a portion of their ramparts to allow its passage, while Laocoon hastened down to the shore to offer sacrifice to the gods. As he stood there by the improvised altar, with one of his sons on either side to assist him in his office, two huge serpents came out of the sea, coiled themselves around him and his sons, and crushed and bit them to death

> " Unswerving they
> Toward Laocoon hold their way;
> First round his two young sons they wreathe,
> And grind their limbs with savage teeth:
> Then, as with arms he comes to aid,
> The wretched father they invade

And twine in giant folds : twice round
His stalwart waist their spires are wound,
Twice round his neck, while over all
Their heads and crests tower high and tall.
He strains his strength their knots to tear,
While gore and slime his fillets smear,
And to the unregardful skies
Sends up his agonising cries."

Virgil (Conington's tr.).

The awestruck witnesses of this terrible scene accepted this as a sure sign that the gods resented his interference concerning the wooden horse, and had justly punished the sacrilegious hand which had dared strike it with a spear, merely to demonstrate, that, being hollow, it might contain an armed band. Ever since then, Laocoon and his sons' struggle with the serpents has been a favourite subject for poets and artists.

The Fall of Troy

Meanwhile the Greeks had been hiding behind Tenedos ; but when night came on they returned to the site of their ten-years' encampment, and were let into the city by Sinon, who also released their companions from their prison within the wooden horse. Although taken by surprise, the city guards made desperate attempts to repel the Greeks ; but it was now too late, for the enemy had already broken into houses and palaces, and were killing, pillaging, and burning all who came in their way.

" The melancholy years,
The miserable melancholy years,
Crept onward till the midnight terror came,
And by the glare of burning streets I saw
Palace and temple reel in ruin and fall,
And the long-baffled legions, bursting in
Through gate and bastion, blunted sword and spear
With unresisted slaughter."

Lewis Morris.

Clytæmnestra

The Triumph of Galatea

The royal family, even, was not exempt from the general massacre; and the aged Priam, who lived to see his last son perish before his eyes, finally found relief in death.

Their object accomplished, the Greeks immediately sailed for home, their vessels heavily laden with plunder and slaves. But the homeward journey was not as joyful as might have been expected; and many, after escaping from the enemy's hands, perished in the waves, or found death lying in wait for them by their own fireside.

Menelaus, with his wife Helen, who, in spite of the added ten years, retained all her youthful beauty, were detained in Egypt by contrary winds, sent to punish them for omitting the usual sacrifice to the gods. He at last consulted Proteus, who revealed how the wrath of the gods could best be allayed, and how favourable winds could be secured to waft him home.

As for Agamemnon, leader of the Greeks, he returned to Argos only to be murdered by his wife Clytæmnestra and her paramour Ægisthus.

> " ' Ægisthus, bent upon my death,
> Plotted against me with my guilty wife,
> And bade me to his house, and slew me there,
> Even at the banquet.' "
>
> *Homer (Bryant's tr.).*

Then, mortally afraid lest Orestes, Agamemnon's son, should avenge his father's death, Ægisthus prepared to slay him too; but Electra, the boy's sister, discovering this intention, helped him to escape, and placed him under the fatherly protection of Strophius, King of Phocis, whose son, Pylades, became his inseparable friend. In fact, their devotion to each other was so great that it has become proverbial in every tongue.

Electra had not forgotten her father's base murder, although years had elapsed since it occurred; and when

Orestes had attained manhood, she bade him come and punish those who had committed the crime. Orestes came, slew Ægisthus and Clytæmnestra, and then, terrified at what he had done, took flight, but only to be pursued by the Furies and Nemesis, goddess of revenge, sent by the gods to punish him for taking justice into his own hands.

Arrived at Delphi, Orestes consulted the oracle, and learned that his crime would be forgiven if he brought a statue of Diana in Tauris back to Greece. The young prince hastened thither, accompanied by the ever faithful Pylades, who never left his side ; and there, in a temple, he found his long-lost sister Iphigenia, who helped him obtain the image he sought, and accompanied him back to his native land, where Nemesis left him for ever.

CHAPTER XXVIII : ULYSSES

The Adventures of Ulysses

THE Greek chiefs, on their return from Troy, were, as we have seen, all more or less visited by the wrath of the gods ; but none of them endured as many hardships as Ulysses (Odysseus), King of Ithaca, the hero of Homer's world-renowned epic the Odyssey. During ten long years he roamed the seas, driven away from his native land by adverse winds, sailing about from place to place, losing his ships and companions, until at last the gods allowed him to return home. His marvellous adventures and numerous mishaps during these ten years form the theme of the Odyssey, which is, shortly, as follows.

After leaving Troy in ruins, Ulysses embarked with his men and spoils, and, favoured by a good wind, soon came within sight of Ismarus, the home of the worthy and wealthy Ciconians. To increase the riches he was carrying home, he proposed to his army to land and storm the city—a proposal which was enthusiastically received and immediately carried out.

But when the men collected near the fleet, instead of embarking as Ulysses urged them to do, they began to drink the rich wine, to roast oxen whole, and to indulge in games and revelry. While they were thus employed and entirely off their guard, the neighbours and allies of the Ciconians came upon them unawares, and put many to death.

The Greeks, although taken by surprise, fought bravely but it was only when the sun was fast sinking that they finally embarked, and left the fatal Ciconian shores.

> " Onward we sailed, lamenting bitterly
> Our comrades slain, yet happy to escape
> From death ourselves."
> *Homer (Bryant's tr.).*

THE CLASSICAL MYTHS

The Lotus-eaters

A hurricane soon arose. The flying clouds blotted the stars from view. The vessels, with broken masts and torn sails, were driven far out of their course, and, after ten days, reached the land of the Lotophagi or Lotus-eaters—a people whose sole food consisted of lotus fruit and blossoms.

Three of Ulysses' best men were sent ashore to reconnoitre; but they had not gone very far before they met the natives, seated under their favourite trees, banqueting on their sweet food. These received the strangers hospitably, and made them partake of the lotus blossoms; but no sooner had the three men done so, than all recollection of their waiting companions or distant homes passed from their minds, while a dreamy, lethargic sensation stole over them, and made them long to recline there and feast for ever.

> " Whoever tasted once of that sweet food
> Wished not to see his native country more,
> Nor give his friends the knowledge of his fate.
> And then my messengers desired to dwell
> Among the Lotus-eaters, and to feed
> Upon the lotus, never to return."
>
> Homer (*Bryant's tr.*).

Ulysses impatiently watched for their return; then, seeing they did not appear, feared some evil had befallen them, and set out, with a few well-armed men, to go in search of them. Instead of finding them in chains, as he fully expected, he soon perceived them feasting among the Lotus-eaters. Their eyes had lost all animation, and rested upon him in a vague, dreamy way, which aroused his suspicions. At the same moment some of the Lotus-eaters advanced to invite him and his troop to join in their feast.

302

THE LOTUS-EATERS

" Branches they bore of that enchanted stem,
  Laden with flower and fruit, whereof they gave
To each, but whoso did receive of them,
  And taste, to him the gushing of the wave
Far, far away did seem to mourn and rave
  On alien shores ; and if his fellow spake,
His voice was thin, as voices from the grave ;
  And deep asleep he seem'd, yet all awake,
And music in his ears his beating heart did make."

Tennyson.

In peremptory tones Ulysses quickly forbade his
men to taste of the magic food, directed them to seize
and bind their unwilling comrades, and forcibly take
them back to their ships. There the magic effect of
the lotus food soon wore away, and the men rowed
steadily westward until they came to the Island of
Sicily, then inhabited by the Cyclopes, a rude race of
one-eyed giants.

" A single ball of sight was fix'd
In their mid-forehead : hence the Cyclops' name :
For that one circular eye was broad enfix'd
In the mid-forehead :—strength was theirs, and force,
And craft of curious toil."

Hesiod (Elton's tr.).

The main part of the fleet was stationed at another
island not far distant, but Ulysses and twelve companions landed in Sicily in search of food. The prospect was promising, for on the plains and hillsides
great flocks of sheep cropped the tender grass ; and
Ulysses and his followers soon came to a great cave
filled with rich stores of milk and cheese. This was
the abode of Polyphemus, son of Neptune, the largest
and fiercest among the gigantic Cyclopean race. The
Greeks' first impulse was to help themselves, since no
one was there to say them nay ; but they finally decided
to await the master's home-coming and courteously

303

ask his assistance. They had moored their vessel under an overhanging cliff, where no one would be likely to find it, and had therefore no fear lest their means of escape should be cut off.

Polyphemus and Galatea

Polyphemus, the ugly giant in whose cave they were waiting, had once seen the charming sea nymph Galatea riding in her pearl-shell chariot drawn by bounding dolphins. Her unsurpassed loveliness made a vivid impression upon him, and he was soon deeply in love with her. He neglected his flocks, shunned his companions, and spent all his time near the seashore, watching for her, and bitterly cursing his fate, which prevented his seeking her in her native element, for the gods had cursed the race of Cyclops with an unconquerable aversion to water. He

> "lov'd
> Not in the little present-making style,
> With baskets of new fruit and pots of roses,
> But with consuming passion. Many a time
> Would his flocks go home by themselves at eve,
> Leaving him wasting by the dark seashore,
> And sunrise would behold him wasting still."
>
> *Theocritus (Hunt's tr.)*.

To induce Galatea to leave the salt sea waves and linger by his side on the white sandy beach, Polyphemus constantly made the most extravagant promises; but the dainty nymph merely laughed at all his professions, and strolled on the shore only when he was sound asleep. Although she made fun of his love, she was not so obdurate to the suit of Acis, a very fascinating young shepherd, who had no need to call her repeatedly, for she always yielded to his first appeal, joyfully joined him, and sat beside him under the shade of some great rock, listening to his tender wooing.

Polyphemus once accidentally came upon them thus, ere they were aware of his proximity. For a moment he glared down upon them ; then, seizing a huge rock, he vowed his rival Acis should not live to enjoy the love which was denied him, and hurled it down upon the unsuspecting lovers. Galatea, the goddess, being immortal, escaped unhurt ; but poor Acis, her beloved, was crushed to death. The stream of blood from his mangled remains was changed by the gods into an exhaustless stream of limpid water, which ever hastened down to the sea to join Galatea.

Ulysses and Polyphemus

Ulysses and his companions, waiting in the cave, soon felt the ground shake beneath their feet, and saw the sheep throng into the cave and take their usual places ; then behind them came the horrible apparition of Polyphemus, who picked up a huge rock and placed it before the opening of the cave, preventing all egress. Ulysses' companions had shrunk with fear into the darkest corners of the cave, whence they watched the giant milk his ewes, dispose of his cheeses, and make his evening meal. But the firelight soon revealed the intruders, and Polyphemus immediately demanded who they were, whence they came, and what they were seeking.

Ulysses, ever wily, replied that his name was No man, that he and his companions were shipwrecked mariners, and that they would fain receive his hospitality. In answer to this statement, the Cyclops stretched forth his huge hand and grasped two of the sailors, whom he proceeded to devour for dessert. Then, his frightful repast being ended, he lay down on the rushes and fell asleep, his loud snores reverberating like thunder through the great cave.

Ulysses silently crept to his side, sword in hand, and was about to kill him, when he suddenly recollected that neither he nor his men could move the rock at the cave's mouth, and that they would never be able to escape. He therefore resolved to have recourse to a stratagem.

When morning came, the giant rose, milked his flock, made his cheese, arranged the vessels, and then, without the least warning, again seized and devoured two of the Greeks. His brawny arm next pushed aside the rock, and he stood beside it with watchful eye, until all his herd had passed out; then, replacing the stone to prevent the escape of his prisoners, he went off to the distant pasture-ground.

During his absence, Ulysses and his men devised a cunning plan whereby they hoped to effect their escape, and made all their preparations to ensure its complete success. A huge pine club which they found in the cave was duly pointed, hardened in the fire, and set aside for future use.

When the darkness began to fall over the earth, Polyphemus again rolled the stone away to admit his flocks, keeping careful guard upon the Greeks. The sheep all in, he replaced the rock, performed his usual evening duties, and then devoured two more of Ulysses' crew.

When this part of the evening meal was over, Ulysses drew near and offered him a leathern flask full of heady wine, which the giant took down at a gulp, little suspecting its effect. Very soon he sank into a deep drunken sleep; and then the men, at a sign from Ulysses, heated the point of the huge club and thrust it into his sole eye, in spite of his frightful cries and execrations. These soon, however, attracted the attention of the other Cyclopes, who thronged without the cave, clamouring to know who was hurting him. "No man!" replied the Cyclops, howling with pain, "No man!" which answer convinced his would-be helpers that he needed no assistance, and made them disperse.

> " ' If no man does thee violence, and thou
> Art quite alone, reflect that none escape
> Diseases ; they are sent by Jove.' "
>
> *Homer (Bryant's tr.).*

Deserted by his companions, Polyphemus spent the night in agony; and, when the anxious bleating of his herd roused him at break of day, he fumblingly milked them, and prepared to let them go forth, as usual, in search of their morning meal. To prevent the Greeks escaping, he rolled the stone only partly aside, and allowed the sheep to pass out a few at a time, carefully running his hand over each broad back to make sure that none of the prisoners were mounted upon them.

Ulysses, meanwhile, having observed this manœuvre, fastened his companions under the rams, reserving one for his own use, and watched them pass out one after the other undetected. Then, clinging to the wool of the largest ram, he too was slowly dragged out, while Polyphemus petted the ram, and inquired how he came to pass out last of all.

> " ' My favourite ram, how art thou now the last
> To leave the cave ? It hath not been thy wont
> To let the sheep go first, but thou didst come
> Earliest to feed among the flowery grass,
> Walking with stately strides, and thou wert first
> At the fresh stream, and first at eve to seek
> The stable ; now thou art the last of all.
> Grievest thou for thy master, who has lost
> His eye, put out by a deceitful wretch
> And his vile crew ?' "
>
> *Homer (Bryant's tr.).*

Ulysses, having thus escaped, sprang to his feet, set his companions free, rushed with them down to the seashore, taking the choice animals on board, and then, when his men had rowed some distance, raised his voice and taunted Polyphemus, revealing at the same time his identity.

> " ' Ha ! Cyclops ! those whom in thy rocky cave
> Thou, in thy brutal fury, hast devoured,
> Were friends of one not unexpert in war ;
> Amply have thy own guilty deeds returned
> Upon thee. Cruel one ! who didst not fear
> To eat the strangers sheltered by thy roof,
> Jove and the other gods avenge them thus !
>
> .   .   .   .
>
> Cyclops, if any man of mortal birth
> Note thine unseemly blindness, and inquire
> The occasion, tell him that Laertes' son,
> Ulysses, the destroyer of walled towns,
> Whose home is Ithaca, put out thine eye.' "
>
> *Homer (Bryant's tr.).*

With a cry of rage, Polyphemus then ran down to the shore, tore up some huge rocks, which he hurled in the direction whence the taunting voice came, and in his rage almost destroyed the Greeks ; for one piece of rock fell very near their vessel, and they were forced to redouble their efforts to row out of reach and prevent disaster.

The Gift of Æolus

The Greeks now sailed on until they reached the Æolian Islands, where dwelt Æolus, king and father of the winds. He had heard of Ulysses' prowess, received him kindly, and at parting gave him a leathern bag containing all the contrary winds, which Ulysses was thus at liberty to retain imprisoned until he had safely reached home.

THE GIFT OF ÆOLUS

Day and night Ulysses' barks now bounded over the blue waves. On the ninth evening the shores of Ithaca were discerned by the eager eyes on board, and all made their preparation for landing early the next morning. For the first time since he had left the Æolian shores, Ulysses now indulged in sleep; and while he was lost in oblivion his sailors opened the leathern bag, intending to rob their master of a portion of his treasure, for they imagined that Æolus had given him much gold.

The bag was no sooner opened than the contrary winds, weary and cramped with their uncomfortable position, sprang out with a rush and a roar, and in a few moments stirred up a terrible storm, which tore the ships from their anchors and soon drove them far out to sea.

After untold suffering, the Greeks landed again upon the Æolian Isle, and Ulysses sought the king, to beseech his aid once more; but this time the god received him coldly, and bade him depart, as his cruelty to Polyphemus had awakened the gods' wrath.

> " ' Hence with thee! Leave our island instantly,
> Vilest of living men! It may not be
> That I receive or aid as he departs
> One who is hated by the blessed gods,—
> And thou art hated by the gods. Away!'"
>
> *Homer (Bryant's tr.).*

Sorrowfully now the Greeks embarked; but, instead of being hurried along by favourable winds, they were obliged to row against wind and waves, and only after many days came to the land of the Læstrygonians, where fresh losses awaited them. These people were cannibals, who were in the habit of slaying all the strangers who visited their shores, to satisfy their horrible appetites. When they saw the vessels enter their harbour, they sunk some of them by casting huge rocks at them from their tall cliffs, and speared and devoured the unfortunate crews.

Ulysses, ever cautious, had lingered without the harbour; and when, from afar, he saw his companions' horrible fate, he bade his men strike the waves with "their sounding oars" and escape.

The Story of Circe

The Greeks went on again until they came to Ææa, an island inhabited by the golden-haired enchantress Circe, sister of Æetes, and aunt of Medea. Here Ulysses' crew was divided into two parties, one of which, led by Eurylochus, set out to explore the island, while the other, headed by Ulysses, remained to guard the ships. Through a dense forest, peopled with strangely gentle wild beasts, Eurylochus led his force, until they came in sight of the beautiful palace home of Circe. From afar they could hear her sweet voice raised in song, as she wove a beautiful web for her own adornment; so they pressed eagerly on, and entered the palace hall, Eurylochus alone lingering on the porch, fearing lest some fraud might suddenly be revealed.

Circe received her self-invited guests most graciously, seated them on tapestry-covered couches, and bade her numerous handmaidens speedily set before them all manner of good cheer—an order which was immediately carried out. The men feasted greedily, for they had fasted for many days, and Circe watched them with ill-concealed disgust. Suddenly she started from her seat, waved her wand over their heads, and bade them assume the form of swine (which obscene animals their gluttony suggested), and hie them to their sties.

> "Then instantly
> She touched them with a wand, and shut them up

Circe

Æneas and Anchises

ULYSSES AND CIRCE

In sties, transformed to swine in head and voice,
Bristles and shape, though still the human mind
Remained to them. Thus sorrowing they were driven
Into their cells, where Circe flung to them
Acorns of oak and ilex, and the fruit
Of cornel, such as nourish wallowing swine."

Homer (*Bryant's tr.*).

Eurylochus, meanwhile, vainly awaited their return, and finally resolved to go back alone to the ships and report what had happened. Sword in hand, Ulysses then set out alone to rescue his comrades; but he had not gone far before he met a youth,—Mercury in disguise,—who warned him not to approach any nearer Circe, and told him of his companions' transformation.

As Ulysses would not be dissuaded from his purpose, Mercury gave him some moly, a herb warranted to preserve him from Circe's magic spells, and sundry important directions, which were all duly listened to and observed.

Ulysses and Circe

Pressing onward, Ulysses reached the palace, and entering the banqueting-room, he accepted the cup proffered by his charming hostess; but Circe's mixture was rendered ineffective by the power of the herb, and, when she waved her wand over his head and bade him join his fellows, he drew his sword and rushed upon her, threatening to take her life if she did not immediately restore his friends to their human forms, and promise to do them no further harm.

Circe, terrified at the threat, agreed to comply with all his demands; and in a few moments Ulysses was again surrounded by his companions, who were exceedingly grateful for their rescue. Circe now prepared

311

a second feast, and entertained them all so well, that Ulysses lingered there for one whole year.

> " And there from day to day
> We lingered a full year, and banqueted
> Nobly on plenteous meats and delicate wines."
>
> *Homer (Bryant's tr.).*

At the end of that time, Ulysses' companions began to long for their own homes, and prevailed upon their chief to leave the fair enchantress. At first Circe was loth to let him go, but, seeing that her efforts to detain him longer would be of no avail, she bade him seek the Cimmerian shores, and there consult the seer Tiresias. This land, which lay on the confines of Pluto's dark realm, was inhabited by shadows, the spirits of the dead, condemned to sojourn there a while ere they were admitted into Hades.

Ulysses embarked, and, according to Circe's directions, let his vessel drift along until its prow grated on a pebbly beach, where he landed. Then, walking straight before him, he came to a spot whence he could hear the roar of the Phlegethon as it joined the Acheron, and here he dug a trench with his sword.

The trench finished, he killed two black victims, furnished by Circe, and made their blood flow into the trench. Immediately all the spirits crowded about him, eager to drink the fresh blood; but Ulysses, with drawn sword, forced them back, until at last Tiresias, the blind seer, approached.

He was allowed to stoop down and drink; and, as soon as he had done so, he recovered the power of human speech, and warned Ulysses of the many trials still awaiting him. Then, his prophecy concluded, he vanished; but Ulysses lingered a little longer to allow his mother to drink some blood, and explain how she came to be here in the spirit land.

CHARYBDIS AND SCYLLA

Many others came and conversed with him; but at last he was forced to depart, and return to Æææa, where he lingered to perform the funeral rites for Elpenor,— one of his followers, a youth who had fallen asleep on one of the palace turrets, and by an inadvertent movement had fallen to the ground, where he had been found dead.

The Sirens

These obsequies over, the Greeks, favoured by a fresh wind, left Circe's isle, and sailed along until they drew near the rocky ledge where the Sirens had their abode. These maidens were wont to sit on the rocks and sing entrancing songs, which allured the mariners until they turned aside from their course, and their vessels were dashed to pieces on the rocks.

According to Circe's advice, Ulysses bade his men bind him fast to the mast, disregard his cries and gestures of command, and keep on their course until the dangerous rocks were lost to view; but, before he allowed them to execute these orders, he stopped their ears with melted wax, so they could not hear a sound, for he alone could hear the Sirens' song and live.

The men then bound him hand and foot to the mast, returned to their oars, and rowed steadily on. Soon the Sirens' melody fell upon Ulysses' charmed ears; but, although he commanded and implored his men to set him free and alter their course, they kept steadily on until no sound of the magic song could reach them, when they once more set their leader free

Charybdis and Scylla

Now, although this danger had been safely passed, Ulysses was troubled in spirit, for he knew he would soon be obliged to steer his course between two dread

monsters, Charybdis and Scylla, who lay so close together, that, while striving to avoid one, it was almost
impossible not to fall an easy prey to the other.

Charybdis' den lay under a rock crowned with a
single wild fig-tree ; and three times daily she en-
gulfed the surrounding waters, drawing even large
galleys into her capacious jaws.

As for Scylla, she too dwelt in a cave, whence her
six ugly heads protruded to devour any prey that came
within reach.

> " No mariner can boast
> That he has passed by Scylla with a crew
> Unharmed; she snatches from the deck, and bears
> Away in each grim mouth a living man."
>
> *Homer (Bryant's tr.).*

This self-same Scylla, once a lovely maiden, had won
the heart of the sea god Glaucus, but coquettishly
tormented him until he implored Circe to give him
some love potion strong enough to compel her love.

Circe, who had long nursed a secret passion for
Glaucus, was angry at him, and jealous of her rival,
and, instead of a love potion, prepared a loathsome
drug, which she bade him pour into the water where
Scylla was wont to bathe. Glaucus faithfully did as
she commanded ; but when Scylla plunged into the
water, her body, and not her feelings, changed, and
she became a loathsome monster, a terror to gods
and men.

When in sight of the fig-tree, Ulysses, clad in armour,
stood on the prow to attack Scylla should she attempt
to seize one of his crew. The sound of the rushing
waters whirling around Charybdis made all on board
tremble with fear, and the pilot steered nearer still to
dread Scylla's den.

Suddenly a piercing cry was heard, as the monster

seized six of the men and devoured them. The rest
passed on unharmed; but since then, in speaking of
conflicting dangers, it has been customary to use the
expression, "falling from Charybdis into Scylla."

The Cattle of the Sun

Only too glad to effect an escape at any price, the
Greeks again rowed on until they sighted Trinacria,
the island of the sun, where Phaetusa and Lampetia
watched over the sun god's sacred herds. The men
wished to land here to rest; but Ulysses reminded
them that Tiresias, the blind seer, had warned them
to avoid it, lest by slaying any of the sacred animals
they should incur divine wrath.

The men, however, worn out with the toil of many
days' rowing, entreated so piteously to be allowed to
rest, voluntarily pledging themselves to be content
with their own provisions and not to slay a single
animal, that Ulysses reluctantly yielded to their
entreaties, and all went ashore.

After they had duly rested, they were still detained
by unfavourable winds, until all their provisions were
exhausted, and the few birds and fishes they managed
to secure no longer sufficed to still the pangs of hunger.

Led by Eurylochus, some of the men, during one of
Ulysses' temporary absences, caught and slew some of
the sun-god's cattle. To the general amazement and
terror, the meat lowed while roasting on the spit, and
the empty skins moved and crawled as if alive. All
these sounds and sights could not, however, deter the
sailors from their feast, which they kept up for seven
days, ere Ulysses could make them leave the Trinacrian
shores.

In the meantime, Lampetia had hastened to her
father to apprise him of the crime committed by

Ulysses' men. In anger Apollo appeared before the assembled gods and demanded vengeance, threatening to withdraw the light of his countenance if he were not properly indemnified. Jupiter, to appease his hot anger, immediately promised that all the offenders should perish.

> " ' Still shine, O Sun ! among the deathless gods
> And mortal men, upon the nourishing earth.
> Soon will I cleave, with a white thunderbolt,
> Their galley in the midst of the black sea ! "
>
> *Homer (Bryant's tr.).*

This promise he immediately fulfilled by drowning all excepting Ulysses, who alone had not partaken of the sacred flesh, and who, after clinging to the rudder for nine weary days, a plaything for the wind and waves, was washed ashore on the Island of Ogygia, where the fair sea nymph Calypso had taken up her abode.

Ulysses and Calypso

There he was kindly and most hospitably entertained during eight long years ; but he could not depart, as he had no vessel or crew to bear him away. At last Minerva, who had always befriended him, prevailed upon Jupiter to allow him to return to Ithaca. Mercury was sent to Ogygia to bid Calypso furnish all things necessary for his comfort, and aid in the construction of a huge raft, whereon our hero found himself afloat after many years of reluctant lingering on the land.

All seemed well now; but Neptune suddenly became aware that his old enemy, the torturer of Polyphemus, was about to escape from his clutches. With one blow of his trident he stirred up one of those sudden tempests whose fury nothing can withstand, shattered Ulysses' raft, and buffeted him about on the waves, until the goddess Leucothea, seeing his distress, helped him to reach the Phæacian shore.

Nausicaa and Ulysses

Too weary to think of aught but rest, Ulysses dragged himself into a neighbouring wood, where he fell asleep on a bed of dry leaves. While he was thus resting, Minerva visited Nausicaa, daughter of Alcinous, King of the Phæacians, in a dream, and bade her go down to the shore and wash her linen robes in readiness for her wedding-day, which the goddess assured her was near at hand. Nausicaa obeyed, and drove with her maidens down to the shore, where, after their labours were duly finished, they all indulged in a game of ball, with the usual accompaniment of shrill cries and much laughter. Their cries awoke Ulysses, who came on the scene just in time to save their ball from the waves, and claimed Nausicaa's protection for a shipwrecked mariner.

She graciously permitted him to follow her to her father's palace, and presented him to Alcinous and Arete, who bade him welcome, and invited him to join in the games then taking place. He did so, and displayed such strength and skill that his identity was revealed. Alcinous then promised to send him safely home in a Phæacian bark, which reached Ithaca in safety, and deposited Ulysses, asleep, on his native shore.

When Neptune discovered that the Phæacians had outwitted him, he was so angry that he changed the returning vessel into a rock, which blocked the harbour and put an end to further maritime excursions on their part.

> " He drew near
> And smote it with his open palm, and made
> The ship a rock, fast rooted in the bed
> Of the deep sea."
>
> *Homer (Bryant's tr.).*

The Return of Ulysses

Disguised as a beggar by Minerva's kindly care, Ulysses sought the lowly dwelling of Eumæus, his swineherd, and from him learned all he wished to know about his wife and son. He heard that Penelope was besieged with suitors, who were even now feasting and revelling in his palace, whence they refused to depart until she had made choice of a second husband ; and also that Telemachus, now a young man, indignant and displeased with the suitors' conduct, and guided and accompanied by his tutor Mentor, had set out in search of the father whom he could not believe to be dead.

Mentor, none other than Minerva in disguise, guided the young man to the courts of Nestor and Menelaus, and finally in a dream bade him return to Ithaca, where he would find the parent he sought. The young prince immediately obeyed, and landed near Eumæus' hut, escaping a clever ambuscade posted by the suitors at the entrance of the port.

Minerva now permitted the father and son to recognise each other, in spite of their twenty years' separation, and together they planned how best to punish the insolent suitors. They finally agreed that Telemachus should return to the palace and make no mention of his father's return, while Ulysses, still in the guise of a beggar, should enter his home and claim the usual hospitality.

All was executed as they had planned. No one recognised the long-expected hero in the miserable old beggar —no one save his aged nurse Euryclea, and his faithful old dog Argus, who died for joy at his long-lost master's feet.

> " While over Argus the black night of death
> Came suddenly as soon as he had seen
> Ulysses, absent now for twenty years."
> *Homer (Bryant's tr.).*

DEATH OF THE SUITORS

Penelope, hearing that a stranger was within her gates, sent for him, to inquire whether he knew aught of her husband. She too failed to pierce his disguise, and languidly continued a piece of work with which she was endeavouring to baffle her suitors; for, when urged to marry, she had replied that she would do so as soon as she had finished the tapestry upon which she was at work.

As she was a diligent worker, the suitors expected soon to hear her decision, little knowing that she undid at night the web so carefully woven during the day.

> " Three full years
> She practised thus, and by the fraud deceived
> The Grecian youths."
>
> *Homer (Bryant's tr.).*

At last the subterfuge was discovered, and the unfortunate Penelope was forced to finish her work; but ere it was quite done, she found another expedient to postpone her choice of a husband. She brought Ulysses' bow, and announced that she would marry the man who could bend it and send an arrow through twelve rings which she pointed out.

> " 'I bring to you
> The mighty bow that great Ulysses bore.
> Whoe'er among you he may be whose hand
> Shall bend this bow, and send through these twelve rings
> An arrow, him I follow hence, and leave
> This beautiful abode of my young years,
> With all its plenty,—though its memory,
> I think, will haunt me even in my dreams.' "
>
> *Homer (Bryant's tr.).*

Death of the Suitors

The suitors all vainly strove to bend the mighty bow, which was then seized by the disguised Ulysses, while the youths laughed aloud in scorn, until Telemachus bade them let the old man try his strength. To the

319

amazement of all, Ulysses easily performed the required feat; and then, turning his aim towards Antinous, the handsomest and most treacherous of all the suitors, he pierced his heart.

A scene of wild commotion ensued, in which Ulysses, Telemachus, Eumæus, and Minerva disguised as Mentor, opposed and slew all the wooers. Penelope, unconscious of all this bloodshed, slept in her room, until she was gently awakened by Euryclea with the announcement of the return of her long-absent husband.

> " ' Awake, Penelope, dear child, and see
> With thine own eyes what thou hast pined for long.
> Ulysses has returned; thy lord is here,
> Though late, and he has slain the arrogant crew
> Of suitors, who disgraced his house, and made
> His wealth a spoil, and dared insult his son.' "
>
> Homer (*Bryant's tr.*).

But Penelope had too long believed her husband dead to credit this marvellous news; and it was only after Ulysses had given her an infallible proof of his identity, by telling her a secret which was shared by her alone, that she received him.

Ulysses' Last Journey

Ulysses was now safe at home, after twenty years of warfare and adventure, and at first greatly enjoyed the quiet and peace of his home life; but after a while these tame joys grew wearisome, and he decided to renew his wanderings. He therefore prepared a fleet, and sailed " out into the West," whence he never returned. The Greeks, however, averred that he had gone in search of the Isles of the Blest, where he dwelt in perfect peace, and enjoyed the constant society of heroes as brave and renowned as himself.

> " ' Come, my friends,
> 'Tis not too late to seek a newer world.

ULYSSES' LAST JOURNEY

Push off, and sitting well in order, smite
The sounding furrows; for my purpose holds
To sail beyond the sunset, and the baths
Of all the western stars, until I die.
It may be that the gulfs will wash us down!
It may be we shall touch the Happy Isles,
And see the great Achilles, whom we knew.
Tho' much is taken, much abides: and tho'
We are not now that strength which in old days
Moved earth and heaven; that which we are, we are;
One equal temper of heroic hearts,
Made weak by time and fate, but strong in will
To strive, to seek, to find, and not to yield.' "

Tennyson.

CHAPTER XXIX : ÆNEAS

The Adventures of Æneas

YOU have already heard how the Greeks entered the city of Troy in the dead of night, massacred the inhabitants, and set fire to the beautiful buildings which had been the king's pride and delight. Now you shall hear Virgil's story of the escape of some of the Trojans from general destruction.

Unconscious of coming danger, Æneas, son of Venus and Anchises, lay fast asleep in his palace; but the gods had not doomed him to perish, and sent the shade of Hector to warn him in a dream to arise, leave the city, and fly to some distant land.

> " ' Ah, goddess-born,' he warns me, ' fly !
> Escape these flames : Greece holds the walls ;
> Proud Ilium from her summit falls.
> Think not of king's or country's claims :
> Country and king, alas ! are names :
> Could Troy be saved by hands of men,
> This hand had saved her then, e'en then.
> The gods of her domestic shrines
> That country to your care consigns :
> Receive them now, to share your fate :
> Provide them mansions strong and great,
> The city's walls, which Heaven has willed
> Beyond the seas you yet shall build.' "
>
> *Virgil* (*Conington's tr.*).

Awakened at last by the ever-increasing tumult without, Æneas seized his arms and hastened forth, attended by many of his fellow citizens, to ascertain the cause of the great uproar. A few minutes later he discovered that the Greek army had entered the town, and was even now killing, plundering, and burning without mercy. The men were all slain, but the fairest women were dragged away to be sold as slaves in Greece; and among them Æneas beheld in the hands of Agamemnon's soldiers the unfortunate daughter of Priam, Cassandra, whom the gods had endowed with prophetic powers, but whom no one would heed.

Æneas, seeing ere long that there was no hope of saving the doomed city, quickly disguised himself in Greek armour which he tore from the corpse of one of his foes, and rushed on to the palace, hoping to save the aged king, who, at the first alarm, had seized his weapons, determined to fight to the very last.

Hecuba, his wife, was clinging to him, imploring him to remain, when suddenly Polites, their son, rushed into their presence, closely followed by Pyrrhus, or Neoptolemus, son of Achilles, who thrust his sword into the youth, and then murdered Priam also.

> " So Priam's fortunes closed at last:
> So passed he, seeing as he passed
> His Troy in flames, his royal tower
> Laid low in dust by hostile power,
> Who once o'er land and peoples proud
> Sat, while before him Asia bowed:
> Now on the shore behold him dead,
> A nameless trunk, a trunkless head."
>
> *Virgil (Conington's tr.).*

Æneas, who arrived just too late to hinder this frightful catastrophe, now suddenly remembered that a similar fate awaited his aged father Anchises, his wife Creusa, and little son Iulus, who were at home without any protector near them. The hero therefore madly cut his way through the foe, and rushed through the once magnificent palace, which was now stripped of its rarest treasures and desecrated by the feet of the enemy.

There, in one of the abandoned halls, he saw Helen, the fair cause of all this war and bloodshed,—who, after Paris' death, had married Deiphobus, his brother, —and for a moment he determined to take her life; but ere he could do so, Venus, his mother, stayed his hand, and bade him remember that the immortal gods had long ago decreed that the city should fall, and that Helen was merely the pretext used to induce the riva' nations to fly to arms.

Further to convince him of the truth of her assertions, she enabled him to see what was hidden from mortal eyes. Neptune, Minerva, Juno, and Jupiter himself were fighting and levelling the walls with mighty blows. She then vehemently implored her son to leave this scene of carnage, and fly, with his family and followers, to some safe place without the city, whence he could embark, and sail away to a more fortunate land; and her entreaties finally prevailed.

Æneas and Anchises

Æneas rushed home and bade his father prepare to leave Troy; but Anchises obstinately refused to leave his post, until he saw a bright flame hover for a moment above his grandson's head, which sign he interpreted as an omen that his race should endure. He no longer resisted; and, as he was too weak to walk, Æneas bade him hold the Lares and Penates, and, taking him on his back, carried him off, while with one hand he led his little son, and bade Creusa closely follow him.

> " ' Come, mount my shoulders, dear my sire:
> Such load my strength shall never tire.
> Now, whether fortune smiles or lowers,
> One risk, one safety shall be ours.
> My son shall journey at my side,
> My wife her steps by mine shall guide,
> At distance safe.' "
>
> *Virgil (Conington's tr.).*

A trysting-place near a ruined temple had already been appointed for his servants, and thither Æneas turned his steps. When he arrived there, he found many awaiting him, and counted them carefully to make sure none were missing. All were there except Creusa, his beloved young wife; and he retraced his steps with anxious haste, hoping to find her still alive. But on the threshold of his once happy home he met her disembodied spirit, and heard her bid him seek the banks of the Tiber, where a beautiful young bride would comfort him for her loss. This speech ended, Creusa's ghost vanished, and Æneas sadly returned to the ruined temple, where he found many fugitives ready to follow him wherever he went, and eager to obey his every command. Their preparations for departure were speedily completed, the sails unfurled, and the little exiled band soon lost sight of the shores of Troy.

> " Weeping I quit the port, the shore,
> The plains where Ilium stood before,
> And homeless launch upon the main,
> Son, friends, and home gods in my train."
>
> *Virgil (Conington's tr.).*

Although they had escaped from burning Troy and the swords of the Greeks, their trials had only just begun. After many days' sailing, they landed in Thrace, viewed the country, decided to settle there, and began to trace the foundations of a new city, which they decided to call Æneades, in honour of their leader.

Their next care was to offer a sacrifice to the gods; but when Æneas, with due ceremony, cut down a sapling, he was startled to see blood flow from its severed stem. At the same time a mysterious voice was heard, bidding him forbear, for his former friend Polydorus, sent to Thrace to conceal some treasures, had been murdered there by an avaricious king, and this grove of trees had sprouted from the spear-handles driven into his unhappy breast.

After paying the customary funeral rites to appease the soul of his unfortunate friend, Æneas easily prevailed upon his followers to leave these inhospitable shores and seek another resting-place. They rowed over the briny deep until they came to Delos, where they stopped to consult the oracle, who bade them seek the cradle of their race, and settle there.

> "'Stout Dardan hearts, the realm of earth
> Where first your nation sprang to birth,
> That realm shall now receive you back:
> Go, seek your ancient mother's track.
> There shall Æneas' house, renewed
> For ages, rule a world subdued.'"
>
> *Virgil (Conington's tr.).*

This obscure command left them uncertain what course to pursue, until the aged Anchises remembered that one of his ancestors, Teucer, had once reigned in Crete. Thither they sailed, and hoped to settle; but a terrible pestilence came upon them, and decimated their already sparse ranks.

The Vision of Æneas

One night Æneas had a vision, in which his household gods bade him seek the Italian or Hesperian shores; and when, on waking, he imparted this advice to Anchises, the latter remembered a long-forgotten prophecy of Cassandra, purporting that they would settle there, and also that Dardanus, their first progenitor, was reported to have come from thence.

> "There is a land, by Greece of old
> Surnamed Hesperia, rich its mould,
> Its children brave and free:
> Œnotrians were its settlers: fame
> Now gives the race its leader's name,
> And calls it Italy.

THE VISION OF ÆNEAS

Here Dardanus was born our king,
And old Iasius, whence we spring:
Here our authentic seat."
Virgil (Conington's tr.).

Ere many days Æneas and his trusty followers were
once more afloat, and forced to battle with fierce storms
sent by Juno to hinder their advance. Exhausted,
they landed on the Strophades Islands, where they proposed to recruit their strength by a hearty meal ; but
no sooner was their table spread, than the meats were
devoured and destroyed by the loathsome Harpies.
A terrible prophecy uttered by Celæno, one of these
monsters—half woman and half bird—made them embark again in great haste, and row on until they came
to Epirus, where they again effected a landing. In
this country they met the sorrowing Andromache,
Hector's widow, the slave of King Helenus, who entertained them royally and sent them on their way again,
with many kindly cautions to beware of the Cyclopes
and avoid Charybdis and Scylla by circumnavigating the
whole island of Sicily.

This advice was duly followed by Æneas, who,
while rounding one of the promontories of the island,
saw and rescued Achemenides, one of Ulysses' companions, accidentally left behind when they escaped
from the rage of Polyphemus, the Cyclops. This
giant now came down to the shore, and was regarded
with unconcealed horror by the Trojans, who rowed
away in haste. Soon after, Æneas moored his ships
in the harbours of Sicania and Drepanum, and while
there lost his aged father Anchises.

" There
I lose my stay in every care,
My sire Anchises ! "
Virgil (Conington's tr.).

327

Juno, in the meanwhile, had not been idle, and gloated over the dangers she had forced the unhappy Trojans to encounter during the seven years which had already elapsed since they first sailed from Troy. She was not yet weary of persecuting them, however; and as soon as she saw them once more afloat, she hurried off to Æolus, and bade him let loose his fiercest children, and scatter the fleet by a terrible storm.

> "'O Æolus! since the Sire of all
> Has made the wind obey thy call
> To raise or lay the foam,
> A race I hate now ploughs the sea,
> Transporting Troy to Italy
> And home gods reft of home:
> Lash thou thy winds, their ships submerge,
> Or toss them weltering o'er the surge.'"
>
> *Virgil (Conington's tr.).*

This request was immediately granted. The vessels, tossed hither and thither, lost sight of each other. Some were stranded, some sank, and still the tempest raged on with unabated fury, and death stared the unhappy Trojans in the face. The commotion on the deep finally aroused Neptune, who came to the surface just in time to see all the misfortunes which had overwhelmed Æneas. He imperiously bade the winds return, and lent a helping hand to float the stranded ships once more.

> "'Back to your master instant flee,
> And tell him, not to him but me
> The imperial trident of the sea
> Fell by the lot's award.'"
>
> *Virgil (Conington's tr.).*

The Trojans, grateful for his timely aid, and re assured by the calm which now reigned supreme steered for the nearest port, where they anchored their

Captive Andromache

Orpheus and Eurydice

seven vessels, all that now remained of their once large fleet.

Æneas and Achates, his faithful friend, immediately set out to view the land, and ere long encountered Venus, disguised as a mortal, who informed them that they had landed upon the Libyan coast, which was under the sway of Dido, a fugitive from Tyre. Dido's husband, Sychæus, King of Tyre, the possessor of untold riches, had been murdered by Pygmalion, his brother-in-law; but the queen was kept in complete ignorance of this crime, until visited in a dream by the shade of Sychæus, which bade her fly with his treasures, whose place of concealment she alone knew.

Dido obeyed the ghost's commands, and, accompanied by a number of faithful subjects, landed on the Libyan coast, where she entreated the inhabitants to sell her as much land as an ox-hide would enclose. This seemingly modest request was immediately granted; but the Libyans regretted their compliance when they saw the ox-hide cut up into thin strips, which enclosed a considerable tract of land, the site of Dido's beautiful capital, Carthage.

Æneas and Dido

Thither Venus advised her son to proceed and claim the queen's protection. Æneas and Achates obediently hastened onward, and entered the town unseen, for Venus had enveloped them both in mist. Their attention was first attracted by the festive appearance of the people assembled together, and by the beauty of the queen, who was giving audience to some of their companions, who also had miraculously escaped from the waves.

These men spoke to the queen of their renowned chief, whose fame had already reached her ear; and she gladly promised to send out a search party to discover him, and aid him if necessary.

> " ' I will send
> And search the coast from end to end,
> If haply, wandering up and down,
> He bide in woodland or in town.' "
>
> *Virgil* (*Conington's tr.*).

At these gracious words, Æneas stepped forward, the mist vanished, and he stood before the queen in all his manly beauty.

Dido then led her guests to the banquet-hall, where they recounted their adventures by land and sea, while partaking of the viands and wines set before them. At this feast, Cupid, by Venus' request, assumed the face and form of Iulus, Æneas' young son, and reclining on the queen's bosom, secretly thrust one of his darts into her heart, and made her fall in love with Æneas.

Day after day now passed in revelry and pleasure, and still Æneas lingered by Dido's side, forgetful of the new kingdom he was destined to found. One whole year passed thus ; and the gods, impatient of delay, finally sent Mercury to remind Æneas of his duty.

To avoid Dido's tears and recriminations, the hero kept his preparations for departure a complete secret, and finally set sail while she was wrapt in slumber. When she awoke and looked out of her palace window, it was only to see the last vessel sink beneath the horizon.

Concealing her grief, and pretending an anger she did not feel, she bade her servants make a funeral pyre, and place upon it all the objects Æneas had used during his sojourn in her palace ; then, having crowned the pile with an effigy of her false lover, she set fire to the pyre, sprang into the midst of the flames, and there stabbed herself.

> " ' Yet let me die: thus, thus I go
> Exulting to the shades below.
> Let the false Dardan feel the blaze
> That burns me pouring on his gaze,
> And bear along, to cheer his way,
> The funeral presage of to-day.' "
>
> *Virgil (Conington's tr.).*

From the mast of his vessel Æneas saw the rising column of smoke, and his heart sank within him, for he suspected its fatal import, and honestly mourned the death of the beautiful queen.

The Trojans sailed onward until the threatening clouds made them take refuge in the Sicanian port, where they celebrated the usual games to commemorate Anchises' death, which had occurred there just one year previous. While the men were engaged in the customary naval, foot, and horse races, boxing, wrestling, and archery matches, the women gathered together, and, instigated by Juno, began to bewail the hard lot which compelled them to encounter again the perils of the sea. Their discontent ultimately reached such a pitch that they set fire to the vessels. When Æneas heard of this new misfortune, he rushed down to the shore, tore his costly festal garments, and cried to Heaven for assistance in this his time of direst need.

> " ' Dread Sire, if Ilium's lorn estate
> Deserve not yet thine utter hate,
> If still thine ancient faithfulness
> Give heed to mortals in distress,
> Oh, let the fleet escape the flame!
> Oh, save from death Troy's dying name!' "
>
> *Virgil (Conington's tr.).*

This prayer was instantly answered by a sudden severe shower, which quenched the devouring flames. Soon

331

after this miracle, Anchises appeared to Æneas, and bade him leave the women, children, and aged men in Sicily, and travel on to Cumæ, where he was to consult the Sibyl, visit the Infernal Regions, and there receive further advice from him.

> " First seek the halls of Dis below,
> Pass deep Avernus' vale and meet
> Your father in his own retreat."
> *Virgil (Conington's tr.).*

Æneas again dutifully obeyed; but when Venus saw him afloat once more, she hastened to Neptune, and bade him watch over her unfortunate son. Neptune listened very graciously to her appeal, and promised to take but one of all the many lives entrusted to his care. That one was Æneas' pilot, Palinurus, who, falling asleep at the helm, fell overboard and was drowned.

As for the fleet, it reached the Cumæan shore in safety; and Æneas hastened off to the Sibyl's cave, made known his wish to visit Hades, and entreated her to serve as his guide in that perilous journey. She consented, but at the same time informed him that he must first obtain a golden twig, which grew in a dark forest.

> "None may reach the shades without
> The passport of that golden sprout."
> *Virgil (Conington's tr.).*

Almost despairing, Æneas now prayed for assistance; for how could he find a tiny golden sprig in the midst of the dense forest foliage without the gods' aid? In answer to this appeal, Venus, ever mindful of her son, sent two of her snowy doves to lead the way and alight on the tree, where Æneas readily found the object of his search.

332

Æneas visits Hades

Armed with this branch as key, he and the Sibyl boldly entered the Lower Regions, where all the ghastly sights and sounds we have already described met them on every side. Charon quickly ferried them over Acheron, on whose bank they saw the wandering shade of Palinurus, who had no obolus to pay his way across, and that of Dido, with a gaping wound in her breast.

They did not pause, however, until they reached the Elysian Fields, where they found Anchises, gravely considering among the unborn souls those who were destined to animate his race and make it illustrious in the future. These he carefully pointed out to Æneas, foretelling their future achievements, and called by name Romulus, Brutus, Camillus, the Gracchi, Cæsar, —in fact, all the heroes of Roman history.

> " Anchises showed Æneas, in long line,
> The illustrious shades of those who were to shine
> One·day the glory of the Italian shore."
> *Tomas de Iriarte.*

After a prolonged conversation with his father, Æneas returned to his companions, and led them to the mouth of the Tiber, whose course they followed until they reached Latium, where their wanderings were to cease. Latinus, king of the country, received them hospitably, and promised the hand of his daughter Lavinia in marriage to Æneas.

Lavinia was very beautiful, and had already had many suitors, among whom Turnus, a neighbouring prince, boasted of the most exalted rank. The queen, Amata, specially favoured this youth's suit; and the king would gladly have received him for a son-in-law, had he not twice been warned by the gods to reserve his daughter for a foreign prince, who had now appeared.

In spite of all the years which had elapsed since Paris scorned her attractions and bribes, Juno had not yet forgotten her hatred of the Trojan race, and afraid lest her enemy's course should now prove too smooth, she sent Alecto, the Fury, down upon earth to stir up war and goad Amata to madness. The Fury executed both commands, and Amata fled to the woods, where she concealed her daughter Lavinia, to keep her safe for Turnus, whom she preferred to Æneas.

War with the Latins

As Iulus and some companions had unfortunately wounded the pet stag of Silvia, daughter of the chief shepherd, a brawl ensued, which, fomented by Alecto, soon developed into a bloody war. Hostilities having thus begun, Turnus, with the various Latin chiefs, immediately besought Latinus to open the gates of Janus' temple. He refused: but Juno, afraid lest even now her plans might be set at naught, came down from Olympus, and with her own hand flung wide the brazen doors. This unexpected apparition kindled a general ardour; new troops enlisted; and even Camilla, the Volscian warrior-maiden, came to proffer her aid to Turnus.

> " Last marches forth for Latium's sake
>   Camilla fair, the Volscian maid,
> A troop of horsemen in her wake
>   In pomp of gleaming steel arrayed;
> Stern warrior queen ! "
>
> *Virgil (Conington's tr.).*

The Story of Camilla

When but a babe in arms, Camilla had been carried off by her father, as he fled before the Volscian troops.

NISUS AND EURYALUS

When he came to the Amasenus River, he found his pursuers close at his heels. Tying his infant daughter to his spear, he hurled her to the opposite bank, which, thanks to Diana's aid, she reached unharmed, while her father plunged into the waves to join her. In his gratitude at finding her safe, he dedicated her to Diana, who trained her to love the chase and all manly pursuits.

Surprised to see Latinus' friendly offers of hospitality so suddenly withdrawn, Æneas made rapid preparations for war, and sailed farther up the Tiber to secure the aid of Evander, king of the Tuscans, the hereditary foe of the Latins. This monarch, too old to lead his troops in person, nevertheless promised his aid, and sent his beloved son Pallas in his stead to command the troops he supplied.

Nisus and Euryalus

Juno, still implacable, had in the meantime sent Iris to apprise Turnus of Æneas' departure, and to urge him to set fire to the remainder of the fleet,—a suggestion which Turnus joyfully obeyed. The Trojans, headed by young Iulus, Æneas' son, defended themselves with their usual courage ; but, seeing that the enemy would soon overpower them, they despatched Nisus and Euryalus, two of their number, to warn Æneas of their danger, and entreat him to hasten with his reinforcements. These unfortunate youths passed through the camp unseen, but farther on fell into the hands of a troop of Volscian horsemen, who cruelly put them to death, and then hurried with the Rutules to lend assistance to Turnus. Next some of the Trojan vessels were fired by the enemy; but, instead of being consumed by the flames, they were changed into water nymphs by the intervention of the gods, and, sailing down the Tiber, met Æneas, and warned him to hasten to his son's rescue.

> " His vessels change their guise,
>   And each and all as Nereids rise."
>
> *Virgil.*

Meanwhile, Venus, who befriended the Trojans, had sought Vulcan's detested abode, and had prevailed upon him to forge a suit of beautiful armour for Æneas. On the shield, which is minutely described in one of the books of Virgil's celebrated epic poem, the Æneid, were depicted many of the stirring scenes in the lives of the future descendants of Æneas, the heroes of Roman history. As soon as this armour was completed, Venus brought it to her son, who donned it with visible pleasure, and, encouraged by his mother's words, prepared to meet the Latins and hold his own.

Venus and Juno were not the only deities interested in the coming struggle, for all the gods, having watched Æneas' career, were anxious about his fate. Seeing this, and fearful lest their interference should still further ;endanger the hero whom he favoured, Jupiter assembled the gods on high Olympus, and sternly forbade their taking any active part in the coming strife, under penalty of his severe displeasure.

Æneas and his Tuscan allies arrived on the battle scene just in time to give the necessary support to the almost exhausted Trojans; and now the fight raged more fiercely than ever, and prodigies of valour were accomplished on both sides, until finally young Pallas fell, slain by Turnus. When aware of the death of this promising young prince, Æneas' heart was filled with grief, for he could imagine the sorrow of the aged Evander when he saw his son's corpse brought

home for burial : and he then and there registered a
solemn vow to avenge Pallas' death by slaying Turnus,
and immediately hastened forth to keep his word.

In the meantime, Juno, suspecting what his purpose
would be, and afraid to allow Turnus to encounter such
a formidable antagonist as Æneas, had determined to
lure her favourite away from the field. To compass this,
she assumed the form of Æneas, challenged Turnus,
and, as soon as he began to fight, fled toward the river,
and took refuge on one of the vessels, closely pursued
by him. No sooner did she see the Rutulian chief safe
on board, than she loosed the vessel from its moorings,
and allowed it to drift down the stream, bearing Turnus
away from the scene of battle. Aware now of the delusion
practised, Turnus raved, and accused the gods, and then
eagerly watched for an opportunity to land, and make his
way, alone and on foot, back to the scene of conflict.

During Turnus' involuntary absence, Æneas had
ranged all over the battlefield in search of him, and
had encountered and slain many warriors, among others
Lausus and his aged father Mezentius, two allies of
Latinus, who had specially distinguished themselves
by their great valour. The dead and dying covered
the field, when Latinus, weary of bloodshed, summoned
a council, and again vainly tried to make peace. But
his efforts were of no avail. The war was renewed
more fiercely than ever ; and in the next encounter,
Camilla, the brave Volscian maiden, fell at last, breathing a fervent entreaty that Turnus should hasten to the
succour of his despairing people, if he would not see
them all slain and the town in the hands of the Trojans.

> " ' Go : my last charge to Turnus tell,
> To haste with succour, and repel
> The Trojans from the town—farewell.' "
>
> *Virgil (Conington's tr.).*

337

Shortly after her death, in the very midst of the fray, Æneas suddenly felt himself wounded by an arrow sent by some mysterious hand. He hastened to seek the aid of the leech Iapis; but, in spite of his ministrations, the barb could not be removed nor the wound dressed, until Venus brought a magic herb, which instantly healed the hero, and enabled him to return to the fight with unabated strength and energy.

The tide was now decidedly turning in favour of the Trojans; and Amata, the Latin queen, sorry for her ill-advised opposition to her daughter's marriage with Æneas, brought Lavinia home and hanged herself in a fit of remorse.

The Death of Turnus

Æneas, appearing once more on the battlefield, finally encountered the long-sought Turnus, who had made his way back, and was now driving about in his chariot, jealously guarded by his sister Juturna, who, the better to watch over his safety, had taken the place of his chariot driver. The two heroes, having met, instantly closed in deadly fight; but, in spite of Turnus' bravery, he was finally vanquished, and sank to the ground, frankly acknowledging himself beaten as he exhaled his last breath.

> " ' Yours is the victory: Latian bands
> Have seen me stretch imploring hands:
> The bride Lavinia is your own:
> Thus far let foeman's hate be shown.' "
>
> *Virgil (Conington's tr.).*

With the death of Turnus the war came to an end. A lasting peace was made with Latinus; and the brave Trojan hero, whose woes were now over, was united in marriage with Lavinia. In concert with Latinus, he ruled the Latins, and founded a city, which he called

Lavinia in honour of his bride, and which became for a time the capital of Latium.

Æneas, as the gods had predicted, became the father of a son named Æneas Silvia, who founded Alba Longa, where his descendants reigned for many a year, and where one of his race, the Vestal Virgin Ilia, after marrying Mars, gave birth to Remus and Romulus, the founders of Rome.

CHAPTER XXX : ANALYSIS OF MYTHS

The Various Theories

"I shall indeed interpret all that I can, but I cannot interpret all that I should like."—*Grimm.*

IN attempting an analysis of the foregoing myths, and an explanation of their origin, it is impossible, in a work of this kind, to do more than give a very superficial idea of the scientific theories of various eminent mythologists, who, on this subject, like doctors, are sure to disagree.

These myths, comprising "the entire intellectual stock of the age to which they belonged," existed as "floating talk among the people" long ere they passed into the literature of the nation : and while to us mythology is merely "an affair of historical or anti-quarian study, we must remember that the interpreta-tion of myths was once a thing full of vital interest to men whose moral and religious beliefs were deeply con-cerned." Received at first with implicit faith, these myths became a stumbling-block as civilisation ad-vanced. Cultured man recoiled from much of the grossness which had appeared quite natural to his an-cestors in a savage state, and made an attempt to find out their primitive meaning, or an explanation which would satisfy his purer taste.

With the latter object in view, the sages and writers of old interpreted all that seemed "silly and sense-less" in mythology as physical allegories—a system subsequently carried to extremes by many heathen philosophers in the vain hope of evading Christian satire.

Learned men have also explained these self-same myths as historical facts disguised as metaphors, or as

moral allegories, which the choice of Hercules undoubtedly is. Euhemerus (316 B.C.) was the pioneer of
the former theory, and Bacon an exponent of the latter.
Euhemerus' method was exaggerated by his disciples,
who declared Zeus was merely a king of Crete; his
war with the giants, an attempt to repress a sedition;
Danae's shower of gold, the 'money with which her
guards were bribed; Prometheus, a maker of clay
images, "whence it was hyperbolically said he created
man out of clay"; and Atlas, an astronomer, who was
therefore spoken of as supporting the weight of the
heavens. This mode of interpretation was carried to
such an extreme that it became ridiculous, and the inevitable reaction took place. In the course of time,
however, the germ of truth it contained was again
brought to light; and very few persons now refuse to
believe that some of the heroic myths have some slig'it
historical basis, the "silly and senseless" element
being classed as accretions similar to the fabulous
tales attached to the indubitably historical name of
Charlemagne. During the seventeenth century, some
philosophers, incited by "the resemblance between
Biblical narrative and ancient myths, came to the conclusion that the Bible contained a pure and the myths
a distorted form of an original revelation." But within
the past century new theories have gradually gained
ground : for the philologists have attempted to prove
that the myths arose from a "disease of language";
while the anthropologists, basing their theory on comparative mythology, declare "it is man, it is human
thought and human language combined, which naturally
and necessarily produced the strange conglomerate of
ancient fable."

As these two last-named schools have either successfully confuted or incorporated the theories of all their

predecessors, a brief outline of their respective beliefs will not be out of place. While philology compares only the " myths of races which speak languages of the same family " (as will shortly be demonstrated), anthropology resorts to all folklore, and seeks for the origin of myths, not in language, which it considers only as a subordinate cause, but in the "condition of thought through which all races have passed."

The anthropologists, or comparative mythologists, do not deny that during the moderate allowance of two hundred and fifty thousand years, which they allot to the human race on earth, the myths may have spread from a single centre, and either by migration, or by slave or wife stealing, or by other natural or accidental methods, may have "wandered all around the globe"; but they principally base their arguments on the fact that just as flint arrowheads are found in all parts of the world, differing but slightly in form and manufacture, so the myths of all nations "resemble each other, because they were formed to meet the same needs, out of the same materials."

They argue that this similarity exists, "not because the people came from the same stock" (which is the philologist's view), "but because they passed through the same savage intellectual condition." By countless examples taken from the folklore of all parts of the earth, they prove that the savage considers himself akin to beasts (generally to the one whose image is used as a tribal or family badge or totem), and "regards even plants, inanimate objects, and the most abstract phenomena, as persons with human parts and passions." To the savage, " sun, moon, and stars are persons, but savage persons"; and, as he believes "many of his own tribe-fellows to have the power of assuming the form of animals," he concedes the same

privilege and power to sun, moon, and stars, &c.
This school further prove that all pre-Christian reli-
gions have idols representing beasts, that all mythologies represent the gods as fond of appearing in animal
forms, and declare that, although the Greeks were a
thoroughly civilised people, we can still find in their
mythology and religion "abundant survivals of savage
manners and savage myths." They claim that, during
the myth-making age, the ancestors of the Greeks were
about on an intellectual level with the present Aus-
tralian Bushmen, and that "everything in civilised
mythologies which we regard as irrational, seems only
part of the accepted and rational order of things to the
contemporary savages, and in the past seemed equally
rational and natural to savages concerning whom we
have historical information." Of course it is difficult,
not to say impossible, for civilised man to put himself
in the savage's place, and regard things from his point
of view. The nearest approach to primitive intelligence
which comes under our immediate observation is the
working of the minds of small children, who, before
they can talk intelligibly, whip the table or chair
against which they have bumped their heads, and later
on delight in weaving the most extraordinary tales.
A little four-year-old seized a book and began to "read
a story"; that is to say, to improvise a very improbable
and highly-coloured tale of a pony. Forced to pause
from lack of breath, she resumed the thread of her
narrative with the words, "Now, this dog"; and,
when it was suggested that the story was about a pony,
she emphatically replied, "Well, this pony was a dog,"
and continued. Now, either because she perceived
that the transformation had attracted attention, or to
satisfy the childish inborn taste for the marvellous, in
the course of the next few minutes the pony underwent

as many transformations as Proteus, all of which apparently seemed perfectly natural to her. The anthropologists explain the tales of the various transformations of Jupiter and his animal progeny " as in many cases survivals of the totemistic belief in descent from beasts," while the mythologists explain them as " allegories of the fruitful union of heaven and earth, of rain and grain." The former school also declare that the myth of Cupid and Psyche, which has its parallel in stories found in all parts of the world, was invented to explain curious marriage customs (for in some countries it is unlawful for the husband to see his wife's face until after she has given birth to her first child, and in others a wife may not speak her husband's name) ; the latter school interpret the same myth as a beautiful allegory of the soul and the union of faith and love.

The philologists' interpretation of myths is not only the most accredited at the present time, but also the most poetical. We therefore give a brief synopsis of their theory, together with an analysis, from their point of view, of the principal myths told at length in the course of this work. According to this school, " myths are the result of a disease of language, as the pearl is the result of a disease of the oyster "; the key to all mythologies lies in language; and the original names of the gods, " ascertained by comparative philology, will be found, as a rule, to denote elemental or physical phenomena," that is, phenomena of the sunshine, the clouds, rain, winds, fire, &c.

To make their process of reasoning plain, it should be explained that as French, Spanish, and Italian are derived from the Latin, even so Latin, Greek, and Sanskrit have a common source in a much older language; that, even if Latin were entirely lost, the similarity of the word " bridge," for instance (*pons* in Latin), in French (*pont*), in Spanish (*puente*), and in Italian (*ponte*) would justify the conclusion that these terms had their origin in a common language, and that the people who spoke it were familiar with bridges, which they evidently called by some name phonetically the same.

Further to prove their position, they demonstrate the similarity of the most common words in all the languages of the same family, showing (as is the case with the word "father" in the accompanying table) that they undergo but few changes in sixteen different languages :

Sanskrit, *pitri.*	Latin, *pater.*
Zend, *paitar.*	Greek, pronounced *pätair.*
Persian, *pader.*	Gothic, *vatar.*
Erse, *athair.*	German, *vater.*
Italian, *padre.*	Dutch, *fader.*
Spanish, *padre.*	Danish, *fader.*
French, *père.*	Swedish, *fader.*
Saxon, *fæder.*	English, *father.*

The most learned of all these philologists argues that during the first or Rhematic period there existed a tribe in Central Asia which spoke a monosyllabic language, in which lay the germs of the Turanian, Aryan, and Semitic forms of speech. This Rhematic period was followed by the Nomadic or Agglutinative age, when, little by little, the languages "received once for all that peculiar impress of their formative system which we still find in all the dialects and national idioms comprised under the name of Aryan or Semitic"; that is to say, in the Hindoo, Persian, Greek, Roman, Celtic, Slavic, and Teutonic languages, and in some three thousand kindred dialects.

After the Agglutinative period, and previous to the

National era and "the appearance of the first traces of literature," he places "a period represented everywhere by the same characteristic features, called the Mythological or Mythopœic age."

It was during this period that the main part of the vast fund of mythic lore is supposed to have crystallised; for primitive man, knowing nothing whatever of physical laws, cause and effect, and the "necessary regularity of things," yet seeking an explanation of the natural phenomena, described them in the only way possible to him, and attributed to all inanimate objects his own sentiments and passions, fancying them influenced by the same things, in the same way. This tendency to personify or animate everything is universal among savages, who are nothing but men in the primitive state; and "in early philosophy throughout the world, the sun, moon, and stars are alive, and, as it were, human in their nature." "Poetry has so far kept alive in our minds the old animative theory of nature, that it is no great effort in us to fancy the waterspout a huge giant or a sea monster, and to depict, in what we call appropriate metaphor, its march across the field of ocean."

As the names of the Greek gods and heroes have in a great measure been found to correspond with the Sanskrit names of physical things, we have been able to read some of the first thoughts of primitive man; and "the obvious meaning" of many words "did much to preserve vestiges of plain sense in classic legend, in spite of all the efforts of the commentators."

According to the philologists, therefore, these thoughts had already assumed a definite form in the remote epoch when many nations, now scattered over the face of the earth, occupied the same country, spoke the same language, and formed but one people. Of course, "as long as such beings as Heaven or Sun are consciously talked of in mythic language, the meaning of their legends is open to no question, and the action ascribed to them will as a rule be natural and appropriate"; but with the gradual diffusion of this one people to various parts of the earth, the original meaning of these words was entirely lost, and they came to be looked upon eventually simply as the names of deities or heroes—very much in the way that the word "good-bye" has long survived its original form as a conscious prayer, "God be with you!" and the word "ostracism" has lost all connection with an oyster shell.

The primitive meaning of a myth died away with the original meaning of a word; and it is because "the Greek had forgotten that Zeus (Jupiter) meant 'the bright sky,' that he could make him king" over a company of manlike deities on Olympus.

We can best explain how the many anomalies occur, and how the myths got so tangled up together that now it is almost impossible to disentangle them and trace them back to their original meanings, by comparing their descent through the ages to the course of a snow-ball, which, rolling down a mountain-side, gathers to itself snow, earth, rocks, &c., until, in the vast agglomeration of kindred and foreign substances, the original nucleus is entirely lost to sight.

The fact that there are many different myths to explain the same phenomenon can readily be accounted for by the old saying, "Circumstances alter cases." Thus the heat of the sun, for example, so beneficial at certain times, may prove baleful and injurious at others.

The philologists, who believe that all myths (except

347

THE CLASSICAL MYTHS

the imitative myths, of which the tale of Berenice is a fair example) were originally nature myths, have divided them into a few large classes, which include the myths of the sky, the sun, dawn, daylight, night, moon, earth, sea, clouds, fire, wind, and finally those of the underworld and of the demons of drought and darkness.

Sky Myths

Taking them in the order in which they are presented in this work, we find among the myths of the sky, Uranus, whose name, like that of the old Hindoo god Varuna, is derived from the Sanskrit root *var* ("to veil, conceal, or cover"). This god was therefore a personification of the heavens, which are spread out like a veil, and cover all the earth; and we are further told that he hurled the thunder and lightning, his Cyclop children, down from his abode into the abyss called Tartarus.

Zeus (or Jupiter), whose name is the same as the Hindoo Dyaus Pitar, the god and personification of the bright sky or the heavens, has likewise been traced to the Sanskrit root *div* or *dyu*, meaning "to shine"; and there is also a noun *dyu* in that language which means either "sky" or "day." In early times the name was applied to the one God, and was therefore "retained by the Greeks and all other kindred people to express all they felt toward God"; but as the word also meant the visible sky, with its ever-changing aspect, some of the phrases used to describe it came, in the course of time, to denote vile and fickle actions, and apparently inconsistent behaviour.

The name of Hera (or Juno), the heavenly light, and therefore the complement and consort of the sky, is supposed to be derived from the Sanskrit *soar* ("the

348

bright sky ") and *surya* (" the sun ") ; and all the manifold changes which at first merely denoted the varying atmosphere, by being personified, gradually gave the impression of the jealous, capricious, vengeful person whom poets and writers have taken pleasure in depicting ever since.

Another personification of the sky, this time under the nocturnal and starry aspect, is Argus, whose many bright eyes never closed all at once, but kept constant watch over the moon (Io)—confided to his care by the heavenly light (Juno)—until at last their beams were quenched by the wind and rain (Mercury).

Sun and Dawn Myths

The myths of the sun, from which it is almost impossible to separate those of the dawn, are probably more numerous than any others, and have some main features of resemblance in all cases. The first sun myth mentioned in the course of this work is the story of Europa, in which Europa is "the broad spreading light," born in Phœnicia (the "purple land of morn"), the child of Telephassa ("she who shines from afar"), carried away from her eastern birthplace by the sky (Jupiter), closely pursued by the sun (her brother Cadmus), who, after passing through many lands, slays a dragon (the usual demon of drought or darkness), and sets (dies) at last without having ever overtaken the light of dawn (Europa).

Apollo, whose name of Helios is pure Greek for " the sun," had therefore not lost all physical significance for the Hellenic race, who worshipped in him the radiant personification of the orb of day. Another of his appellations, Phœbus (" the lord of life and light "), still further emphasises his character ; and we are informed that he was born of the sky (Jupiter) and

349

of the dark night (Leto), in the " bright land "(Delos), whence he daily starts on his westward journey.

Like all other solar heroes, Apollo is beautiful and golden-haired, radiant and genial, armed with unerring weapons, which he wields for good or evil, as the mood sways him. He is forced to labour, against his will at times, for the benefit of man, as, for instance, when he serves Admetus and Laomedon; and the cattle, by which he evidently sets such store, are the fleecy clouds, pasturing "in the infinite meadows of heaven," whose full udders drop down rain and fatness upon the land, which are stolen away either by the wind (Mercury), or the storm demon (Cacus), or the impious companions of Ulysses, who pay for their sacrilegious temerity with their lives.

The sun's affinity for the dawn is depicted by his love for Coronis, who, however beloved, falls beneath his bright darts; and, as "the sun was regarded naturally as the restorer of life" after the blighting influence of winter and disease, so their offspring (Æsculapius) was naturally supposed to have been endowed with marvellous curative powers.

The sun, for the same reason, was supposed to wage continual warfare against cold, sickness, and disease, and to use his bright beams or arrows against the demon of drought, darkness, or illness (Python), which in some form or other inevitably appears in every solar myth.

In the story of Daphne, a name derived from *Dahana*, the Sanskrit *dawn*, we find another version of the same story, where the sun, although enamoured with the dawn, causes her death. As some mythologists have interpreted it, Daphne is a personification of the morning dew, which vanishes beneath the sun's hot breath, and leaves no trace of its passage except in the luxuriant verdure.

SUN AND DAWN MYTHS

In Cephalus and Procris the sun again appears, and his unerring spear unwittingly causes the death of his beloved Procris " while she lingers in a thicket (a place where the dew lingers longest)." This interpretation has been further confirmed by philological researches, which prove that the name " Procris " originated from a Sanskrit word meaning "to sprinkle"; and the stories evidently arose from three simple phrases,—" ' the sun loves the dew,' ' the morning loves the sun,' and ' the sun kills the dew.' "

In the tale of Orpheus and Eurydice, while some mythologists see in him a personification of the winds, which "tear up trees as they course along, chanting their wild music," others see an emblem of "the morning, with its short-lived beauty " Eurydice, whose name, like that of Europa, comes from a Sanskrit word denoting " the broad spreading flush of the dawn across the sky," is, of course, a personification of that light, slain by "the serpent of darkness at twilight."

Orpheus is also sometimes considered as the sun, plunging into an abyss of darkness, in hopes of overtaking the vanishing dawn, Eurydice ; and as the light (Eurydice) reappears opposite the place where he disappeared, but is no more seen after the sun himself has fairly risen, "they say that Orpheus has turned around too soon to look at her, and so was parted from the wife he loved so dearly."

His death in the forest, when his strength had all forsaken him, and his severed head floated down the stream murmuring " Eurydice," may also, perchance, have been intended to represent either the last faint breath of the expiring wind, or the setting of the sun in blood-tinged clouds.

In the story of Phaeton, whose name means "the bright

and shining one," a description of the golden palace and car of the sun is given us. We are told that the venturesome young charioteer, by usurping his father's place, causes incalculable mischief, and, in punishment for his mismanagement of the solar steeds (the fleecy white clouds), is hurled from his exalted seat by a thunderbolt launched by the hand of Jupiter.

"This story arose from phrases with spoke of drought as caused by the chariot of Helios, when driven by some one who knew not how to guide his horses; and the smiting of Phaeton by the bolt of Zeus is the ending of the time of drought by a sudden storm of thunder."

The story of Diana and Endymion has also been interpreted as a sun myth, in which the name "Endymion" refers specially to the dying or setting sun, who sinks to rest on Mount Latmus ("the land of forgetfulness," derived from the same root as "Leto"). Müller, the great authority on philology, tells us that, in the ancient poetical and proverbial language of Elis, people said, "Selene loves and watches Endymion," instead of saying, "It is getting late"; "Selene embraces Endymion," instead of, "The sun is setting and the moon is rising"; "Selene kisses Endymion into sleep," instead of, " It is night."

These expressions remained long after their real meaning had ceased to be understood; and, as the human mind is generally as anxious for a reason as ready to invent one, a story arose without any conscious effort, that Endymion must have been a young lad loved by a young maiden, Selene.

In the story of Adonis some mythologists find another sun myth, in which Adonis, the short-lived sun, is slain by the boar, the demon of darkness, and passionately mourned by the dawn or twilight (Venus), who utterly refuses to exist without him.

352

SUN AND DAWN MYTHS

In the story of Tantalus (the sun), who in time of drought offers to Jupiter the flesh of his own offspring, Pelops (the withered fruits), and in punishment for his impiety is doomed to hunger and torturing thirst, we have again merely a story founded upon an expression used in time of drought, when the sun's heat, becoming too intense, burns up the fruit his fostering rays had produced, and men exclaimed, "Tantalus is slaying and roasting his own child!"

In the same way the stone which Sisyphus painfully forced up a steep ascent, only to see it go rolling down and plunge into a dark abyss enveloped in a great cloud of dust, has been interpreted to represent the sun, which is no "sooner pushed up to the zenith, than it rolls down to the horizon."

The name of Ixion has been identified with the Sanskrit word *Akshanah*, denoting one who is bound to a wheel, and has been proved akin "to the Greek *axôn*, the Latin *axis*, and the English *axle*." This whirling wheel of fire is the bright orb of day, to which he was bound by order of Jupiter (the sky) because he dared insult Juno (the queen of the blue air); while Dia, his wife, is the dawn, the counterpart of Europa, Coronis, Daphne, Procris, Eurydice, and Venus, in the foregoing illustrations.

One of the greatest of all the solar heroes is doubtless the demi-god Hercules, born at Argos (a word signifying "brightness") from the sky (Jupiter) and the dawn (Alcmene), who, in early infancy, throttles the serpents of darkness, and who, with untiring strength and patience, plods through life, never resting, and always on his journey performing twelve great tasks, interpreted to represent either the twelve signs of the Zodiac, or the twelve months of the solar year, or the twelve hours of daylight.

353

Like Apollo and Cadmus, Hercules is forced to labour for mankind against his will. We see him early in life united to Megara, and, like Tantalus, slaying his own offspring in a sudden fit of madness. He loves and is soon forced to leave Iole, the violet-coloured clouds. He performs great deeds, slays innumerable demons of drought and darkness on his way, and visits the enchanted land of the Hesperides,—a symbol of the western sky and clouds at sunset.

The main part of his life is spent with Deianeira ("the destroying spouse"), a personification of the daylight; but toward the end of his career he again encounters Iole, now the beautiful twilight. It is then that Deianeira (the daylight), jealous of her rival's charms, sends him the bloody Nessus robe, which he has no sooner donned, than he tears it from his bleeding limbs, ascends the burning pile, and ends his career in one grand blaze,—the emblem of the sun setting in a framework of flaming crimson clouds.

Like all solar heroes, he too has unerring poisoned weapons ("the word *ios*, 'a spear,' is the same in sound as the word *ios*, ' poison ' "), of which he is shorn only at death.

Perseus also belongs to this category of myths. Danae, his mother, either the earth (*dano* means " burnt earth") or the dawn, a daughter of Acrisius (darkness), is born in Argos (brightness). Loved by Jupiter, the all-embracing sky, she gives birth to the golden-haired Perseus, a personification of the radiant orb of day; and he, like many another solar hero, is cast adrift immediately after his birth, owing to an ominous prophecy that he will slay the darkness from which he originally sprang.

As soon as Perseus attains manhood, he is forced to journey against his will into the distant land of the

Perseus and Andromeda

mists (the Grææ), and conquer the terrible Medusa, "the starlit night, solemn in its beauty, but doomed to die when the sun rises." He accomplishes this by means of his irresistible sword, the piercing rays of the sun, and then passes on to encounter the monster of drought, and to marry Andromeda, another personification of the dawn, the offspring of Celeus and Cassiopeia, who also represent night and darkness.

In company with Andromeda, Perseus, whose name also signifies "the destroyer," revisits his native land, and fulfils the prophecy by slaying Acrisius (the darkness), whence he originally sprang.

In the Athenian solar myth, Theseus is the sun, born of Ægeus (the sea, derived from *aisso*, "to move quickly like the waves") and Æthra (the pure air). He lingers in his birthplace, Trœzene, until he has acquired strength enough to wield his invincible sword, then journeys onward in search of his father, performing countless great deeds for the benefit of mankind. He slays the Minotaur, the terrible monster of darkness, and carries off the dawn (Ariadne) ; whom he is, however, forced to abandon shortly after on the Island of Naxos.

In his subsequent career we find him the involuntary cause of his father's death, then warring against the Centaurs (personification of the clouds, through which the victorious sun is sometimes forced to fight his way), then again plunging for a short space of time into the depths of Tartarus, whence he emerges once more ; and finally we see him uniting his fate to Phædra (the twilight), a sister of the beautiful dawn he loved in his youth. He ends his eventful career by being hurled headlong from a cliff into the sea,— an emblem of the sun, which often seems to plunge into the waves at eventide.

THE CLASSICAL MYTHS

In the story of the Argonautic expedition we have Athamas, who marries Nephele (the mist). Their children are Phryxus and Helle (the cold and warm air, or personifications of the clouds), carried off to the far east by the ram—whose golden fleece was but an emblem of the rays of the sun—to enable them to escape from the baleful influence of their stepmother Ino (the broad daylight), who would fain encompass their destruction.

Helle, an emblem of the condensation of vapour, falls from her exalted seat into the sea, where she is lost. The ship *Argo* "is a symbol of the earth as a parent, which contains in itself the germs of all living things." Its crew is composed mainly of solar heroes, all in quest of the golden fleece (the rays of the sun), which Jason recovers by the aid of Medea (the dawn), after slaying the dragon (the demon of drought). Æetes, Medea's father, is a personification of the darkness, which vainly attempts to recover his children, the dawn and light (?), after they have been borne away by the all-conquering sun.

Glauce (the broad daylight) next charms Jason; and the poisoned robe which causes her death is woven by Medea, now the evening twilight, who mounts her dragon car and flies to the far east, forsaking her husband (the sun) in his old age, when he is about to sink into the sleep of death.

Meleager is also a solar hero. After joining the Argonautic expedition, and wandering far and wide, he returns home, slays the boar (or drought fiend), loves, but parts from, Atalanta (the dawn maiden), and is finally slain by his own mother, who casts into the flames the brand upon which his existence depends.

In the Theban solar myth, Laius (derived from the

356

same root as "Leto" and "Latmus") is the emblem
of darkness, who, after marrying Jocasta (like Iole, a
personification of the violet-tinted clouds of dawn),
becomes the father of Œdipus, doomed by fate to be
the murderer of his father. Early in life Œdipus is
exposed on the barren hillside to perish,—an emblem
of the horizontal rays of the rising sun, which seem
to lie for a while upon the mountain slopes, ere they
rise to begin their journey.

He too, like Cadmus, Apollo, Hercules, Perseus,
Theseus, and Jason, is forced to wander far from home,
and, after a prolonged journey, encounters and slays
Laius (the darkness), from whom he derived his
existence, and kills the dread monster of drought, the
Sphinx, whose very name means "one who binds fast,"
—a creature who had imprisoned the rain in the clouds,
and thus caused great distress.

Urged on by unrelenting fate, he marries his own
mother, Jocasta, now the violet-tinted twilight, and
ends his life amid lightning flashes and rolls of thunder,
after being accompanied to the end of his course by
Antigone ("the pale light which springs up opposite
the sun at his setting"). This story—which at first
was merely intended to signify that the sun (Œdipus)
must slay the darkness (Laius) and linger for a while
beside the violet-coloured clouds (Jocasta)—having
lost its physical meaning, the Thebans added the
tragic sequel, for it seemed but poetic justice that
the author of such crimes should receive signal
punishment.

As the Eumenides, or Erinnyes, were at first merely
the searching light of day, from which nothing can
be hidden, they came gradually to be considered the
detectives and avengers of crime, and were therefore
said to take possession of a criminal at the end of his

course, and hurry him down into darkness to inflict horrible torments upon him.

In the story of Bellerophon, although the name originally came from *Bellero* (some "power of darkness, drought, winter, or moral evil") and from *phon* or *phontes* (a word derived from the Sanskrit *han-tâ*, "the killer,"), the Greeks, having forgotten the signification of the first part of the word, declared this hero was the murderer of Bellero, his brother, for which involuntary crime he was driven from home, and forced to wander about in search of shelter.

We find this hero, although enticed by Anteia (the dawn), virtuously hastening away, then sent against his will to fight the Chimæra (the monster of drought), whom he overcomes, thanks to his weapon and to Pegasus (the clouds), born from the mist of the sea, beneath whose hoofs fresh fountains were wont to spring.

Bellerophon, after many journeys, is finally united to Philonoe, a personification of the twilight, and ends his career by being hurled from the zenith into utter darkness by one of Jupiter's deadly thunderbolts.

"The fall of Bellerophon is the rapid descent of the sun toward evening, and the Alein plain is that broad expanse of sombre light through which the sun sometimes seems to travel sullenly and alone to his setting."

In the story of the Trojan war there are several sun myths; for Paris, Menelaus, Agamemnon, and Achilles have equal claims to be considered personifications of the sun. They love Œnone, Helen, Clytæmnestra, Briseis, various impersonations of the dawn, and forsake, or are forsaken by, their lady-loves, whom they meet again at the end of their career: for Paris sees Œnone, and expires with her on the burning pile; Menelaus recovers Helen, with whom he vanishes in the far west; Agamemnon rejoins Clytæmnestra, and dies by her hand in a bloody bath; while Achilles, after a period of sullen gloom, meets with an untimely death shortly after recovering the beautiful Briseis.

Like Perseus and Œdipus, Paris is exposed in early infancy and lives to fulfil his destiny, and cause, though indirectly, the death of his parents.

In this myth, Helen (the beautiful dawn or twilight), whose name corresponds phonetically with the Sanskrit *Sarama*, born of the sky (Jupiter) and of the night (Leda, derived from the same root as " Leto," " Lat-mus," and " Laius "), is carried away by Paris, whom some mythologists identify with the Hindoo *Panis* (or " night demons ") instead of the sun. In this character he entices away the fickle twilight (Helen) during her husband's temporary absence, and bears her off to the far east, where, after struggling for a while to retain possession of her and her treasures, he is finally forced to relinquish her, and she returns to her husband and her allegiance.

The siege of Troy has thus been interpreted to signify " a repetition of the daily siege of the east by the solar powers, that every evening are robbed of their brightest treasures in the west."

Achilles, like several of his brother heroes, " fights in no quarrel of his own; his wrath is the sun hiding his face behind the clouds; the Myrmidons are his attendant beams, who no longer appear when the sun is hidden; Patroclus is the feeble reflection of the sun's splendour, and stands to him in precisely the same relation as Phaeton to Helios," and, like him, meets with an early death.

In the story of Ulysses we find a reproduction of the story of Hercules and Perseus : for Ulysses, early in life, after wedding Penelope, is forced to leave her to fight for another; and on his return, although longing to rejoin his mourning bride, he cannot turn aside from the course marked out for him. He is detained by Circe (the moon), who weaves airy tissues, and by Calypso (the nymph of darkness); but neither can keep him for ever, and he returns home enveloped in an impenetrable disguise, after having visited the Phæacian land (the land of clouds or mists). It is only after he has slain the suitors of Penelope (the weaver of bright evening clouds) that he casts aside his beggar's garb to linger for a short time beside her ere he vanishes in the west.

The greater part of the dawn myths have been explained simultaneously with the sun myths, with which they are inextricably interwoven. One personification of the dawn, however, stands apart. It is Minerva, whose Greek name, Athene, is derived, like Daphne, from the Sanskrit *Dahana*, or *ahana* (meaning "the light of daybreak"), and we are thus enabled to understand why the Greeks described her as sprung from the forehead of Zeus (the heavens). She gradually became the impersonation of the illuminating and knowledge-giving light of the sky; for in Sanskrit the same word also means "to wake" and "to know," while the Latins connected her name of Minerva with *mens*, the same as the Greek *mēnos* and the English *mind*.

Moon Myths

In the moon myths the most important personification is first Diana, the horned huntress, "for to the ancients the moon was not a lifeless ball of stones and clods." Diana, like Apollo, her twin brother, was also a child of the sky (Jupiter) and of night (Latona), and, like him, was born in the "bright land" (Delos). She also possessed bright and unerring arrows, and in the course of her nightly journey she looked lovingly down upon the sleeping face of the setting sun (Endymion).

Io and Circe, already mentioned, are also personifications of the moon, and Io's wanderings represent its journeys across the sky.

Earth Myths

In the earth myths, beside those already mentioned in connection with the sun myths, we have Gæa and Rhea, the mothers and consorts of the Sky and of Time, who swallows his own children, "the Days, as they come each in order."

We have also Ceres or Demeter, "the mother of all things," and more particularly of "the maiden" Cora (or Proserpina), whose loss she grievously mourned; for she had been carried away by Pluto to the underworld, whence she could only emerge at the command of Jupiter. During the time of Ceres' mourning, the earth remained barren, and it seemed as though all mortal things must die. But when Proserpina (the spring or vegetation) returned from her sojourn under the ground, people said "that the daughter of the earth was returning in all her beauty; and when summer faded into winter, they said that the beautiful child had been stolen away from her mother by dark beings, who kept her imprisoned beneath the earth." The sorrow of Ceres was therefore merely a poetical way of expressing "the gloom which falls on the earth during the cheerless months of winter."

Danae, as a personification of the earth, was quickened by the golden shower, the light of the morning, which streamed in upon the darkness of the night. Semele has also been interpreted as the earth, the chosen bride of the sky, who brings forth her offspring in the midst of the thunder and lightning of a summer storm.

Sea Myths

The myths of the sea comprise, of course, Oceanus and Neptune (the earth shaker), whose name is connected with such words as " potent " and " despot," and whose " green hair circles all the earth." We are further informed that he loves the earth (Ceres), whom he embraces, and that he marries the graceful undulating Amphitrite, whose gliding charms appeal to him. Neptune's palace is beneath the deep waters near Greece, and he is said to ride about his realm in a swift chariot drawn by golden or white-maned steeds.

Nereus, another personification of the sea, whose name is derived from *nao* (" to flow "), is quite inseparable from his native element, even in the Greeks' conception of him, as are also the Tritons, Oceanides, Nereides, and the alluring Sirens ; who, however, have also been viewed as personifications of the winds.

Cloud Myths

The cloud myths, to which frequent allusion has already been made, comprise not only the cattle of the sun, the Centaurs, Nephele, Phryxus, Helle, and Pegasus, but as " in primitive Aryan lore, the sky itself was a blue sea, and the clouds were ships sailing over it," so Charon's boat was supposed to be one of these vessels, and the gilded shallop in which the sun daily made his pilgrimage back to the far east, another.

As the ancient Aryan had the same word to denote cloud and mountain (" for the piles of vapour on the horizon were so like Alpine ranges "), the cloud and mountain myths are often the same. In the story of Niobe we have one of the cloud myths. According to some mythologists, Niobe herself is a personification of the clouds. Her many children, the mists, are fully as beautiful as Apollo and Diana, by whose bright darts they are ruthlessly slain. Niobe grieves so sorely at their untimely death, that she dissolves in a rain of tears, which turns into hard ice on the mountain summit. According to other authorities, she was a personification of winter, and her tears represented the thaw occasioned by the sunbeams (Apollo's arrows).

Fire Myths

The fire myths also form quite a large class, and comprise the Cyclopes (the thunder and lightning), children of Heaven and Earth, whose single blazing eye has been considered an emblem of the sun. They forge the terrible thunderbolts, the weapons of the sky (Jupiter), by means of which he is enabled to triumph over all his enemies and rule supreme.

The Titans are emblems of the subterranean fires and the volcanic forces of nature, which, hidden deep underground, occasionally emerge, heave up great masses of rock, and hurl them about with an accompaniment of deafening roars, while their ponderous tread causes the very earth beneath them to tremble.

In this group we also find Prometheus, whose name has been traced to the Sanskrit *pramantha* (or " fire drill "). Learned men have therefore proved that the "beneficent Titan, who stole fire from heaven and bestowed it upon mankind as the richest of boons," was originally nothing but the lightning (" the celestial drill which churns fire out of the clouds ") ; but the Greeks had so entirely forgotten this etymological meaning, that they interpreted his name as the " forethinker," and considered him endowed with extraordinary prophetic powers.

Vulcan (or Hephæstus), strictly "the brightness of the flame," another fire hero, is represented as very puny at birth, because the flame comes from a tiny spark. His name is derived from the Hindoo *agni*, whence come the Latin *ignis* and the English verb *to ignite*. Vulcan dwells by preférence in the heart of volcanoes, where the intense heat keeps the metals in fusion, and so malleable that he can mould them at will; and, as "the association of the heavenly fire with the life-giving forces of nature is very common," the Hindoo Agni was considered the patron of marriage as well as of fire; and the Greeks, to carry out this idea, united their fire god, Hephæstus, to the goddess of marriage, Aphrodite.

The Greek Hestia (or Latin Vesta) was also a personification of fire ; and, her name having retained its primitive meaning to a great extent, "she continued to the end, as she had been from the beginning, the household altar, the sanctuary of peace and equity, and the source of all happiness and wealth." Her office was not limited merely to the hearths of households and cities, for it was supposed "that in the centre of the earth there was a hearth which answered to the hearth placed in the centre of the universe."

Wind Myths

In the myths of the wind, Mercury (or Hermes) was one of the principal personifications. According to the ancients, he was born of the sky (Jupiter) and the plains (Maia), and after a very few hours' existence assumed gigantic proportions, stole away the cattle of the sun (the clouds), and, after fanning up a great fire in which he consumed some of the herd, glided back into his cradle at dawn. With a low, mocking chuckle at the recollection of the pranks he had played, he sank finally into rest.   His name, derived from the Sanskrit *Sarameias*, means " the breeze of a summer morning " ; and it is in his capacity of god of the wind that he is supposed to waft away the souls of the dead ; for " the ancients held that in the wind were the souls of the dead."   Mercury is the " lying, tricksome wind-god who invented music," for his music is but " the melody of the winds, which can awaken feelings of joy and sorrow, of regret and yearning, of fear and hope, of vehement gladness and utter despair."

Another personification of the wind was Mars (or Ares), born of the sky (Jupiter) and of the heavenly light (Juno) in the bleak land of Thrace, rejoicing in din and in the noise of warfare.   His nature is further revealed by his inconstancy and capriciousness ; and whenever he is overcome, he is noted for his great roar.   His name comes from the same root as Maruts, the Indian god, and means the " grinder " or " crusher."   It was first applied " to the storms which throw heaven and earth into confusion, and hence the idea of Ares is confined to mere disorder and tumult."

Otus and Ephialtes, the gigantic sons of Neptune, were also at first merely personifications of the wind and hurricanes.   The name of the latter indicates " one who leaps."   Although very short-lived, these giants were supposed to increase rapidly in size, and assume colossal proportions, which inspired the hearts of men and gods with terror, until they saw them finally slain by the unfailing arrows of the sun.

Pan, Æolus, his numerous progeny, and the Har-pies, were also wind divinities who never entirely lost their original character with the Greeks, and were therefore worshipped merely as personifications of the elements.

Underworld Myths

The myths of drought, darkness, and of the underworld have sufficiently been dwelt upon as personified by Python, the Hydra, Geryones, the Gorgons, Grææ, Minotaur, Sphinx, Chimæra, &c. ; but their main personifications were Cerberus (the grim three-headed guardian of the nether world) and Pluto or (Aïdes), whose name means " the wealth-giver," or "the unseen," who greedily drew all things down into his realm, never to relinquish his grasp upon them.

Such is the physical explanation of the various poetical myths which form the staple of classic literature, and which have been a fount of inspiration for poets and artists of all ages.

INDEX TO POETICAL QUOTATIONS

INDEX TO POETICAL QUOTATIONS

GLOSSARY AND INDEX

A

AB-SYR'TUS. Son of King Æetes of Colchis ; slain by Medea, 238

A-BY'DUS. A city of Asia Minor ; the home of Leander, 89–94

A-CHÆ'US. Grandson of Hellen and ancestor of the Achaians, 26

A-CHA'I-ANS. Inhabitants of the province of Achaia, 26, 285

A-CHA'TES. Friend and inseparable companion of Æneas, 329

ACH-E-LO'US. River in Greece, bearing the name of its god, 202

ACH-E-MEN'I-DES. Ulysses' sailor, rescued from Polyphemus by Æneas, 327

ACH'E-RON. 1. River in Hades, 138 ; Ulysses visits, 312 ; Æneas crosses, 333. 2. Father of Furies, 139

A-CHIL'LES. Son of Peleus and Thetis, 278–280 ; surrenders Briseis, 283, 284 ; the Greeks appeal to, 288–289 ; slays Hector, 290–292 ; death, 293 ; in Happy Isles, 321 ; father of Pyrrhus, 323 ; significance, 358, 359

A'CIS. Youth loved by Galatea, and slain by Polyphemus, 304, 305

A-CRIS'I-US. King of Argos, and father of Danæ, 208, 209, 216 ; significance, 354, 355

A-CROP'O-LIS. Hill in Athens, the site of the Parthenon and Theseus' temple, 229

AC-TÆ'ON. Hunter changed to a stag by Diana, 79–81

AD-ME'TE. Daughter of Eurystheus ; covets Hippolyte's girdle, 194

AD-ME'TUS. King of Thessaly, served by Apollo, and saved from death by Alcestis, 47, 48 ; Hercules restores Alcestis to, 200 ; one of the Argonauts, 234 ; in Calydonian Hunt, 241 ; significance, 350

A-DO'NIS. Hunter loved by Venus and slain by a boar, 86–88 ; significance, 168, 352

A-DRAS'TUS. King of Argos ; his horse Arion, 130 ; father of Hippodamia, 227 ; sends expedition against Thebes, 253

Æ'A-CUS. One of the three judges of the dead in Hades, 139

Æ-Æ'A. Island inhabited by Circe and visited by Ulysses, 310–313

Æ-E'TES. King of Colchis, father of Medea and Absyrtus, 236–238 ; brother of Circe, 310 ; significance, 356

Æ-GE'AN SEA. Delos chained in, 45 ; Arion borne by dolphins in, 63, 64 ; named after Ægeus 226

Æ-GE'US. King of Athens ; father of Theseus, 218, 220, 221 ; drowns himself, 226 ; significance, 355

Æ'GIS. Shield or breastplate of Minerva and Jupiter, 41 ; lent to Perseus, 211 ; bears Medusa's head, 216

Æ-GIS'THUS. Murderer of Agamemnon ; slain by Orestes, 299

ÆG'LE. One of the Heliades ; changed to a poplar tree, 68

Æ-GYP'TUS. Brother of Danaus, 142

Æ-NE'A-DÆ. City which Æneas proposed to found in Thrace, 325

Æ-NE'AS. Son of Venus and Anchises, 88 ; Æneas' descendants, 118 ; worship introduced into Italy by, 171 ; hero of Virgil's Æneid, 322· 339

Æ-NE'AS SIL'VI-A. Son of Æneas ; founder of Alba Longa, 339

Æ-NE'ID. Virgil's epic poem on the adventures of Æneas, 336

Æ-O'LI-A. 1. Same as Æolian Islands. 2. In Asia Minor, near Ægean Sea, 185

Æ-O'LI-AN ISLANDS. The home of

Æolus, god of the winds, 184, 308 ; supposed to be Lipari Islands, 184

Æ-O'LI-AN RACE. Descendants of Æolus, son of Hellen, 26

Æ'O-LUS. 1. God of the winds, 184–186 ; Juno's bargain with, 234 ; gift to Ulysses, 308 ; destruction of Æneas' fleet, 328 ; significance, 365. 2. Son of Hellen, founder of the Æolian race, 25

ÆS-CU-LA'PI-US. Son of Apollo and Coronis, 46, 47 ; Machaon, son of, 295 ; significance, 350

Æ'SON. Father of Jason, 230 ; rejuvenated by Medea, 239

Æ'THER. God of light, 3 ; dethroned, 6

Æ'THRA. Princess of Trœzene, 218 ; mother of Theseus, 221 ; Helen intrusted to, 227 ; significance, 355

ÆT'NA. Volcano in Sicily, 158 ; the tomb of Enceladus, 13 ; forge of Vulcan, 123, 125, 290 ; Ceres' visit to, 162

Æ-TO'LI-A. Country between Epirus and Locris, 241

AF'RI-CA. Hercules' visit to, 196, 197

AFTERTHOUGHT. Name given to Epimetheus, 14

AG-A-MEM'NON. Chief of the expedition against Troy, 278–284 ; return of, 299 ; troops of, 323 ; significance, 358, 359

A-GA'VE. Mother of Pentheus ; infuriated by Bacchus, slays her son, 157

A-GE'NOR. Father of Europa, Cadmus, Cilix, Phœnix, 31, 32

AG-LA'IA. One of the Graces ; an attendant of Venus, 83

A-Ï'DES. Same as Pluto ; significance, 366

A-I-DO'NEUS. Same as Pluto, god of the Infernal Regions, 136

A'JAX. Greek hero in Trojan war, 278 ; Patroclus' corpse recovered by, 291 ; insanity of, 294

AL'BA LON'GA. City in Italy founded by Æneas Silvia, 339

AL-CES'TIS. Wife of Admetus ; dies to save his life, 47, 48 ; restored by Hercules, 200

AL-CI'DES. Same as Hercules, 188 ; lion skin of, 191 ; Deianeira accompanies, 203 ; Deianeira's charm for, 204 ; pose of, 207

AL-CIM'E-DE. Queen of Iolcus ; mother of Jason, 230

AL-CIN'O-US. Phæacian king, enables Ulysses to reach Ithaca, 317

AL-CIP'PE. Daughter of Mars ; carried off by Halirrhothius, 117

ALC-ME'NE. Wife of Jupiter, and mother of Hercules, 17, 188 ; significance, 353

A-LEC'TO. One of the Furies, 139 ; sent by Juno to kindle war between Æneas and the Latins, 334

A-LEC'TRY-ON. Servant of Mars ; changed to a cock, 84, 85

AL'EIN PLAIN. Significance of, 358

AL-PHE'US. 1. River of Peloponnesus ; dammed to clean Augean stable, 193. 2. The river god who pursued Arethusa, 164–167

AL-THÆ'A. Mother of Meleager, 241, 242

AM-AL-THE'A. Goat which nursed Jupiter, 9

AM-A-SE'NUS. River over which Metabus flung Camilla, 335

A-MA'TA. Wife of Latinus, 333 ; driven mad by Alecto, 334 ; suicide of, 338

AM'A-ZONS. Nation of warlike women ; Hercules visits, 194, 195 ; Theseus visits, 226 ; Bellerophon visits, 259 ; Queen of the, 293

AM-BRO'SI-A. Celestial food used by the gods, 27 ; gods deprived of, 66

AM'MON. Temple of Jupiter in Libya, 34

A'MOR. Same as Eros, Cupid, &c. ; god of love, 3 ; son of Venus and Mars, 85

AM-PHI'ON. Son of Jupiter and

GLOSSARY AND INDEX

GLOSSARY AND INDEX

CIM-ME'RI-AN SHORES. Land visited by Ulysses to consult Tiresias, 312

CIR'CE. Sister of Æetes; sorceress who changes Ulysses' men into swine, 310–314; significance, 360, 361

CLE'O-BIS. Brother of Biton; a devoted son, 38

CLE-O-PA'TRA. Daughter of Boreas and Orithyia, 187

CLI'O. One of the nine Muses, presided over history, 69

CLO'THO. One of the Fates; she spins the thread of life, 141

CLYM'E-NE. 1. Wife of Iapetus; an ocean nymph, 14. 2. Nymph loved by Apollo; mother of Phæton, 64, 65, 68

CLYT-ÆM-NES'TRA. Wife of Agamemnon; slain by Orestes, 299; significance, 358, 359

CLYT'I-E. Maiden who loves Apollo, and is changed into a sunflower, 54

CO-CY'TUS. River in Hades, formed of tears of the condemned, 137, 138

CŒ'US. One of the Titans; son of Uranus and Gæa, 6

COL'CHI-AN LAND. Ram bears Phryxus to, 130; Argonauts arrive at, 236; Argonauts depart from, 237; sailors of, 238

COL'CHIS. Land in Asia ruled by Æetes, where the golden fleece was kept, 232, 233; return from, 240

CO-LO'NUS. Forest sacred to Furies, where Ædipus vanished in a storm, 252

CO-LOS'SUS. Statue of Apollo in the Island of Rhodes, 72

CO-MA'TAS. A goatherd, servant of the Muses, 70

CON-SEN'TES. Same as Pan, god of the universe and of nature, 265

CO'PRE-US. Son of Pelops; owner of the marvellous horse Arion, 129

CO'RA. Same as Proserpina, goddess of vegetation, 158; significance, 361

COR'INTH. City and isthmus between Greece proper and the Peloponnesus, 128, 134, 258; Sisyphus, king of, 144, 256; Sciron at, 219; Polybus, king of, 246–248, 251

CO-RO'NA. Constellation, also known as Ariadne's Crown, 156

CO-RO'NIS. Maiden loved by Apollo; mother of Æsculapius, 45, 46; significance, 350, 353

CO'RUS. North-west wind; son of Æolus and Aurora, 184–186

COR-Y-BAN'TES. Same as Curetes; Rhea's priests, 9

COT'TUS. One of the Centimani; son of Uranus and Gæa, 7

CRE'ON. Father of Jocasta and of Megara, 190; King of Thebes, 253

CRE'TAN BULL. Hercules captures, 193–194

CRETE. Island home of Minos, 193, 223, 225; Menelaus' journey to, 277; Æneas' sojourn in, 326; Zeus, king of, 341

CRE-U'SA. 1. Wife of Æneas; killed in attempting to fly from Troy, 323–325. 2. Same as Glauce; maiden loved by Jason, 239

CRI'US. One of the Titans; son of Uranus and Gæa, 6

CRO'NUS. Same as Saturn, Time; a Titan who rules supreme; father of Jupiter, 6–10, 12, 14, 22; daughters of, 36, 158, 171; son of, 136

CRU'MIS-SA. Island where Neptune carried Theophane; birthplace of the golden-fleeced ram, 130

CU'MÆ. Cave where the Sybil gave her prophecies, 332

CU'PID, or CU-PI'DO. Same as Amor, god of love; son of Venus and Mars, 85, 118; growth of, 86; darts of, 89, 124, 330; Psyche and, 99–106, 344

CU-RE'TES. Same as Corybantes; Rhea's priests, 9

GLOSSARY AND INDEX

CY'A-NE. River which tried to stop Pluto when he abducted Proserpina, 160

CYB'E-LE. Same as Rhea, goddess of the earth, 8 ; chariot of, 243

CY-CLO'PES. Three children of Uranus and Gæa, 7 ; thunderbolts forged by, 11, 47, 124 ; Orion visits the, 79 ; Vulcan and the, 123, 124 ; Island of the, 303, 307 ; Æneas warned against, 327 ; significance, 348, 363

CY'CLOPS. Polyphemus the, 303–309, 327

CYC'NUS. Intimate friend of Phæton, 68

CYL-LE'NE. Mountain upon which Mercury was born, 109, 110

CYN'THI-A. Same as Diana, goddess of the moon and the chase, 73–81

CYN'THI-US. Name given to Apollo, god of the sun and fine arts, 44

CYP-A-RIS'SUS. Friend of Apollo ; turned to a cypress tree, 50

CY-PRUS. Island in the Mediterranean sacred to Venus, 82, 98, 102

CYTH-E-RE'A. Name given to Venus, goddess of beauty, love, and laughter, 82

D

DÆD'A-LUS. An architect who planned the Cretan Labyrinth, 221, 222 ; the inventor of sails, 185

DAN'A-E. Maiden visited by Jupiter as a golden shower ; mother of Perseus, 208–210 ; significance, 341, 354, 361

DA-NA'I-DES. Daughters of Danaus, who slay their husbands, 142, 143

DAN'A-US. King of Argos ; father of the fifty Danaides, 142

376

DAN'UBE. River of Europe ; Medea slays Absyrtus near its mouth, 238

DAPH'NE. Maiden loved by Apollo, and changed into a laurel tree, 50, 51 ; significance, 350, 353, 360

DAR'DA-NUS. Ancient king Troy, who gives his name to his race, 326 ; mares of, 187

DE-I-A-NEI'RA. Wife of Hercules, 201–205 ; causes Hercules' death by using the Nessus robe, 205, 206 ; significance, 354

DE-IPH'O-BUS. Son of Priam and Hecuba ; married Helen after the death of Paris, 324

DE'LOS. Floating island ; birthplace of Apollo and Diana, 62 ; shrine of Apollo at, 71, 326 ; significance, 350, 360

DEL'PHI. Shrine of Apollo, famed for its oracles, 25, 32, 71 ; Ceyx visits, 181 ; Œdipus consults oracle at, 247, 248, 251, 255 ; Orestes at, 300

DEL'UGE. Caused by Jupiter's wrath, 23 ; slime from, 48

DE-ME'TER. Same as Ceres ; goddess of agriculture, 158, 163 ; significance, 361

DE'MI-OS (Dread). Attendant or son of Mars, 116

DES'TI-NY. One of the ancient deities not subjected to Jupiter, 27

DEU-CA'LI-ON. Only male survivor of Deluge ; son of Prometheus and father of Hellen, 24–26

DI'A. Maiden loved and deserted by Ixion, king of the Lapithæ, 145 ; significance, 353

DI-A'NA. Goddess of the moon and chase ; daughter of Jupiter and Latona, 73–81 ; birth of, 45 ; nymphs of, 52, 163 ; arrows of, 117 ; Arethusa protected by, 164 ; Œneus neglects, 241 ; Iphigenia saved by, 280 ; temple of, 300 ; Camilla rescued by, 334, 335 ; significance, 352, 360, 363

GLOSSARY AND INDEX

380

GLOSSARY AND INDEX

Hy-met'tus. Mountain in Attica, 71

Hyp-er-bo're-an Mountains. The mountains separating the land of the Hyperboreans from Thrace, 186

Hyp-er-bo're-ans. People north of Oceanus, a virtuous race, 4

Hy-pe'ri-on. The Titan who had charge of the sun chariot, 6, 8, 10

Hyp-erm-nes'tra. Daughter of Danaus ; saves her husband, 143

I

I-ap'e-tus. One of the Titans ; father of Prometheus, 6, 14, 199

I-a'pis. Leech consulted by Æneas ; cures Æneas with Venus' aid, 338

I-a'si-us. Same as Iasion ; father of Atalanta, 241, 327

Iby'cus. Avenged by the Furies, 140 ; the murderers of, 141

Ic'a-rus. Son of Dædalus ; fell into the Icarian Sea, 222

I'da. Mountain in Crete, and near Troy also, 9, 285

I'das. A mortal befriended by Neptune ; elopes with Marpessa, 131, 132

Il'i-a. 1. One of the Titanides ; daughter of Uranus and Gæa, 6. 2. Priestess of Vesta ; wife of Mars ; mother of Romulus and Remus, 118, 339

Il'i-ad. Homer's epic poem on the Trojan war, 282, 286, 293

Il'i-um. Same as Troy, whence comes the Iliad's name, 282, 322, 325, 331

In'a-chus. River god (father of Io), 111, 113

In'dia. Bacchus' visit to, 151

Infernal Regions. Judges in the, 32 ; Orpheus visits, 59–61 ; Adonis visits, 87 ; Pluto's realm, 136 ; Proserpina's sojourn in, 167 ; Æneas visits, 332

I'no. Same as Leucothea ; second wife of Athamas ; daughter of Cadmus and Harmonia, 150, 232 ; significance, 356

I'o. Maiden loved by Jupiter ; changed into an heifer, 111–114 ; significance, 349, 361

I-ob'a-tes. King of Lycia ; recipient of the sealed letter carried by Bellerophon, 256–259

I-o-la'us. Friend of Hercules ; helped to slay the Hydra, 192

I-ol'cus. Kingdom of Æson and Jason ; usurped by Pelias, 230

I'o-le. Maiden loved by Hercules, 205, 206 ; significance, 354, 357

I'on. Grandson of Hellen ; ancestor of Ionian race, 25

I-o'ni-an Race. Race descended from Ion, grandson of Hellen, 26

I-o'ni-an Sea. Sea west of Greece, named after Io, 114

Iph-i-ge-ni'a. Daughter of Agamemnon : sacrificed to Diana, 280, 281 ; Orestes finds, 300

I'ris (the Rainbow). Attendant of Juno, 37, 292, 335

Iron Age. Fourth and last age previous to the Deluge, 23

Isles of the Blest. Islands west of Oceanus, inhabited by the virtuous dead, 5, 6 ; Ulysses searches for, 321

Is'ma-rus. Town in Thrace, spoiled by Ulysses, 301

Is-me'ne. Daughter of Œdipus and Jocasta, 250 ; dies of grief, 255

Isth'mi-an Games. Games held in honour of Neptune, at Corinth, every four years, 134

It'a-ly. Saturn retires to, 12, 22 ; statues of Juno, 38 ; Neptune worshipped in, 133 ; Ceres returns to, 163 ; Vesta's shrine in, 171 ; Janus, king of, 176

Ith'a-ca. Ulysses' island kingdom, 185, 277, 301, 308 ; Ulysses arrives in sight of, 309 ; Ulysses returns to, 316, 317 ;

GLOSSARY AND INDEX

K

KA'KIA. Goddess of vice ; tries to mislead Hercules, 189

L

LAB'Y-RINTH. A maze in Crete, constructed by Dædalus for the Minotaur, 221, 222

LAC-E-DÆ-MO'NI-A. Province in Peloponnesus; capital of Sparta, also name of Sparta, 277

LAC-E-DÆ-MO'NI-ANS. Inhabitants of Lacedæmonia, or Sparta, 182

LACH'E-SIS. One of the Fates ; twists the thread of life, 141

LA'DON. Dragon which guarded golden apples of Hesperides, 196

LA-ER'TES. Father of Ulysses, 279, 308 ; Penelope weaves his shroud, 319

LÆS-TRY-GO'NI-ANS. Cannibals visited by Ulysses, 309

LA'IUS. Father of Œdipus, 246 ; slain by him, 248 ; significance, 356–359

LAM-PE'TIA. One of the Heliades, 68 ; guards the cattle of the sun, 315

LA-OC'O-ON. Trojan priest ; crushed to death by two serpents, 297, 298

LA-OD-A-MI'A. Wife of Protesilaus ; dies of grief, 281, 282

LA-OM'E-DON. King of Troy ; employs Neptune and Apollo to build walls, 126–128 ; Hesione, daughter of, 195 ; significance, 350

LAP'I-THÆ. People who dwelt in Thessaly and fought the Centaurs, 201, 227 ; Ixion, king of, 145 ; Pirithous, king of, 226

LA'RA. Wife of Mercury ; mother of the two Lares, 174

LA'RES. Two tutelary divinities of ancient Roman households, 174 ; saved by Anchises, 324

384

LAT'IN. Names of days in 178

LAT'INS. People of Latinus and Æneas, 335, 336, 338, 360 ; Æneas fights, 334

LA-TI'NUS. King of Latium, 333; welcomes and then wars against Æneas, 334, 335, 337 ; Æneas makes peace with, 338

LA'TI-UM. Province of Italy, ruled by Latinus, 335 ; Æneas comes to, 333

LAT'MUS. Mountain in Asia Minor, where Endymion lies asleep, 77 ; significance, 352, 357, 359

LA-TO'NA. Same as Leto ; wife of Jupiter ; mother of Apollo and Diana, 44, 45, 129 ; boast of, 73 ; significance, 360

LAU'SUS. Hero slain by Æneas during wars against the Rutules, 337

LA-VIN'I-A. Daughter of Latinus, 333, 334 ; Æneas' second wife, 338, 339

LE-AN'DER. Youth of Abydus ; Hero's lover, who swam the Hellespont, 89–94

LE-AR'CHUS. Son of Athamas and Ino ; slain by his father, 150

LE'DA. Mother of Castor and Pollux, Helen and Clytæmnestra, 276 ; significance, 359

LE'LAPS. The tireless hunting dog given by Procris to Cephalus, 52

LEM'NOS. Island in the Grecian Archipelago ; Vulcan landed there, 122 ; Philoctetes on, 294

LER'NA. Marsh where the Hydra lay concealed, 191

LE'THE. River of forgetfulness, which separated the Elysian Fields from Hades, 139, 179, 180

LE'TO. Same as Latona ; mother of Apollo and Diana, 61 ; significance, 352, 357, 359, 360

LEU-CO'THE-A. Same as Ino, Athamas' wife ; sea goddess, 151 ; Ulysses rescued by, 317

LI'BER. Same as Bacchus, god of wine and revelry, 151

GLOSSARY AND INDEX

LIB-ER-A'LI-A. Festivals in honour of Liber, or Bacchus, held in the autumn, 157

LIB'Y-A. Ancient name of Africa; coast upon which Æneas landed, 34, 329

LI'CHAS. Bearer of the Nessus robe; slain by Hercules, 205, 206

LIGHT. Same as Æther, 3

LIP'A-RI ISLANDS. Same as Æolian Islands, where Ulysses landed, 184

LITTLE BEAR. Arcas changed into the constellation of the, 37

LO'TIS. Nymph changed into a lotus blossom, 263

LO-TOPH'A-GI. People whose food was the lotus; the Lotus-eaters, 302

LOVE. Same as Eros, Cupid, &c., 3, 4; Psyche courted by, 99–106

LOVES. Attendants of Venus, 125

LOWER WORLD. Pluto receives sceptre of, 14; Adonis leaves, 88; Pluto conveys Proserpina to, 160; visited by Æneas, 333

LU'NÆ. Same as Diana, 178

LYC'I-A. Land ruled by Iobates, who sends Bellerophon to slay the Chimæra, 256, 259

LYC-O-ME'DES. King of Scyros; treacherously slays Theseus, 229; shelters Achilles, 279, 280

LY'CUS. Antiope's second husband; slain by Amphion and Zethus, 62, 63

LYD'I-A. Kingdom of Midas, in Asia Minor, 153, 201

LYN'CEUS. Husband of Hypermnestra, who spared his life, 143

LYN'CUS. King of Scythia; changed into a lynx by Ceres, 169

LY'RA. Orpheus' lute; placed in heavens as a constellation, 62

M

MA-CHA'ON. Celebrated leech, son of Æsculapius, 47; Philoctetes healed by, 295

MA'IA. Goddess of the plains; mother of Mercury, 109; significance, 364

MAN. The creation of, 14, 15

MA'NES. Tutelary divinities of Roman households, with the Lares and Penates, 174

MAR-PES'SA. Daughter of Evenus; marries Idas, 131, 132

MARS. Same as Ares; son of Jupiter and Juno, 37; god of war, 116–121; Venus courted by, 84–86; day of, 178; descendants of, 339; significance, 365

MAR'SY-AS. 1. Shepherd who enters into competition with Apollo, 55, 56. 2. Name of river, 56

MAR'TI-US, CAM'PUS. Roman exercising grounds, 121

MAT-RO-NA'LI-A. Festivals in honour of Juno, in Rome, 38

ME-DE'A. Daughter of Æetes, 236, 237; wife of Jason, 237–240; wife of Ægeus, 220, 221; significance, 356

ME'DI-A. Country in Asia Minor, where Medea took refuge, 221

MED-I-TER-RA'NE-AN. Sea dividing world in two, 4

MEDU'SA. Gorgon slain by Perseus, whose hair was turned into snakes, 210–216; Neptune marries, 130; Pegasus, offspring of, 258; significance, 355

ME-GÆ'RA. One of the Furies, Eumenides, or Erinnyes, 139

MEG'A-RA. First wife of Hercules, whose three children he burns in his madness, 190; significance, 354

ME-LE-A'GER. Son of Œneus and Althæ; leader of Calydonian Hunt, 241, 242; significance, 356

ME'LI-AN NYMPHS. Nymphs who nursed Jupiter in infancy, 9

2 B

385

GLOSSARY AND INDEX

GLOSSARY AND INDEX

NY-SI'A-DES. Nymphs who cared for Bacchus, and form a constellation, 150

NYX. Same as Nox, goddess of night; mother of Day and Light, 2, 3, 4, 6; mother of Furies, 139

O

O-CE-AN'I-DES. Daughters of Oceanus; nymphs of the ocean 14, 82, 269; significance, 362

O-CE'A-NUS. 1. River surrounding the earth, according to ancients, 4, 5, 200. 2. One of the Titans; son of Uranus and Gæa, 6, 8, 10, 14, 126; significance, 362

O-CRIS'I-A. A slave; wife of Vulcan; mother of Servius Tullius, 125

O-DYS'SEUS. Same as Ulysses; hero of the Odyssey, 301

OD'YS-SEY. Epic poem of Homer on the adventures of Ulysses, 301

ŒD'I-PUS. Son of Laius and Jocasta; King of Thebes, 246–255; significance, 357, 359

ŒNEUS. Father of Meleager and Deianeira; husband of Althæa, 201, 241

Œ-NO'NE. Wife of Paris, son of Priam, 273, 275; she dies on his funeral pyre, 295; significance, 358

Œ-NO'PI-ON. Father of Merope; blinds Orion, 78

Œ'TA. Mountain on whose summit Hercules builds his funeral pyre, 206

O-GYG'I-A. Island where Calypso detains Ulysses seven years, 316

O-LYM'PI-A. City in Elis noted for its temple and games, 34, 200, 207

O-LYM'PI-AD. Time between Olympian Games; i.e., four years, 35

O-LYM'PI-AN DIVINITIES. Name given to the gods of Olympus,

388

27.—GAMES. Games instituted by Hercules in honour of Jupiter, 35, 207

O-LYM'PUS. Mountain north of Greece; the abode of the gods, 4, 6, 8, 9, 11, 12, 16, 17, 27, 29, 36, 39, 41, 52, 59, 66, 74, 75, 84, 87, 91, 98, 106, 110, 112, 115, 123, 124, 129, 147, 208, 259, 334, 336, 347; gods fly from, 12; Prometheus visits, 16; Ganymede transported to, 29; Vulcan expelled from, 122; Ceres visits, 167; Bellerophon storms, 260; Pan carried to by Mercury, 266; Thetis visits, 284; significance, 347

OM'PHA-LE. Queen of Lydia; the taskmistress of Hercules, 201

O-NE-I-CO-POM'PUS. Name borne by Mercury as conductor of dreams, 109, 114

OPS. Same as Cybele; name given to Rhea, and also to Ceres, 8

O-RE'A-DES. Mountain nymphs who guided travellers, 261

O-RES'TES. Son of Agamemnon and Clytæmnestra; friend of Pylades, 299, 300

O-RI'ON. Youth loved by Diana, and accidentally slain by her, 77–79

OR-I-THY'I-A. Wife of Boreas; mother of Calais, Zetus, Cleopatra, and Chione, 186

OR'PHEUS. Musician; son of Apollo and Calliope, 58–62, 234; significance, 351

OS'SA. Mountain in Thessaly, upon which the Titans piled Pelion, 12

O'TUS. Giant son of Neptune; slain by Diana and Apollo, 117, 130; significance, 365

P

PAC-TO'LUS. River in Asia Minor in which Midas washed, to remove his golden plague, 154

PA-LÆ'MON. Son of Athamas and Ino; changed into sea god, 151

PAL-A-ME'DES. Messenger sent to summon Ulysses to war against Troy, 277, 278

PAL-I-NU'RUS. Æneas' pilot; lost at sea off Cape Misenum, 332, 333

PAL-LA'DI-UM. Statue of Minerva, 43; stolen from Troy by Ulysses and Diomedes, 171, 296

PAL'LAS. 1. Name given to Minerva in Athens, 15, 39. 2. Son of Evander; slain by Turnus, while fighting for Æneas, 336, 337

PAL'LOR. Special attendant of Mars; lover of strife, 116

PAN. Same as Consentes, god of nature and the universe, 57, 105, 265, 266; significance, 365

PAN-ATH-E-NÆ'A. Festivals held in honour of Minerva, 43

PAN-DO'RA. First woman; created in heaven, she brings evil into the world, 18–22, 24

PAR'CÆ. The Fates, or Mœræ; they spin the thread of destiny, 141

PAR'IS. Son of Priam and Hecuba, 273; judgment of, 274; visits Troy, 274, 275; elopes with Helen, 277; duel with Menelaus, 285; in battle, 287; Achilles slain by, 294; death of, 295; significance, 358, 359

PAR-NAS'SUS. Mountain in Greece, 24–26; sacred to Apollo and the Muses, 69

PAR-THE'NI-UM. Mountain upon which Atalanta was exposed, 241

PAR'THE-NON. Temple dedicated to Minerva at Athens, 43

PA-TRO'CLUS. Friend of Achilles; slain by Hector, 288–292; significance, 359

PEG'A-SUS. Steed born from the sea foam and the blood of Medusa, 130, 213; Bellerophon rides, 258–260; significance, 358, 362

PE'LEUS. Husband of Thetis; father of Achilles, 234, 241, 271, 278

PE'LI-AS. Uncle of Jason; brother of Neleus, 130; usurps the throne of Æson, 230–233, 238–239

PE'LI-ON. A high mountain in Thessaly, piled upon Ossa by the giants to reach Olympus, 12, 234

PEL-O-PON-NE'SUS. The peninsula south of Greece, 34, 143

PE'LOPS. Son of Tantalus; gave his name to the Peloponnesus, 143; father of Copreus, 129; significance, 353

PE-NA'TES. Household gods worshipped in Rome with the Lares, 174, 175; Æneas saves the, 324

PE-NEL'O-PE. 1. Wife of Ulysses, 277; suitors of, 318–320; significance, 359, 360. 2. A nymph, the mother of Pan, 265

PE-NE'US. 1. River god; father of Daphne; changes Daphne into a laurel, 50. 2. Name of a river in Greece, 50

PEN-THE-SI-LE'A. Queen of Amazons; slain during Trojan war, 293

PEN'THEUS. King of Thebes; refuses to receive Bacchus, and is slain, 156, 157

PER-I-PHE'TES. Son of Vulcan, 125; encountered and slain by Theseus, 219

PER-SEPH'O-NE. Same as Proserpina, goddess of vegetation, 158, 161, 167

PER'SEUS. Son of Jupiter and Danae; slays Medusa, 209–217; significance, 354, 355, 357, 359

PET'A-SUS. Name given to the winged cap worn by Mercury, 111

PHÆ-A'CI-ANS. People who dwelt in Scheria, and sent Ulysses home, 317; significance, 360

PHÆ'DRA. Daughter of Minos; wife of Theseus, 228; significance, 355

GLOSSARY AND INDEX

PHA'E TON. Son of Apollo and Clymene ; drives the sun car, and is slain, 64–68 ; significance, 351, 352, 359

PHA-E-TU'SA. Sister of Phaeton ; one of the Heliades, 68 ; Apollo's flocks guarded by, 315

PHE-RE-PHAT'TA. Name given to Persephone, or Proserpina, 158

PHID'I-AS. Noted Greek sculptor ; made statues of the gods, 35, 43

PHI-LE'MON. Husband of Baucis changed into an oak, 29, 30

PHIL-OC-TE'TES. Friend of Hercules ; receives his arrows, 206, 294, 295

PHI-LON'O-E. Daughter of Iobates ; wife of Bellerophon, 257 ; significance, 358

PHIN'E-US. 1. Rival to Perseus for Andromeda, 215. 2. The blind king of Thrace ; annoyed by the Harpies, 235

PHLEG'E-THON. One of the rivers of Hades ; a river of fire, 138, 140, 312

PHO'BOS. One of the attendants of Mars, god of war, 116

PHO'CIS. Province in Greece, bounded by Doris, Locris, and the Gulf of Corinth, 299

PHŒ'BE. One of the Titanides, 6, 8 ; same as Diana, 73–81, 106

PHŒ'BUS. Name given to Apollo, god of the sun and of medicine, 44, 50, 70, 74, 76, 283 ; significance, 349

PHŒ-NIC'I-A. Province in Asia Minor, named after Phœnix, 32 ; significance, 349

PHŒ'NIX. Brother of Europa, who gave his name to Phœnicia, 31, 32

PHRYX'US. Son of Athamas and Nephele ; rides on golden-fleeced ram to Colchis, 130, 232 ; significance, 356, 362

PHTH'IA. Peleus, king of, 278

PI-RE'NE. Fountain near Corinth, where Pegasus drinks, 258

PI'RATES. Bacchus borne off by, 152

390

PI-RITH'O-US. King of the Lapithæ ; friend of Theseus, 221, 227, 241

PLE'IA-DES. Seven of Diana's nymphs ; pursued by Orion and changed into stars, 78

PLU'TO. Same as Hades, Dis, Orcus, Aïdoneus, &c., 136–146 ; god of the Infernal Regions, 14, 59, 60, 87, 179, 312 ; birth of, 10 ; Proserpina abducted by, 136–141 ; Arethusa sees, 165 ; Ceres visits, 167 ; Perseus aided by, 211 ; Theseus punished by, 228 ; significance, 361, 366

PLU'TUS. Son of Jason and Ceres, the god of riches, 136

POD-A-LIR'I-US. Son of Æsculapius ; skilled in medicine, 47

PO-DAR'CES. Same as Priam, King of Troy ; slain by Pyrrhus, 128

PO-LI'TES. Last of Priam's sons ; slain at his feet by Pyrrhus, 323

POL'LUX. Son of Jupiter and Leda ; brother of Castor, Helen, and Clytæmnestra, 227, 234, 241, 244, 245

POL'Y-BUS. King of Corinth ; adopted Œdipus when forsaken by the servant, 246–248

POL-Y-DEC'TES. King of Seriphus ; sends Perseus in quest of Medusa, 210, 216

POL-Y-DO'RUS. Trojan youth, murdered in Thrace ; his grave discovered by Æneas, 325

POL-Y-HYM'NI-A. Muse of rhetoric ; daughter of Jupiter and Mnemosyne, 69

POL-Y-NI'CES. Son of Œdipus, 250 ; slain by Eteocles, 253 ; buried by Antigone, 254

POL-Y-PHE'MUS. Giant son of Neptune, 130 ; Ulysses visits, 301–310 ; Galatea loved by, 304 ; blinded by Ulysses, 306 ; Achemenides escapes from, 327

PO-LYX'E-NA. Daughter of Priam ; affianced wife of Achilles, 29, 294

GLOSSARY AND INDEX

PO-MO′NA. Goddess of the orchards ; wife of Vertumnus, 268, 269

PON′TUS. Name given to the sea when first created, 3, 4

PO-SEI′DON. Same as Neptune, god of the sea and of horse trainers, 126

PO′THOS. God of the amities of love ; one of the numerous attendants of Venus, 84

PRI′AM. Same as Podarces, 128 ; King of Troy, 273 ; Paris received by, 275 ; duel witnessed by, 285 ; Hector, son of, 285, 289 ; Hector's death seen by, 292 ; Mercury leads, 293 ; Polyxena, daughter of, 293 ; death of, 299, 323

PRI-A′PUS. God of the shade ; pursues the nymph Lotis, 263, 268

PRO′CRIS. Wife of Cephalus ; slain by his unerring javelin, 52, 53 ; significance, 351, 353

PRO-CRUS′TES (The Stretcher). Encountered and slain by Theseus, 220

PRŒ′TUS. Husband of Anteia, and kinsman of Bellerophon, 256, 257

PRO-ME′THEUS (Forethought). Son of Iapetus, 14–17 ; man created by, 14 ; Olympus visited by, 16 ; Pandora taken to, 18 ; chained to Caucasian Mountains, 16 ; Hercules delivers, 16, 197 ; Deucalion, son of, 24 ; significance, 341, 363

PRO-SER′PINA. Same as Proserpine and Persephone ; goddess of vegetation, 105, 158–170 ; Orpheus visits, 60 ; Adonis welcomed by, 87 ; Pluto abducts, 136, 159 ; emblem of death, 182 ; condemned by Jupiter, 167 ; significance, 361

PRO-TES-I-LA′US. First Greek who landed on Trojan coast, 281, 282

PRO′TEUS. Inferior sea divinity ; shepherd of the deep, 132, 133 ; Menelaus consults, 299 ; significance, 344

PSY′CHE. Fair princess loved by Cupid ; the emblem of the soul, 99–106 ; significance, 344

PSY-CHO-POM′PUS. Name given to Mercury as leader of souls to Hades, 109, 114

PYG-MA′LI-ON. 1. Celebrated sculptor, who loves a statue, 98, 99. 2. Brother of Dido ; murderer of Sychæus, Dido's husband, 329

PYG′MIES. Race of small people in Africa ; defended by Antæus, 197, 198

PYL′A-DES. Son of Strophius ; intimate friend of Orestes, 299, 300

PYR′A-MUS. Faithful lover of Thisbe ; commits suicide, 94, 95

PYR′RHA. Wife of Deucalion and daughter of Epimetheus and Pandora ; the only woman who survives the Flood, 24–26

PYR′RHUS. Same as Neoptolemus ; son of Achilles, 294, 323

PYTH′E-US. Surname given to Apollo as python slayer, 48, 49

PYTH′I-A. Name given to Apollo's priestess at Delphi, 71

PYTH′I-AN GAMES. Games celebrated at Delphi every three years, 72

PY′THON. Serpent born of the Deluge slime ; slain by Apollo, 48, 49 ; significance, 350, 366

Q

QUEEN OF HEAVEN. Name given to Juno, 38, 113, 124

QUIN-QUA′TRI-A. Festivals in honour of the goddess Minerva, 43

QUIR′I-NAL. One of the seven hills on which Rome is built, 120

QUIR-I-NA′LI-A. Festivals in Rome in honour of Quirinus, 120

QUI-RI′NUS. Name given to Romulus when deified, 120

391

GLOSSARY AND INDEX

R

RE-GIL'LUS. Lake in Italy where occurred the battle in which the Dioscuri were supposed to assist, 244

RE'MUS. Son of Mars and Ilia; twin brother of Romulus, 119, 120, 339

RHAD-A-MAN'THUS. Son of Jupiter and Europa; judge in Hades, 32, 139

RHE'A. Female Titan; daughter of Uranus and Gæa, 6; wife of Cronus, 8; Jupiter saved by, 9; Corybantes, priests of, 9; Cronus defeated by, 9; Juno, daughter of, 36; Pluto, son of, 136; Ceres, daughter of, 158; Vesta, daughter of, 171; significance, 361

RHODES. Island in the Mediterranean, where the Colossus stood, 72

RHŒ'CUS. Lover of the Hamadryad, 264, 265, 300

ROMAN DIVINITIES, 27, 176

ROME. City founded by Romulus; it comprises seven hills, 119; worship of Juno, 37; worship of Mercury,115; temple to Vesta in, 171

ROM'U-LUS. Son of Mars and Ilia; founder of Rome, 119, 120, 333, 339

RU'TU-LES. Nation in Italy governed by Turnus, 335, 337

S

SA-GIT-TA'RI-US. The constellation formed by Chiron, the Centaur who taught Hercules, 193

SA-LA'CI-A. Same as Amphitrite; wife of Neptune, 130

SA'LI-I. Priests appointed to watch the sacred shields in Rome, 120

SAL-MO'NEUS. King who wished to emulate Jupiter, 144

SAR-PE'DON. Son of Jupiter and Europa, 32; slain during the Trojan war, 289

SAT'URN, or CRONUS. Son of Uranus and Gæa, 7; father of Jupiter, 9; Italy ruled by, 12, 22; husband of Rhea, 14; day of, 178

SA'TYRS. Male divinities of the woods, half man, half goat, 265

SCÆ'AN GATE. Gate which led from Troy to the plain, 286

SCI'RON. Giant encountered by Theseus on the Isthmus of Corinth, 219, 220

SCYL'LA. Sea nymph changed to monster by Circe. She lived under rock of same name, 314, 315, 327

SCY'ROS. Island in the Archipelago, the home of Lycomedes, visited by Achilles and Theseus, 229

SCYTH'I-A. Country north of the Euxine Sea, 169

SEASONS. The four daughters of Jupiter and Themis, 82

SEC'U-LAR GAMES. Games in honour of Pluto every hundred years, 137

SE-LE'NE. Name given to Diana as moon goddess, 73–81; significance, 352

SEM'E-LE. Daughter of Cadmus; wife of Jupiter; mother of Bacchus, 147–150; significance, 361

SE-RI'PHUS. Island where Danae and Perseus were cast ashore, 210, 216

SER'VI-US TUL'LI-US. Sixth king of Rome; son of Vulcan and Ocrisia, 124

SES'TUS. City opposite Abydus; the home of Hero, 89,.93

SEVEN WONDERS OF THE WORLD, 35, 72

SHEET-LIGHTNING. Same as Arges, 7

SIB'YL. Prophetess of Cumæ, who led Æneas down to the Infernal Regions, 332, 333

GLOSSARY AND INDEX

GLOSSARY AND INDEX

394

GLOSSARY AND INDEX